ISTANBUL

Edited and Directed by Thomas Goltz
Produced by Hans Hoefer

APA PUBLICATIONS

THE INSIGHT GUIDES SERIES RECEIVED SPECIAL AWARDS
FOR EXCELLENCE FROM THE PACIFIC AREA TRAVEL
ASSOCIATION.

ISTANBUL
First Edition

© 1988 APA PUBLICATIONS (HK) LTD
Printed in Singapore by APA Press Pte. Ltd.
Colour Separation in Singapore by Colourscan Pte Ltd

APA PUBLICATIONS

Publisher: Hans Johannes Hoefer
General Manager: Henry Lee
Marketing Director: Aileen Lau
Editorial Director: Geoffrey Eu
Editorial Manager: Vivien Kim
Editorial Consultants: Adam Liptak (North America)
Brian Bell (Europe)
Heinz Vestner (German Editions)

Project Editors

Helen Abbott, Diana Ackland, Mohamed Amin, Ravindralal Anthonis, Roy Bailet, Louisa Cambell, Jon Carroll, Hillary Cunningham, John Eames, Janie Freeburg, Bikram Grewal, Virginia Hopkins, Samuel Israel, Jay Itzkowitz, Phil Jarratt, Tracy Johnson, Ben Kalb, Wilhelm Klein, Saul Lockhart, Sylvia Mayuga, Gordon MaLauchlan, Kal Müller, Eric Oey, Daniel P. Reid, Kim Robinson, Ronn Ronck, Robert Seidenberg, Rolf Steinberg, Sriyani Tidball, Lisa Van Gruisen, Merin Wexler.

Contributing Writers

A.D. Aird, Ruth Armstrong, T. Terence Barrow, F. Lisa Beebe, Bruce Berger, Dor Bahadur Bista, Clinton V. Black, Star Black, Frena Bloomfield, John Borthwick, Roger Boschman, Tom Brosnahan, Jerry Carroll, Tom Chaffin, Nedra Chung, Tom Cole, Orman Day, Kunda Dixit, Richard Erdoes, Guillermo Gar-Oropeza, Ted Giannoulas, Barbara Gloudon, Harka Gurung, Sharifah Hamzah, Willard A. Hanna, Elizabeth Hawley, Sir Edmund Hillary, Tony Hillerman, Jerry Hopkins, Peter Hutton, Neil Jameson, Michael King, Michele Kort, Thomas Lucey, Leonard Lueras, Michael E. Macmillan, Derek Maitland, Buddy Mays, Craig McGregor, Reinhold Messner, Julie Michaels, M.R. Priya Rangsit, Al Read, Elizabeth V. Reyes, Victor Stafford Reid, Harry Rolnick, E.R. Sarachandra, Uli Schmetzer, Ilsa Sharp, Norman Sibley, Peter Spiro, Harold Stephens, Keith Stevens, Michael Stone, Desmond Tate, Colin Taylor, Deanna L. Thompson, Randy Udall, James Wade, Mallika Wanigasundara, William Warren, Cynthia Wee, Tony Wheeler, Linda White, H. Taft Wireback, Alfred A. Yuson, Paul Zach.

Contributing Photographers

Carole Allen, Ping Amarand, Tony Arruza, Marcello Bertinetti, Alberto Cassio, Pat Canova, Alain Compost, Ray Cranbourne, Alian Evrard, Ricardo Ferro, Lee Foster, Manfred Gottschalk, Werner Hahn, Dallas and John Heaton, Brent Hesselyn, Hans Hoefer, Luca Invernizzi, Ingo Jezierski, Wihlhelm Klein, Dennis Lane, Max Lawrence, Lyle Lawson, Philip Little, Guy Marche, Antonio Martinelli, David Messent, Ben Nakayama, Vautier de Nanxe, Kal Müller, Günter Pfannmuller, Van Philips, Ronni Pinsler, Fitz Prenzel, G.P. Reichelt, Dan Rocovits, David Ryan, Frank Salmoiraghi, Thomas Schollhammer, Blair Seitz, David Stahl, Bill Wassman, Rendo Yap, Hisham Youssef.

While contributions to Insight Guides are very welcome, the publisher cannot assume responsibility for the care and return of unsolicited manuscripts or photographs. Return postage and/or a self-addressed envelope must accompany unsolicited material if it is to be returned. Please address all editorial contributions to Apa Publications, P.O. Box 219, Orchard Point Post Office, Singapore 9123.

Distributors:

Australia and New Zealand: Prentice Hall of Australia, 7 Grosvenor Place, Brookvale, NSW 2100, Australia. **Benelux:** Utigeverij Cambium, Naarderstraat 11, 1251 AW Laren, The Netherlands. **Brazil and Portugal:** Cedibra Editora Brasileira Ltda, Rua Leonidia, 2-Rio de Janeiro, Brazil. **Denmark:** Copenhagen Book Centre Aps, Roskildeveji 338, DK-2630 Tastrup, Denmark. **Germany:** RV Reise-und Verkehrsuerlag Gmbh, Neumarkter Strasse 18, 8000 Munchen 80, West Germany. **Hawaii:** Pacific Trade Group Inc., P.O. Box 1227, Kailua, Oahu, Hawaii 96734, U.S.A. **Hong Kong:** Far East Media Ltd., Vita Tower, 7th Floor, Block B, 29 Wong Chuk Hang Road, Hong Kong. **India and Nepal:** India Book Distributors, 107/108 Arcadia Building, 195 Nariman Point, Bombay-400-021, India. **Indonesia:** Java Books, Box 55 J.K.C.P., Jakarta, Indonesia. **Israel:** Steimatzky Ltd., P.O. Box 628, Tel Aviv 61006, Israel (Israel title only). **Italy:** Zanfi Editori SRL. Via Ganaceto 121, 41100 Modena, Italy. **Jamaica:** Novelty Trading Co., P.O. Box 80, 53 Hanover Street, Kingston, Jamaica. **Japan:** Charles E. Tuttle Co. Inc., 2-6 Suido 1-Chome, Bunkyo-ku, Tokyo 112, Japan. **Kenya:** Camerapix Publishers International Ltd., P.O. Box 45048, Nairobi, Kenya. **Korea:** Kyobo Book Centre Co., Ltd., P.O. Box Kwang Hwa Moon 1 658, Seoul, Korea. **Philippines:** National Book Store, 701 Rizal Avenue, Manila, Philippines. **Singapore:** MPH Distributors (S) Pte. Ltd., 601 Sims Drive #03-21 Pan-l Warehouse and Office Complex, S'pore 1438, Singapore. **Switzerland:** M.P.A. Agencies-Import SA, CH. du Croset 9, CH-1024, Ecublens, Switzerland. **Taiwan:** Caves Books Ltd., 103 Chungshan N. Road, Sec. 2, Taipei, Taiwan, Republic of China. **Thailand:** Asia Books Co. Ltd., 5 Sukhumvit Road Soi 61, P.O. Box 11-40, Bangkok 10110, Thailand. **United Kingdom, Ireland and Europe (others):** Harrap Ltd., 19-23 Ludgate Hill, London EC4M 7PD, England, United Kingdom. **Mainland United States and Canada:** Graphic Arts Center Publishing, 3019 N.W. Yeon, P.O. Box 10306, Portland OR 97210, U.S.A. (The Pacific Northwest title only); Prentice Hall Press, Gulf & Western Building, One Gulf & Western Plaza, New York, NY 10023, U.S.A. (all other titles).

French editions: Editions Gallimard, 5 rue Sébastien-Bottin, F-75007 Paris, France. **German editions:** Nelles Verlag GmbH, Schleissheirner Str. 371b, 8000 Munich 45, West Germany **Italian editions:** Zanfi Editori SLR. Via Ganaceto 121 41100 Modena, Italy. **Portuguese editions:** Cedibra Editora Brasileira Ltda, Rua Leonidia, 2-Rio de Janeiro, Brazil.

Advertising and Special Sales Representatives

Advertising carried in Insight Guides gives readers direct access to quality merchandise and travel-related services. These advertisements are inserted in the Guide in Brief section of each book. Advertisers are requested to contact their nearest representatives, listed below.

Special sales, for promotion purposes within the international travel industry and for educational purposes, are also available. The advertising representatives listed here also handle special sales. Alternatively, interested parties can contact Apa Publications, P.O. Box 219, Orchard Point Post Office, Singapore 9123.

Australia and New Zealand: Harve and Gullifer Pty. Ltd. 1 Fawkner St. Kilda 3181, Australia. Tel: (3) 525 3422; Tlx: 523259; Fax: (89) 4312837.
Canada: The Pacific Rim Agency, 6900 Cote Saint Luc Road, Suite 303, Montreal, Quebec, Canada H4V 2Y9. Tel: (514) 9311299; Tlx: 0525134 MTL; Fax: (514) 8615571.
Hawaii: HawaiianLMedia Sales; 1750 Kalakaua Ave., Suite 3-243, Honolulu, Hawaii 96826, U.S.A. Tel: (808) 9464483.
Hong Kong: C Cheney & Associates, 17th Floor, D'Aguilar Place, 1-30 D'Aguilar Street, Central, Hong Kong. Tel: 5-213671; Tlx: 63079 CCAL HX.
India and Nepal, Pakistan and Bangladesh: Universal Media, CHA 2/718, 719 Kantipath, Lazimpat, Kathmandu-2, Nepal. Tel: 412911/414502; Tlx: 2229 KAJI NP ATTN MEDIA.
Indonesia: Media Investment Services, Setiabudi Bldg. 2, 4th Floor, Suite 407, Jl. Hr. Rasuna Said, Kuningan, Jakarta Selatan 12920, Indonesia. Tel: 5782723/5782752; Tlx: 62418 MEDIANETIA; Mata Graphic Design, Batujimbar, Sanur, Bali, Indonesia. Tel: (0361) 8073. (for Bali only)
Korea: Kaya Ad Inc., Rm. 402 Kunshin Annex B/D, 251-1 Dohwa Dong, Mapo-Ku, Seoul, Korea (121). Tel: (2) 7196906; Tlx: K 32144 KAYAAD; Fax: (2) 7199816.
Philippines: Torres Media Sales Inc., 21 Warbler St., Greenmeadows 1, Murphy, Quezon City, Metro Manila, Philippines. Tel: 722-02-43; Tlx: 23312 RHP PH.
Taiwan: Cheney Tan & Van Associates, 7th Floor, 10 Alley 4, Lane 545 Tun Hua South Road, Taipei, Taiwan. Tel: (2) 7002963; Tlx: 11491 FOROSAN; Fax: (2) 3821270.
Thailand: Cheney, Tan & Van Outrive, 17th Floor Rajapark Bldg., 163 Asoke Rd., Bangkok 10110, Thailand. Tel: 2583244/2583259; Tlx: 20666 RAJAPAK TH.
Singapore and Malaysia: Cheney Tan Associates, 1 Goldhill Plaza, #02-01, Newton Rd., Singapore 1130, Singapore. Tel: 2549522; Tlx: RS 35983 CTAL.
Sri Lanka: Spectrum Lanka Advertising Ltd., 56 1/2 Ward Place, Colombo 7, Sr Lanka. Tel: 5984648/596227; Tlx: 21439 SPECTRM CE.
U.K., Ireland and Europe: Brian Taplin Associates, 32 Fishery Road, Boxmoor, Hemel Hempstead, Herts HP 1ND, U.K. Tel: (2)215635; Tlx: 825454 CHARMAN.

APA PHOTO AGENCY PTE. LTD.

The Apa Photo Agency is S.E. Asia's leading stock photo archive, representing the work of professional photographers from all over the world. More than 150,000 original color transparencies are available for advertising, editorial and educational uses. We are linked with Tony Stone Worldwide, one of Europe's leading stock agencies, and their associate offices around the world:

Singapore: Apa Photo Agency Pte. Ltd., P.O. Box 219, Orchard Point Post Office, Singapore 9123, Singapore. **London:** Tony Stone Worldwide, 28 Finchley Rd., St. John's Wood, London NW8 6ES, England. **North America & Canada:** Masterfile Inc., 415 Yonge St., Suite 200, Toronto M5B 2E7, Canada. **Paris:** Fotogram-Stone Agence Photographique, 45 rue de Richelieu, 75001 Paris, France. **Barcelona:** Fototec Torre Dels Pardais, 7 Barcelona 08026, Spain. **Johannesburg:** Color Library (Pty.) Ltd., P.O. Box 1659, Johannesburg, SOuth Africa 2000. **Sydney:** The Photographic Library of Australia Pty. Ltd., 7 Ridge Street, North Sydney, New South Wales 2050, Australia. **Tokyo:** Orion Press, 55-1 Kanda Jimbocho, Chiyoda-ku, Tokyo 101, Japan.

The book you hold in your hands is the younger of a pair of "Irish twins" conceived and born within the same year at Apa Publications in Singapore.

It was a tough task, as the parents of any set of human Irish twins can tell you. How to devote sufficient attention to the first born, while at the same time insuring that the second is sufficiently "individual"? In the case of a book, the problem is made more acute when the subjects are a country, Turkey, which finds its richest cultural expression in its primary city, Istanbul.

Hoefer   Goltz   Nişanyan

Somewhere in the middle of his 17th year of publishing the award-winning Insight Guide series, and with over 60 titles under his belt, publisher **Hans Hoefer** began toying with the idea of a new series of sophisticated guides to the Great Cities of the world. Hoefer, the managing director and founder of the APA Publications, had long wanted to do a book on Istanbul, the Janus-faced metropolis that strides both Europe and Asia. A graduate in printing, book production and photography in Krefeld, West Germany, Hoefer had more than an academic interest in the city: he had first visited Istanbul during his youth as an itinerant car merchant plying the highways between his native Stuttgart and the Middle East, and, with the prospect of the Cityguide Guides on the table, and especially due to the keen German interest in the city, Istanbul absolutely had to be included.

The first step to realizing the task was to find a project editor who knew the turf, and Hoefer was able to turn to **Thomas Goltz**, a writer and journalist resident in Turkey for the past five years who was also the editor of *Insight Guide: Turkey*. An MA from New York University's Near East department, Goltz has a long and variegated resume

indeed, ranging from such bizarre credits as having wandered through Africa as a one-man Shakespeare show to testifying before the US Congress on the plight of the Turkish minority in Bulgaria. Inundated with the material and photographs for the country-guide, he nonetheless accepted the challenge to organize and edit *Cityguide: Istanbul*, and, taking a six month leave of absence from his regular duties as a writer for such variegated publications as *Business Week*, *Playboy* and *Reader's Digest*, he next enlisted the help of assistant editor **Sevan Nisanyan** to put together a new conceptual framework the book on Istanbul. After days—nay, weeks!—of "creative tension," they finally came up with the leitmotif of "the big bazaar"—a radical departure from all other guides to the City of the Sultans astride the Bosphorus.

Goltz, who studied under Orientalist-cum-urbanologist Frank Peters at NYU, and translator of Eugen Wirth's twin studies *Zum Problem des Bazaars* and *Die Orientalische Stadt*, undertook the leading chapter on the development of the city as seen through the experience of the bazaar, with research assistance from **Raoul Perez**, the nom-de-plume of one of the faceless observers of the modern Turkish economy.

Nişanyan, a graduate in political science from Yale and an amateur historian (whose reflections on the North-East and Black Sea readers of the Turkey guide are familiar with), undertook the writing of the historical walk-around chapter on the traces of lost Byzantium. Put on your most comfortable walking shoes when strolling through the city with Nişanyan, as he leaves few stones unturned, even if hidden in the depths of the more "popular" quarters of the city. **Yorgo Paseaus**, currently a professor of journalism at the University of Alabama, chipped in with material on the pre-Byzantine era.

Nisanyan also wrote the essay on Ottoman Istanbul, while **Lyle Lawson** wrote the important piece on the Topkapi Palace Museum. **Marian Ellingworth**, a graduate in oriental studies from Oxford who delights in nothing more than deciphering weather-worn inscriptions in Persian, Arabic and Old Turkish, pitched in with writing the tour of mosques and minarets in the city. She also was a major contributor to the Turkey book. The feature on Muslim cemeteries was written by **B. Samantha Stenzel**. A resident of Athens where she writes for a variety of publications, Stenzel also contributed to both *Insight Guide: Turkey* and *Insight Guide: Greece*.

Goltz teamed up with Istanbul novelist/translator and general "intellectual at large" **Alev Alatli** to write the chapter on Living Islam—a subject of recent political interest, as more and more young Turks attempt to integrate the Islamic heritage into their daily lives. Alatli also added a separate feature on the Turkish bath, which, beyond being a symbol of the Muslim way of life, is also a great place to go and get a scrub-down. Writer Alatli and editor Goltz also jointly wrote the chapter on the darker days of the city, as it declined in status from Imperial Capital to that of a provincial town during the middle decades of this century. Alatli also teamed up with Stenzel to write the section on food, with the former regarding all important subject from the kitchen out, while the latter took to the bars, bistro's and restaurants of the city to see what was on the bill of fare.

Murat Belge, owner of Iletisim Publishing House (his contributions to the Turkish Encyclopedia Britannica are the least of his literary credits, which also include numerous reviews, articles and books) collaborated with Goltz on the chapter on Istanbul during the 19th century, with Goltz giving a flavor of the times in his sub-chapter on La Belle Epoque, and Belge directing the curious to the fascinating remnants of old Pera. Belge also wrote the feature on music in Istanbul, a subject which he has more than a casual interest in.

Assistant editor Nişanyan also penned the chapter on the Living City—an excursion into the modern town seldom seen by visitors, while feature writer **Engin Ardiç**, familiar to Turkish readers of *Nokta* and *Tempo* magazines for his iconoclastic articles on such subjects as the Zoo in Istanbul and public toilets, penned the lively feature on policemen and con-artists, as well as "Sailing within Byzantium" (it has nothing to do with boats!) and on the restricted clubs maintained for the ever elusive Istanbul elite. *Sehir* staff writer **Sevin Okyay** contributed the informative guide to hotels, bars and discos in the city—a subject that she has been studying for years. The mysterious Raoul Perez, meanwhile, looked into the subject that everyone wants to know about but is afraid to inquire into: sex and sleaze in the city of the sultans.

Ellingworth

Stenzel

Ardiç

Okyay

The all-important Bosphorus tour was written by Nişanyan (who grew up on it), with a special "strategic" feature added by Goltz. **Metin Demirsar**, veteran Turkey correspondent of the *Wall Street Journal* and *Voice of America*, meanwhile, chipped in the associated feature on Ethnic Remnants of the Greeks, Armenians and Jews in the city, and the villages where they once lived in concentration—all of which are lovely old haunts and worth a look-see. **Gabriele Ohl**, of West Germany's ARD television network, wrote on Istanbul's Black Sea beaches and Polonezköy, or the Polish Village—the strange, historic anomaly that continues to exist right outside the city.

Rounding out the writers' list are **Jak Deleon**, associate professor at Bosphorus University and the leading dance and ballet critic in the country, and **Biltin Toker**, au-

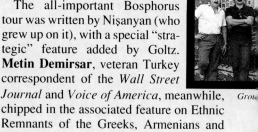
Grou

thor of the classic *Spot on Istanbul*. A culture-vulture who traces his roots back to the arrival of the Sephardic Jews from Spain in 1492. Deleon wrote the chapter on culture and arts as well as the annual Istanbul Festival—an important event in the calender of the city's cultural life. Toker compiled and wrote the vital Travel Tips.

Of equal importance to the writing—if not, indeed, more—was photography, and Goltz and Nişanyan gave highest priority to finding new and exciting pictures to illustrate the book. The two went through a dozen different archives and files of both international and locally recognized photographers, and were disquieted by what they found: most photographers, it seemed, were content with shooting the standard monuments of the city (Goltz swears he never wants to see another photograph of the St. Sophia again), or portrayed an Istanbul peopled exclusively by rustics—unending numbers of quaint, old men and cute, dirty kids. Where were the real people?

Alatli

Belge

Demirsar

Deleon

FOG

Through a quirk of fate, Goltz found himself directed to an obscure address in the old city, where, he was told, a group of young amateur photographers were known to congregate on Saturday afternoons. The IFSAK, or Istanbul Amateur Photographers' Association, turned out to be a goldmine—but of black and white photography, with only a few members that shot color. Discussion with members soon resulted in the mention of another name: Group Fog, a collective of six "amateur" photographers, who, though they had mounted such displays as their year-long work on the City Walls of Istanbul, had never released one of the photographs professionally. The first stop was an appointment with the groups leader, **Nevzat Çakir**, a dentist who maintains a light table right next to his swivel chair. As Çakir went about cleaning the dentures of a young patient, Goltz started going through a sample of Group Fog's work. Goltz sighed in relief upon the first glimpse of the selection. After months of wading through identical cliche pictures, here, at last, was something very special indeed. A second meeting with Çakir and another Fog photographer, **Mehmet Kismet**, only confirmed the first impression: Group Fog simply had to be in the book. Still, acquiring the pictures for use in the Istanbul Guide proved close to pulling teeth. Although the recipient of a dozen awards, Çakir and Group Fog were reluctant to release their work to Apa, until finally, weeks later, another member of the group— **Izzet Keribar**—arrived home from a photographic safari to Kenya. His guide? None other than *Insight Guide: Kenya*. A deal was soon sealed, and to the great relief of Goltz (and hopefully, to the great pleasure of Apa Guide-lovers), Group Fog is now appearing commercially for the first time in the Cityguide. Additional pictures were supplied by IFSAK, as well as from the archives of Cengiz Civa, Şemsi Güner, and Nermi Erdur of *Tempo* magazine.

Special thanks to the preparation of this book are due to a variety of people, among them **Çelik Gülersoy**, and mayor **Bedrettin Dalan**, who might well be the subject of a book himself. Thanks, too, go to **Hakki Aris** of *Savunma ve Havacilik* for communications assistance beyond the call of duty.

Lastly, but hardly the least, inordinately special thanks and credit are due to **Vivien Kim** in Singapore, who might be considered the mid-wife to the Irish twins—*Insight Guide: Turkey*, and the younger sibling, *Cityguide: Istanbul*. Assisting Kim in this delivery are APA's editorial team of **Marion Reincastle**, **Eileen Lim**, **Noor Hayati** and **Johnny Chng**.

TABLE OF CONTENTS

TABLE OF CONTENTS

OTHER INSIGHT GUIDES TITLES

COUNTRY/REGION

ASIA
Bali
Burma
Hong Kong
India
Indonesia
Korea
Malaysia
Nepal
Philippines
Rajasthan
Singapore
Sri Lanka
Taiwan
Thailand
Turkey

PACIFIC
Hawaii
New Zealand

NORTH AMERICA
Alaska
American Southwest
Northern California
Southern California
Florida
Mexico
New England
New York State
The Pacific Northwest
The Rockies
Texas

SOUTH AMERICA
Brazil
Argentina

CARIBBEAN
Bahamas
Barbados
Jamaica
Puerto Rico
Trinidad and Tobago

EUROPE
Channel Islands
France
Germany
Great Britain
Greece
Ireland
Italy
Portugal
Scotland
Spain

MIDDLE EAST
Egypt
Israel

AFRICA
Kenya

GRAND TOURS
Australia
California
Canada
Continental Europe
Crossing America
East Asia
South Asia

GREAT ADVENTURE
Indian Wildlife

CITYGUIDES
Bangkok
Berlin
Buenos Aires
Dublin
Istanbul
Lisbon
London
Paris
Rio de Janeiro
Rome
San Francisco
Venice
Vienna

CITY ON THE STRAITS

Somewhere near the middle of the old Galata Bridge there is a special spot which commands the entire city of Byzas the Megarian, Constantine the Great, Justinian, Mehmet the Conqueror and Süleyman the Magnificent.

To the right is the imposing edifice of the New Mosque, obscured by the swirling clouds of pigeons always wheeling between its steps and the Egyptian Bazaar nearby. Both are misnomers, for the mosque was built over four centuries ago, while the so-called Egyptian bazaar takes its name from the Turkish word for the land of the pharaohs—Misir, or "corn".

These are some of the lesser confusions and contradictions of Istanbul, a city of some two-score historical names, and which even today is referred to by many as "Constantinople"—a label about as appropriate as referring to New York as "New Amsterdam".

Yes, the confusions and misnomers are legion. The Golden Horn, for example, is not the Bosphorus. Let the ignorant be forgiven, as countless others have made that perfectly honest error. It follows that the bridge you are standing on is not the Bosphorus Bridge linking Europe and Asia; that is usually obscured in the mist to your left, some five miles up-stream towards the Black Sea.

To your right, through the belching smoke of the line of white ferry-boats (with such station names as Bebek, Beşiktaş and Beykoz) are the walls of the Topkapi Palace and the bulge of Seraglio Point, where the giraffes, lions and elephants of the sultans' private zoo once roamed. There is still a zoo in the district, but its menagerie consists mainly of chickens, cats and dogs behind bars. The coastal road and the Sirkeci railway station—the final terminal of the Orient Express of Eric Ambler and Agatha Christie fame—have reduced the original palace grounds to a third of their original extent. But the Topkapi itself remains impressive, and still exudes a sense of the absolute power wielded by the sultans during the centuries of Ottoman supremacy in the medieval world, when Europe was a collage of feudal (and feuding) states, Asia a distant realm visited by only the most adventurous.

Behind the stark walls of the Topkapi arise the needle-like minarets and grandiose domes of the St. Sophia and Blue Mosque— one of the most memorable skylines in the world. If the palace wielded temporal power, it was tampered by the check and balance of Islam: even the mightiest of sultans were obliged to pray, fast and repent in the same manner as the most ordinary bootblack. In the domains of Islam, it was also an unspoken law that the powerful and mighty try to outdo one another in the way of pious endowments and buildings, and it is natural that Istanbul, the center of temporal and religious power during high Islamic times, should be the venue where the "rivalry" between such master builders finds its greatest expression.

For those who prefer mulling over their history, the ruins of ancient Byzantium give testimony to a lost age of splendor and decay. Here one encounters the remains of an ancient cistern, there the crumbling shell of a monastery or church, or the traces of old sculpture or wall incorporated into the structure of a ramshackle tenement block of flats.

To the left and on the other side of the bridge in Pera stands the conical Galata Tower, the launching pad by a Turkish "Icarus" in the 16th century. It was the center of the Levantine community—Genoese, Venetians and other Europeans who settled in and around the city for commercial gain before the Turkish conquest of 1453. Pera remained the commercial hub of the city over five centuries until the Great War of 1914-1918, replacing the traditional bazaar as the economic hub of the city. The removal

Preceding pages: Descendants of Byzantium; a blast of ferry smoke near the Galata Bridge; interior tiles of the dome of the Sultan Ahmet, or "Blue" Mosque; Egyptian obelisk and minarets; Yali's on the Bosphorus; Pillow merchant with wares. Left, a view from the bridge into old Pera.

of the royal family from the Topkapi to the flamboyant Dolmabahce palace attests to this shift. Built by the westernizing sultan Abdülmecid in imitation of the palaces of imperial Europe, the construction of the Dolmabahce played a major role in bankrupting the empire. And it was from here, too, following the disintegration of the Empire, that the last sultan slunk off into the night to a waiting British warship, which spirited him to Malta and exile.

The last resident of the Dolmabahce, strangely enough, was Atatürk, the man who banished the sultan, and signaled the end of Istanbul's role as capital when he had the seat of power of the Turkish Republic re-

freighters, tankers and cruisers waiting their turn to navigate the tricky currents of the Bosphorus toward the Black Sea. Flocks of tiny fishing barques pull in *lüfer*, or bluefish, as the shoals rush down stream toward the Princes' Islands and the Aegean beyond, determined, it would seem, to find their way to your table that evening.

There is that spot on the Galata bridge, but it is difficult to find. Too often, it has already been taken by an itinerant salesman of nylon socks, polyester shirts or useless do-hinkies and thing-a-ma-jigs; sometimes it is obscured by a sudden exhaust blast of a passing bus, forcing one to move on, or the crush of the crowds—pretty girls in jeans, mus-

moved to Ankara, deep in the Anatolian hinterland.

Asia. For Europeans and North Americans, at least, the word itself is rich with exotic romance. But in Istanbul, it is embraced within the same city, only somewhat more than a stone's throw away from Europe's shore. (Some people swim between the two continents, although it cannot be advised. There is also an annual marathon across the first bridge for those inclined to run between Europe and Asia.)

And all around is water, from the Sea of Marmara, dotted with the silhouettes of huge

tachioed *hamals* or porters bent double under immense loads, shrouded women walking three feet behind their skull-capped husbands, businessmen with their briefcases rushing across on foot, tired of waiting in the constant traffic jam on the bridge, or aggressive gypsies leading their semi-tame bears over to another group of camera-carrying tourists to bang the tambourine and pull the chain piercing the animal's nose to make it rear up on its hind feet and dance.

Still at other times it is the weather that hides the essence of the city: the fog (none dare call it smog) that envelopes Istanbul on a December evening, burning the eyes with lignite dust of half a million coal-burning apartment blocks, or the heat glare and oppressive humidity that seems to melt the earth to the horizon in July when you know beyond any shadow of a doubt that this is really a city of seven million souls. The only relief to be found then is to abandon the minaret-spiked skyline and flee through the surrounding chock-a-block squatters' sub-urbs to the beaches of the Black Sea or across the Bosphorus to the more tolerable dry heat of Asia.

But sometimes, usually in Spring, when the rains have washed away the coal dust of winter, and lawns of the city's parks have

dent and Orient, and is the synthesis of both.

The book in your hands, the editor hopes, has been organized along the lines that stress the variegated cultural heritage of the Janus-faced city that is Istanbul: Byzantine history has been incorporated into a walking tour of the remaining monuments and ruins; the same approach has been used for the Otto-man centuries as well, with tours focusing on the Topkapi as well as the mosques. The little known cultural effervescence of 19th-century Pera has a separate chapter devoted to it, as well as the grim reality of Istanbul following World War I, as the city devolved from being a world capital to the status of a provincial city, and the more recent efforts to

turned their livid green and the mulberry and cherry trees lining the hills, slopes and cliffs of the Bosphorus are in bloom, or in early Fall, when the riot of fallen leaves blows across Sultan Ahmet Square, it is possible to find that special spot and see the city for what it was and is: Istanbul, surrounded by a garland of waters, the throbbing metropolis that has ever been the bridge between Occi-

restore itself as the preeminent metropolis in the Middle East. Particular emphasis, too, has been placed on that often neglected part of any "touristic" destination—the living city of real people with problems as opposed to inert stones and strangers with peculiar customs.

But throughout its history—be it Megar-ian, Roman, Byzantine, Ottoman or Turkish Republican—Istanbul has been primarily a city of trade, and it is on that note that we

Left, the Süleymaniye Complex from the Golden Horn. Above, a cruise ship under the first Bosphorus Bridge.

begin our journey: from the City on the Straits, deep into the all enveloping laby-rinth of the Big Bazaar.

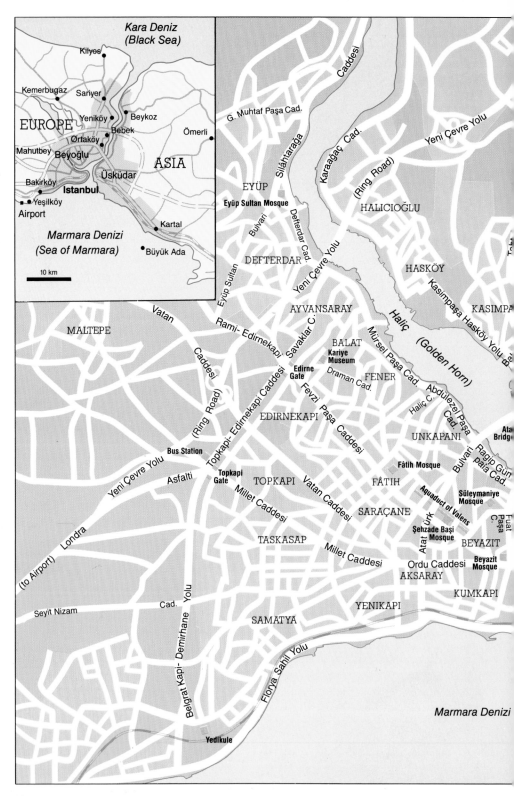

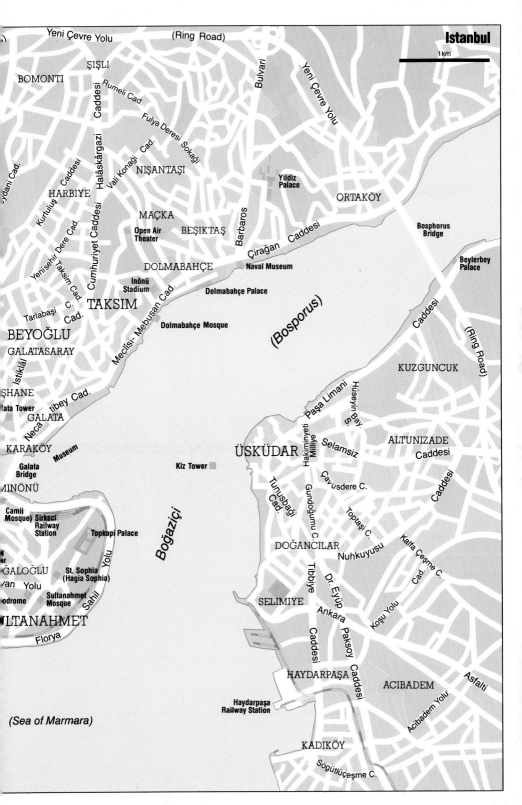

1 km

Yeni Çevre Yolu   (Ring Road)

BOMONTI

ŞİŞLİ

Rumeli Cad.

Caddesi

Bulvari

Yeni Çevre Yolu

Fulya Deresi Sokağı

Halâskârgazi

Vali Konaği Cad.

NİŞANTAŞI

Yildiz
Palace

ORTAKÖY

Kurtuluş Caddesi

HARBIYE

Yenişehir Dere Cad.

Cumhuriyet Caddesi

MAÇKA

Open Air
Theater

BEŞIKTAŞ

Barbaros

Çirağan Caddesi

Bosphorus
Bridge

Taksim Cad.

DOLMABAHÇE

Naval Museum

Beylerbey
Palace

İnönü
Stadium

Dolmabahçe Palace

Tarlabaşi

C.

Cad.

TAKSIM

Meclisi- Mebusan Cad.

Dolmabahçe Mosque

(Bosporus)

BEYOĞLU

GALATASARAY

Caddesi

KUZGUNCUK

(Ring Road)

İstiklâl

tibey Cad.

ŞHANE

ata Tower

GALATA

Neca

KARAKÖY

Museum

Galata
Bridge

MINÖNÜ

Kiz Tower

Paşa Limani

Hüseyin bey

Hakimiyeti
Milliye

Selamsiz

ALTUNIZADE

Caddesi

ÜSKÜDAR

Caddesi

Camii
Mosque)

Sirkeci
Railway
Station

Topkapi Palace

Tunusbağı
Cad.

Çavusdere C.

Gundoğumu C.

Toptaşi C.

Boğaziçi

DOĞANCILAR

Nuhkuyusu

Kalfa Çeşme C.

ar

GALOĞLU

St. Sophia
(Hagia Sophia)

Tibbiye

Dr. Eyüp

Koşu Yolu

Cad.

an Yolu

odrome

Sultanahmet
Mosque

SELIMIYE

Ankara Paksoy

LTANAHMET

Florya

HAYDARPAŞA

Caddesi

ACIBADEM

Asfalti

Haydarpaşa
Railway Station

Acibadem Yolu

(Sea of Marmara)

KADIKÖY

Sögütlüçeşme C.

THE BIG BAZAAR

Forget about street signs. Disregard all maps. Your compass and watch are useless here. Cancel all appointments and abandon all plans—just plunge in and go. The labyrinth awaits you, a rabbit warren of alleyways, cul de sacs and dimly lit, narrow winding streets, peopled by characters and scenes that would make an Alice green with jealousy. This is the real Wonderland of the Grand Bazaar: hookah-smoking merchants (they call them *nargile's* here), indifferent to the world; *hamals* or porters, bent like hinges under incredible loads of paper, fruit, carpets or spice; hawkers and stalkers, whose vocabulary remains the same in a dozen different tongues (the more languages they try, the less to trust their wares); gawking rustics in town for the day in search of the inflation-proof gold (the rustic togs are deceptive—look for the gold capped teeth); conservative women, whose enveloping black shrouds belie the twinkle in their massacred eyes; tourists groups and individual travelers staring wide-eyed with nostrils stretched and ears deafened by the cacophony of the sounds and sights and smells of the market: the pungent odor of fresh vanilla beans from Madagascar mixed with the nearly acrid smell of cloves from Zanzibar; brilliant flash of color tempting one into an alley lined from end to end and top to bottom with identical plastic shoes; the sound you hear drumming in your ears is not the rain, but the timpani of a thousand tiny hammers on a thousand hand-held awls, giving shape and definition to a soon-to-be ancient platter or would-be pewter plate.

There are many things for sale in the bazaar, everything. And if it is not here now, it will be in five minutes. Just sip another tea. Need a cigarette holder hidden in a Dom Perignon champagne bottle, or a mechanical

ape that does flips when you wind it? How about a bottle of Opium perfume for $25? Walk away from the itinerant merchant and watch the price plunge to $5, buy it and send it to your first wife or the suspected lover of your husband, with his name on it.

Stained your original Lacoste tennis shirt with your dinner last night? Its replacement is here in two qualities—the $4 variety, which is so close as to be indistinguishable from the original, and the poor man's ver-

sion for half that price, guaranteed to sustain two washings. Levi's or Calvin Klein's? No problem. You are only paying for the signature anyway, and there is a large, specialized market for fake labels in Istanbul to assist the equally large textile market where the name brands place their orders. Who will notice that your Ferrara sunglasses, purchased for $10, have the name spelled "Ferarra"?

Meerschaum pipes, carved into ridiculous shapes and sizes by some dwarf-laboratory gone mad; 19th-century Junghans clocks with the original Arabic numerals on the dial; fashion leather coats and skirts which would flood the world were it not for the cut-throat tactics of Korea; gloves and socks and shirts and slacks and brass and trinkets and giftables of a thousand shapes and sizes, some for your friends, others for your lover, still others for your in-laws to let them know, perhaps with unnecessary candor, that you never once thought of them during your entire stay in Istanbul. There are gifts and kitsch for everyone and every possible occasion in the Grand Bazaar.

Into the labyrinth: Every carpet tells a story, say the merchants, but so do even the lowliest items for sale in the bazaar. Select a multi-colored shawl, and follow it back from its outlet shop through the maze of alley-

the sound of two dozen ancient looms claw-ing away at ell after ell of wool. Make your way through the huge, metal-studded gates and walk the shuddering stairs. Select a door—any door. They all lead to the same postage-stamp sized rooms, each containing three machines tended by a soon-to-be-deaf lad from Rize on the Black Sea. All the machines look the same, as do all the boys. But each shawl being ripped and clawed into shape is an exquisite explosion of color.

Or demand of the carpet merchant who dragged you in off the street to be shown to the carpet repair shop. He will resist at first, maintaining that all of his merchandise comes in ancient, perfect, and has never seen

ways to the outskirts of the bazaar and be-yond, to cobblestone side streets where tour-ists seldom go. These obscure arteries are the very life-line of the bazaar: streets of huge synthetic suitcases good for one coming and one going before they fall apart, or avenues of cheap fabric shops, all selling the same reams of identically electric material. Who buys such things? Who knows, but there must be tremendous demand to support two dozen identical outlets on the very same street.

One can hear the Büyük Yeni Han a block away. A dull thumping permeates the air—

repair. Squeeze him, and he might order his boy (there is always a 10- or 12-year-old present to bring tea or carry thousands of dollars to and from the black market or run other errands as part of his apprenticeship in the bazaar) to lead you there. Follow him out through the Mercan Gate to a tiny alleyway pinched between two buildings and up a rickety flight of stairs. The obscure door opens a crack to reveal three should-be Turkish school boys defying labor laws, two 20-year-old Kurds and one ancient Sephar-dic Jew, cramped into their respective cubby holes beneath cascades of old yarn, delicately and expertly patching the burns and bruises and blights of time from 100-year-old carpets—some of which have been shipped from England and Argentina to be deftly made as good as new.

The oriental city: The call of the *muezzin* to the faithful for prayer five times a day may seem romantic and strange to those visiting the Islamic cultural sphere for the first time, but it is, in fact, nothing more than a vocal counterpart to the chiming of church bells from belfries across Christendom. The minarets spiked skyline of Istanbul—immediately identifiable as "Islamic" to most of us, would probably look surprisingly similar to the cathedral spires of "Catholic" Rome to

delberg in Germany or Taxico in Mexico. Palaces, schools, residential areas, harbors, policemen, docks, houses of ill repute and traffic—all have their counterparts in East and West.

There is, in fact, only one thing that distinguishes the Oriental city from its cousin in the Occident: the bazaar, that uniquely "eastern" (or more precisely, Islamic) system of human interaction in commerce that truly sets the two worlds apart. And the Grand Bazaar in Istanbul is perhaps the most striking (if arguably best) example of this cultural difference.

An ancient tradition: The historical emergence of the bazaar, predictably, goes back

someone with no previous contact with either religion. Covered ladies and bearded men are found throughout the world, and the meandering rabbit warren of streets associated with such "Oriental" cities as Cairo or Damascus—aside from the relative question of hygiene—would find their counterparts in the quaint old lanes of the older towns of Europe or South America—be they Hei-

Left, shopping for inflation-proof gold. Above left, an itinerate perfume merchant. Right, a wandering pair of cloth salesmen.

to the dawn of time in the Middle East and Mesopotamia, where civilization as we know it began. The first towns and then cities were founded here, and with them, that quintessential element of urban life—interdependency based on trade and the concomitant establishment of a definable market.

The organization of the markets of the ancient Orient, however, are shrouded in obscurity. Some scholars suggest that the ruins of Dura Europos in northeastern Syria might well contain the world's first proto-bazaar. But the agoras of the ancient Greeks and Romans are the best surviving examples of the markets of antiquity, and archaeological evidence at such sites as Ephesus, Perge and Aspendos suggests that most agoras were large public squares serviced by wide, colonnaded streets, usually leading from the temple or to the theater, with simple awnings hung to protect the public from the elements.

The camel and the wheel: The transition from the rigorous design of cities in the Hellenic period to the state of apparent controlled chaos in the "oriental" city has been attributed to a variety of different causes, but can perhaps be most succinctly expressed as the victory of the camel and its load over the wheel and its wagon. In terms of inter-city transport and trade, the amazingly evolved

network of roads built by the Roman corps of engineers in the Middle East fell into disuse soon after the Muslim conquests of the 7th century. In the cities of the region, a similar transformation occurred: the wide streets, constructed for wagon traffic with adjacent arcades for pedestrians, slowly disintegrated as wheeled traffic was replaced by that of the camel, allowing for a helter-skelter growth of booths and shops in the street itself until the colonnades as such disappeared. With more and more business conducted *al fresco*, the next logical step was to roof the remaining open space. Initially, protection

from the elements was affected by cloths and thatchwork mats, later to be replaced by some sort of wooden construction, until finally (and after repeated fires) merchants banded together to construct uniform rows of shops in stone with vaulted passageways for their customers.

The Byzantine bazaar: Surprisingly little is known about the market in Constantinople itself, however. A debate concerning its very location continues in scholarly circles even today. Some suggest that the main commercial district flanked the port in the area of what today is the Egyptian or "spice" bazaar; others maintain that the market—whether covered or open to the elements—stood on the present site of the Grand Covered Bazaar, and that the Old Bedesten is essentially a Byzantine structure rebuilt by the Turks, citing a Byzantine eagle carved in stone above one of the entrances as evidence. Still others maintain that the colonnaded main thoroughfare—today's *Divan Yolu*—was lined with shops and represented the commercial hub of the city.

But if the location of the city's market is obscure, the high level of commercial activity in it is not: Constantinople was a veritable luxury supermarket in its day, the vortex that greedily consumed all and any manner of products to a degree only dreamed of by the most hedonistic Roman. As Gibbon informs the readers:

"Whatever rude commodities were collected in the forests of Germany and Scythia, as far as the sources of the Tanias and the Borysthenes; whatsoever was manufactured by the skill of Europe or Asia; the corn of Egypt, and the gems and spices of farthest India, were brought by the varying winds into the port of Constantinople, which, for many ages, attracted the commerce of the ancient world."

Middlemen, especially, had it good. Through them, Constantinople delivered silks, spices, drugs and grains to a hungry world via the quays and customs houses of Neorion (modern Sirkeci), the major port of the city. The specialization of labor required an orderly pattern of production, resulting in institutionalized guilds through which the state could easily control supply, price, and profit.

More than all else, Constantinople hungered for silk, an addiction which kept the city at the mercy of its ancient rival, Persia, through which caravans on the Silk Road were obliged to pass. The illicit transfer of the silkworm and the discovery of the manufacturing process freed the city of its more odious obligations, but the over-taxation of the peasantry as well as the creation of inefficient state monopolies through the guild system effectively insured economic decay.

Religion also played a major factor in the market: the massive diversion of productivity and wealth to the glory of God may make for good tourism nowadays, but at the time it resulted in the equivalent of a war economy:

however owes more to the city-state of Venice than indigenous entrepreneurs. Having been granted trade and tax exemptions as well as generous port capacity in return for coming to the rescue of Constantinople when the city was attacked by Normans in 1082, Venetian fortunes soon became intertwined with those of the city. Spices, soaps, wax, timber and silks were just some of the commodities in which the Venetians speculated, using the city as an entrepot and transshipment point.

Muslim merchants: By 1453 and the siege of the once and future city by the Ottoman Turks, commerce—and indeed, communion—with the world had virtually ceased to

it was icons, not swords, that needed to be turned into plowshares. The Iconoclastic movement of the 7th century did exactly that: it also served the positive and pedestrian function of freeing a large share of this church-hoarded wealth for more productive uses, as well as a contemporary equivalent of war-reparations induced inflation.

The real commercial flowering of the city,

Left, a *hamal*—the men who carry the bazaar on their backs. Above, money talks when bargaining.

exist. Not only were Turkish cannons aimed at the city's ancient walls, but the life-line that had sustained Constantinople for centuries—the Bosphorus—had been closed. Turkish forts on both the European and Asian sides effectively stopped all trade from getting out and all aid from getting in.

But far from signaling the death-knell of Constantinople as a world market, the Ottoman conquest ushered what is arguably its most splendid age as the capital city—and market—of a vigorous, young power which commanded a hinterland spreading from the Yemen in the South to Vienna in the North,

and from Algiers in the West to the Persian Gulf in the East.

More to the point, it was an Islamic empire, which, unlike the unspoken onus attached to business in medieval Christianity—the most salient Biblical reference to commerce being the money-changers who Jesus evicted from the Temple—actually encouraged trade. According to pious tradition, the Prophet Muhammad (himself a merchant who plied the sands between Mecca and Damascus) extolled good Muslims to seek business as far as China.

And they did. Caravansaries—many still to be seen along the cameltier trade routes criss-crossing the Dar ul-Islam (or "The Abode of Peace")—shuttled in security across the vast area of the Islamic cultural sphere, carrying the silks of China, the spices of India, the ebony, ivory and black slaves of Africa and the timber, furs and white slaves of the Caucuses to market cities whose names still give a thrilling tingle to the ear: Samarkand, Baghdad and Aleppo in the East, and Cairo, Fez and Cordoba in the West, with many lesser bazaar cities scattered in between.

Ibn Battuta, although he died before the conquest of Istanbul, is an excellent example of a medieval Muslim traveler-cum-businessman: he was born in Spain, and he studied religion in Cairo before making his first pilgrimage to Mecca, where he remained for some years to set up a business. Ibn Battuta proceeded to explore; the Ottoman lands around Bursa before dropping into the Byzantine capital of Constantinople, from where he made his way by camel caravan to Iran, then by ox-cart across the Gobi desert to China, from whence he sailed to India to fight the war for Islam against the Hindus. Returning to Mecca again, he next set sail for East Africa, possibly crossing the continent to West Africa, where he was offered human flesh to eat (which he refused), before returning to Morocco once more to write his memoirs. And Battuta was not hitch-hiking camels and eating in soup kitchens: he traveled in style, trading all the way.

The bazaar is built: Upon the Turkish conquest of Constantinople, the city instantly became the primary metropolis of the Muslim world. Politically, this meant that it was to be a city of administrators and bureaucrats. It also meant that it was to be the primary market of the Middle East, and the final depot of a thousand caravans.

To address the needs of the exploration of commerce, one of Mehmet the Conqueror's first tasks was to be build a *"Bedesten"*—a large, covered market hall of some 60 small shops, with storage space used as a depository for valuables. With the addition of a second market hall—the Sandal Bedesten—

devoted primarily to silks and textiles but which also served as the auction house for slaves—the bazaar began to take real form, soon mushrooming into an emporium of 60 streets with 16 separate gates.

Mehmet had ample experience to draw on in creating his market. The Ottoman Turks, as relative late comers to Islam and the Middle East, had managed to absorb both the organic phenomenon of the bazaar in the Muslim cities they had conquered, as well as to impose a certain structure on the market which had hitherto been lacking.

Both Bursa in Anatolia and Edirne in

Left, Mahmut Paşa Aclivity Street—a major artery outside the bazaar. Above, tabulating the day's take in Tahtakale.

Thrace—the first and second Ottoman capitals, respectively—had bazaars predating that of Istanbul, the revenues of which were used for the maintainance of sacral buildings and institutions ranging from mosques to mental hospitals. This tradition was continued with the construction of the Grand Bazaar in Istanbul as well.

Despite such pretensions of piety, the bazaar was ultimately a shopping center. But unlike other similar commercial districts in the West (or even in the Far East), where most individual shops are privately owned and represent the individual architectural tastes of the various owners, the bazaar is of a uniform construction over long stretches

by a monopoly of watchmen, the bazaar is more than a deserted part of town at night. Wall Street in New York is like a carnival at Rio in comparison between dusk and dawn. The moment business stops, the bazaar is as quiet and lifeless as it it had been struck by a neutron bomb.

Hans and caravansaries: If the architecture of the bazaar was provided by imperial decree, the development of the bazaar as the market par excellence of the Islamic world is the direct result of the twin factors of the guild system and long distance trade.

Trade routes with their ultimate destination at the *hans* or warehouses in the Grand Bazaar linked a score of traditional mercan-

on both sides of the street due to the vaulting which binds shops on either side into an architectural whole. The total absence of residential housing in the bazaar—either along side streets or above shops—is another unique characteristic—the bazaar exists for commerce and for commerce alone, with profits—after a healthy tithing for the owners and operators—devoted to religion or related good works. There is no "leisure time"; no sauntering around on a Sunday afternoon (or Friday, as the case may be); no window shopping; no afterhours bars or movie theaters; opened and closed abruptly

tile cities of the Islamic cultural sphere and many outside it.

The centerpiece of long distance trade was the caravansary outside the city, and its intra-muros cousin, the *han* inside. Both consist of an open courtyard surrounded by several stories of rooms, used both for warehousing and as temporary residence. Typically, the *hans* of Istanbul form a recognizable ring around the bazaar, although the larger and supposedly older *hans* are found in their own district near the Golden Horn.

Many of these *hans* can still be seen today, although most are in a rather sorry state of repair and have usually acquired the function of sweat-shops when not completely given over to the storage of plastic shoes and tons of yarn. By far the best preserved—and currently undergoing repair—is the Zincerli Han, just inside the Mercan Gate, which, if given over primarily to the sale of carpets and gold, still gives a taste of what an intimate *han* used to look like. Other good examples of larger *hans* would include the Büyük Yeni Han, the Büyük Yildiz Han, and the Kürkçü Han—all down Mahmut Paşa Aclivity Street on the way to the Egyptian Bazaar.

It was in such *hans* that the big-money moved. Transparency, good faith, extended

Greeks. The ability to place and send orders over long distances on blind trust played a significant role in the successful operations of these traders.

Gold itself—then as now—was a highly valued commodity, made more so by the Sultan's tendency to remove large amounts of the precious metal to his treasury. This led to a value of gold significantly higher in the Ottoman Empire than in the rest of Europe and the expected development of the bazaar as a major center of currency arbitrage. Merchants were virtually assured as much as 20 percent profit simply by transporting their gold and silver coins to the Istanbul market. Thus it was that despite the decline

families and cash on the barrelhead were the means by which business was conducted. Gold and silver were the medium of exchange, with credit accorded only via foreign intermediaries—usually the Venetian *balio*. A notable exception to this cash economy was the family-credit network set up by Jewish merchants, as well as those from other minorities like the Armenians and

of Venice in the 17th and 18th centuries, there was no relenting in its striking of sequins for export to Istanbul.

The guilds: Rather like the Byzantine system of commercial organization, the Ottoman market revolved around guilds. These were no mere collections of related laborers or purveyors of certain services, but tightly knit communities of experts in their respective fields, with initiation rights, apprenticeships, cradle-to-grave security, and collective religious habits. Certain guilds were often identical with sufi mystical orders, so that acceptance into a guild meant accep-

Left, the Grand Bazaar, empty as a graveyard at night. Above left, a whole range of pails for your pleasure. Right, a *yorganci*, or quilt-maker.

tance into not only a trade, but into a very specific—some might suggest a narrow—way of life.

Each trade had its own street, where its goods were displayed to the exclusion of all others, and even today one can stroll down the "Street of the Cotton Printers," the "Street of the Quilt-Makers" or "Street of the Spoon-makers". Herein lies a peculiar feature of the bazaar: the collection of all the retailers of a certain line of goods into a given area clearly allowed for greater government control, especially in the way of consumer protection, a concept which reached a surprisingly high degree of development in traditional Islamic society. But at

Bedesten, which was given over to textiles, in the main. Çelebi's litany includes everyone from the 300 *hamals* or porters, who are allowed to monopolize inner-bazaar transport (their parade uniform included their load supports), the 300 Jewish gold and satin sellers, to the 1,000 cloth merchants, separate from the 70 cloth weavers, and the 800 men who sell weapons in 500 arms shops in the bazaar.

Today, very little remains of the guild-system. Crushed by cheaper European goods—especially textiles in the 19th century—the guilds ineluctably dissolved, and with them, an entire way of life. Some social scientists go so far as to suggest that the

the same time, it clearly resulted in price-fixing; but if so, why then the tradition of bargaining?

Turkish miniature paintings and writers of the period give very colorful accounts of the guilds in action. One such account by the peripatetic chronicler Evliya Çelebi gives a blow-by-blow of the entire bazaar, decked out in its finest, on parade for Sultan Murad IV before his campaign to capture Baghdad. Çelebi exhaustively lists the various guilds, noting whether they ply their trade in the Noble Bedesten (which was built by Mehmet the Conqueror) or the newer Sandal

breakdown of the guild system hastened the end of the empire itself, as what formerly had represented a wholistic lifestyle (to borrow the modern phrase) was replaced with a complete loss of identity.

Demise of the bazaar: By the 17th century, the Grand Covered Bazaar contained upwards of 3,000 shops. If one includes shops associated with the 30 major *hans*, the number totals nearly 4,000. Most were small—tiny by modern standards—and consisted essentially of two cupboards which could be opened into a street stand during the day and locked at night. Lighting was entirely natural, filtering in through the glass nobs and ventilation shafts on the cupolaed ceiling. There were no advertisements. The wares did the talking, with the merchant perched silently among his merchandise, his feet quite literally in the street. The psychological distance between consumer and the object to be consumed was nil.

But the monopoly position of the guilds, while effective in medieval times, could neither compete with the growing industrialization of Europe in the 18th and 19th centuries, and ineluctably, manufactured goods in the factories of England, France and Germany began to flood the bazaar, when foreign countries were allowed special

exemptions for services rendered to the faltering Ottoman state. It was a case of commercial *deja vu*, with the Great Powers in the role of the Genoese and Venetians in the fading days of Byzantium.

Once again Galata, on the other side of the Golden Horn, became the preferred place to do business, and banks and trading companies flourished. Devastating fires encour-

Left, worry beads of every shade and strip. Above, brooms for sale, made just outside the bazaar.

aged other merchants to leave the traditional bazaar area, and the great earthquake of 1894 insured that only those without money to go elsewhere remained with their increasingly shoddy goods among the rubble.

Rebuilt in 1898, the bazaar continued to decline as fewer and fewer traditional crafts were passed on from father to son, and fewer foreign and luxury goods appeared on the shelves, first due to the territorial disintegration of the Ottoman Empire itself, and next by protectionist measures issued in the new Turkish capital at Ankara following World War I meant to insure the economic viability of the state.

Two fires this century—one in 1943, and the more devastating conflagration of 1954 sealed the doom of the traditional bazaar, and today, it is difficult to find one merchant who has descended from a family resident in the bazaar for longer than a single generation. Those few individuals who can remember the Bazaar in the '40s and '50s recall a dimly lit, uninhabited wasteland, with shops which formerly sold luxury goods being used as casual urinals, nests of rats and general squalor. The poverty of the city—and indeed, the nation—was reflected in the commercial activity in the Bazaar, which was effectively zero.

The bazaar today: Happily, much, has changed over the past two decades, and today the bazaar reflects the secret prosperity of the country. The sale of gold alone gives the lie to official statistics of a per capita income of $1,000. The bazaar is not only a major touristic attraction for Arabs, Germans, Poles and Japanese, but also the very real commercial hub of the city: despite government efforts to regulate market speculation within the confines of a stock exchange (described by observers as being as lively as the periodicals check-out counter at a provincial town library), Tahtakale, the unofficial currency market in the country, continues to thrive. The streets in the area are alive with frenetic bidding on dollars, deutsch mark and yen. In true bazaar fashion, the offices of the roving crowds of speculators are the rag-tag looking storefronts lining the streets—an effort at self-effacement that goes back to the 15th century, when even the wealthiest bazaar merchant would content himself with a hole-in-the-wall to avoid a high profile from rapacious tax collectors and jealous dignitaries. Then, as now, it is a ruse that fools none, but remains as essential tradition nonetheless.

Of the 5,000 odd shops that now make up the bazaar area, perhaps only 3,000 are devoted to the weighing, shaping and selling of gold. Kalpakçilar, the main vaulted street in the bazaar, fairly shimmers with earrings, bracelets, rings and chains worked into intricate designs that appeal to three distinct groups of potential customers. The thick bracelets and large gaudy pieces hanging in most windows are specifically designed for Middle Eastern tourists, who like to have

quality worksmanship.

The center of goldsmithing is the Cuhaza Han, an old *han* that contains over 300 crackerbox ateliers, as well as nine gold smelting forges and scores of wholesale outlets. The market maintains a rigorous system of control over the karatage, which ranges from the standard 14 karat for earrings and baubles to 20 karats for super-light rope-chains and up to 22 karats for heavy bracelets. When buying gold, be sure to check for the stamp of both the karatage as well as the number of the goldsmith; obviously, if one of the two stamps is lacking, the material is of questionable value.

Still, much has been irretrievably lost.

their gold with the stamp of the prophet on it. The standard bracelets and earrings—nothing very fancy, but gold nonetheless—are directed at the local market, where gold has long been regarded as an immediate convertible bank account, and as a hedge against inflation. Pious Muslims, too, prefer dealing in the gold market—where the price can double over a year—to sullying their hands with interest bearing bank accounts which only return half the profit as gold in any case. Westerners also purchase substantial amounts of gold sold in the bazaar, but usually for the sake of the inexpensive but

Repairs and restorations (including the installation of public toilets cleaner than those in most banks downtown), might mean a cleaner bazaar, but the old atmosphere of guilds and specialized streets is largely gone, with most stores with their neon signs and credit-card advertisements a far cry from the traditional shops.

There are exceptions. Johanes Muradiyan, who still makes steel engravings by hand for everything from the buttons for naval officers' uniforms to reliefs of Atatürk, still plies his craft as he has for the past 45 years in his museum-atelier at the

Zincirli Han. The world famous Ziliciyan cymbals, too, are once again being produced by hand in workshops near the bazaar under the label of "Istanbul", and it is a pleasant surprise to find some world-famous drummer snooping around the brass shops of the old Bedesten looking for the source. The Sandal Bedesten, formerly the venue for silks and slaves, still functions as an auction house three days a week, but more than half the available space has been devoted to new carpet shops—as if the bazaar needed more.

Indeed, to acquire a contemporary taste of what the bazaar once was, it is perhaps advisable to leave the center and move to the periphery. The spice trade—especially

ber that Istanbul is where the tulip got its start.

Mysteriously, lawn mowers are also on sale here, although the city presents a singular dearth of private greens to be shorn.

In and around the flower market are the sellers of birds and pets—pigeons, partridges, parakeets and parrots, as well as doves, quail, pheasant and fighting cocks. A one-eyed man who first appeared in the area century or two ago still sells fortunes by having his rabbit nibble one out of lettuce-spiked board.

Most interesting of all, perhaps, is the scene immediately outside the Grand Covered Bazaar at closing time, when scores of

those herbs and roots that allegedly possess some medicinal value—remains lively, albeit in the Egyptian Bazaar near the Galata Bridge. In back are miles of kitchen utensils—in case you wanted to know—and in the square pinched between the spice market and the Yeni Camii is the flower market, where all manner of plants, flowers and bulbs can be purchased for a song: remem-

itinerant salesmen, invisible until then, collect down Mahmut Paşa Aclivity Street to spread out their merchandise for those last-minute shoppers who come late, or the bazaar trader on his way home. In a scene that could be from a 17th-century engraving, the merchant sets out his wares in a semi-circle around him, feet in the street. His collection of batteries, portable radios, combs, prophylactics, socks and underwear might not seem that impressive at first glance, but when a potential customer approaches, the merchant lets the goods do the talking. The bargaining, of course, is up to you.

Left, spices for sale in the "Egyptian" Bazaar. Above left, a lemonade salesman. Right, leathersmith plying an ancient craft in the back-alleys of the Bazaar.

THE SAHAFLAR

A fragile remnant of handsome paper, preserved with egg-white, from a 450-year-old Quran with a 22K gold leaf motif decorations in the margins. A four volume black leather bound 1876 version of *Les Miserables* printed in French. *Gone With The Wind* in a 1938 British edition. And if those don't whet your reader's curiosity there are thousands of other literary pleasures, treasures and eccentricities awaiting you in the exotic but dwindling world of Istanbul's second-hand bookshops.

Beginning at the historical center point, every traveler's itinerary in Istanbul obviously includes a visit to the boisterous and endlessly fascinating Kapali Çarşi. However, frequently overlooked in the overwhelming hurly-burly is the historically important **Sahaflar Çarşisi**, the nearby market of the secondhand booksellers quietly tucked away between the splendid Beyazit Mosque and the bazaar.

To gain entrance, first treat yourself to a leisurely walk through the sprawling outdoor teahouse along side the mosque wall. Here a colorful panoply of muted students lingering over their tulip glasses of Turkish tea eternally discussing urgent personal, academic and political questions, vendors of all descriptions in the background plying their diverse wares (electrical tools, plastic toys and antique or cheap pocket watches) and old Turkish men seated in chairs along the periphery laughing and relating the news of the day.

Passing through this scene and under the gracefully ornamented Gate of the Spoon-Makers in the Northeast corner, you enter the Sahaflar Çarşisi. This small and peaceful tree shaded courtyard is lined with over 40 bookshops (check the numbers above the doors) with outdoor stalls filled to overflowing with books on every imaginable subject. From a rare turn-of-the-century Library of

Famous Literature to outdated medical texts, romance novels, westerns and old movie magazines, the market will satisfy even the most idiosyncratic tastes. Once this was the paper and book center of Constantinople. The market then served from the beginning of the 18th century to the advent of Turkish public libraries as a primary source of books for Istanbul.

As you begin your stroll, however, you immediately notice that the Secondhand Booksellers Market now deals primarily in new books. Not to worry for it is still worth a visit. Ten different shops still carry a good sampling of old books and periodicals while three fully devote their entire stock to the dusty old tomes from the past.

Elif No. 4 is the most well known shop in the Sahaflar Çarşisi. It is widely recognized that owner Mr. Aslan Kayhardağ's knowledge of Turkish books, old and new, is unsurpassed. If the book exists in Turkey, he is said to be the man to find it for you.

Across the way at No. 27 is **Güzen Kitap Ve Yayinevi** run by brothers Ünal and Sinan. Started over thirty years ago by their father, they usually obtain their books from library closings in Europe and Turkey or buy them from estates being settled.

After you've seen what the shop offers, ask one of the brothers to take you across the courtyard to the upstairs storeroom at No. 2. It's perfectly safe and there you will be pleasantly surprised to discover another 5,000 volumes hidden in storage including some unexpected Greek religious texts and the gold leaf decorated pages of a centuries old Quran.

A jaunt across the Galata Bridge to Tünel is well worth the bookworm's while. The **Librarie de Pera** (Galip Dede Caddesi 22), offers the book browser an experience steeped in tradition and a selection of over 10,000 books in major European languages. Or stroll up the street and duck into the **Librarie d'Orient** (Galip Dede Caddesi 16) and find a stunning selection of books and magazines from all corners of the world.

Left, the Sahaflar, or used book market.

CARPETS GALORE

Of the 4000-odd shops in the bazaar district, arguably a quarter are devoted to carpets, and it is a rare visitor to the city who won't allow him or herself to be seduced into the cool interior of one of the bazaar's hundred retail outlets by a suave and multilingual "roper". Many have seen you somewhere before, in Rome last Christmas, perhaps, or was it New Orleans at Carnival? Come in anyway. No obligation to buy.

Sit back and drink tea in tulip glasses or a demitasse of thick Turkish coffee as the friendly merchant rolls out rug after luscious rug on the floor. There are big rugs, small rugs, square rugs, runner rugs. Rugs for your walls and rugs for your table tops, rugs for the office and rugs for the cabin. Silk rugs, wool rugs, shag rugs, worn rugs, dear rugs, cheap rugs, good rugs, bad rugs.

The top of the line tend to be the wall to wall *Hereke Silk Carpets*, advertised as having the most knots per square inch of any carpet in the world. This, the merchants will tell you, is highly desirable, and will insure that your grandchildren have an opportunity to experience vicariously grandpa and grandma's trip to the Orient. Be prepared to pay for the pleasure of future generations.

Even the most mundane carpet, of course, tells a story: This *Yagcibedir* was made in Kayseri by the daughter of the last whirling dervish, and that *Van Kilim* by the wife of a fierce Kurdish tribal leader in the East. None has yet broken the secret code in the geometric floral designs on the border of this *Milas* carpet, and that *Bergama* (the same as Yagcibedir) is at least 125 years old. All of them, of course, contain only natural dyes and will last forever.

Have no illusions, you are being bamboozled, but pleasantly. This is an intrinsic part of the bazaar. Bargain. Especially with those merchants who say they don't. You will be amazed at how prices can drop (and perhaps simultaneously appalled at how that friendly young man with the seamless smile can lie through his teeth so shamelessly). One can never be sure of the real price, and if you finally make a purchase, you will have to live with your doubt forever. If you do make a purchase, never ever show your new acquisition to another carpet merchant, or price what you think is a similar piece. Rival carpet dealers are like older brothers, wiser friends and used car salesmen: they like to make you feel like they know better and that you've been had.

A last warning: You have gone through 50 carpets, and the colors and patterns have started to merge into one. You like them all. The friendly merchant helps you by separating out those you like best from the heaping pile on the floor. Indecision rears its expensive head and you think about buying two, or three, or maybe even four. The narrowed field, in the eyes of the merchant, represent his personal favorites as well. They are also part of his personal collection, and not for sale. But for you, well, all right. American Express or Visa will do just fine.

If you find yourself in this situation, keep your hand away from your wallet and leave the bazaar area immediately. You have been stricken with that seldom fatal, but extremely expensive disease known as "carpetitis". Many a traveler has gone home overburdened, paying extra freight at the airport, only to discover that the six carpets picked up for a song in the bazaar neither fit in the den nor bedroom nor match the drapes in the living room. The sad alternative to putting them in eternal storage is to become a reluctant carpet merchant yourself, and spin yarns about the rugs as you roll them out before family and friends, in a last-ditch attempt to break even on your purchases made while under the influence of the bazaar.

There are, in fact, wonderful carpets to be had in the bazaar, but no unique deals or steals. One rug is usually enough to remember the experience with pleasure, provided your purchase fits in the study.

Right, carpets in the Bazaar—credit cards accepted.

41

Sexta etas mūdi

Onstātinopolis imperialis ac famosissima ciuitas: olim bizantiū (vt supra scriptū est) appellata. τ
cū admodū parua esset: eā postmodū constātinopolim noiarūt. Constātin⁹ em̄ impator cognomi̅
ne magn⁹: dum statuisset imperij sedē ex vrbe roma in oriēte trāsferre: quo facili⁹ parthoꝛ excur
sationes cōpesceret. Tradūt aliqui autores in troadē pfectū: ibi regie vrbis fundamēta iecisse: vbi quon
dam agamenon: ceteriꝗ grecoꝛ principes aduersus priamū fixere tentoria. Sed admonitū in somnis a
xpo saluatore loci aliū designāte: ceptū opus (cui⁹ diu mansere vestigia) infectū reliquisse. atꝗ in tracia na
uigante bizantiū petiisse. Cūꝗ sibi loci diuinitus ostensum dixisse: mox vrbem ampliasse: noua menia
erexisse: sublimes excitasse turres magnificētissimis tuꝗ priuatis: tuꝗ publicis operib⁹ exornasse. Tātuꝗ
illi decoris adiecisse: vt altera roma nō imerito dici posset. Scriptores vetusti qui florentē videre: deoꝛum
poti⁹ in terris habitaculū ꝗ impatoris putauere. Nomē vrbi noua roma impator indidit: sed vicit obsti
natio vulgi: vt a cōditore poti⁹ Constātinopolis vocicaret. Quā ei⁹ successores impatores passim tuꝗ pu
blicis edib⁹: tuꝗ priuatis ciuiū pallacijs ꝗ quidē supbissimis exoꝛnare curarūt. Et adeo vt exteri eo venię
res vrbis splēdore admirati: nō tam mortaliū ꝗ celestiū eā domiciliū dixerint. Erant muri vrbis τ altitu
dine τ crassitudine toto oꝛbe celebres. antemuralia vero opportune cōmunita. Triangularē pene vrbis
formā fuisse tradūt. Duas partes alluit mare. nec muri desunt: ad ppulsandos nautales impetus idonei
qd reliquū est ad terras vergens: post alta menia τ antemuralia. ingēti claudiꝰ fossa. Habetꝗ hec ciuitas
vndeciꝰ portas: dignitate ipsi⁹ pre se ferētes. quarū noia hec sunt: aurea: pagea: sancti romani: carthasea
regia: caligaria: rilina: bacmagona: phara: theodosia: τ sylaca. Extāt in ea preter cetera magnificētissima
edificia templū Sophie iustiniani cesaris opus: toto oꝛbe memorabile nongētis quondā sacerdotib⁹ ce
lebratū: mirabili ope: pciosa materia cōstructū. Ea deniꝗ vrbs tanto splēdore insignis fuit vt toti⁹ oꝛien
tis columen: τ vnici docte grecie domiciliū habita fuerit. vbi tria magna cōcilia celebrata fuerūt: videlicet
sub theodosio seniore: sub agathone papa: τ sub iustiniano principe. Eam cū thurci ppter ei⁹ dignitatem
diu exosam habuissent. Anno salutis nre. 1093. a belzete quodā eoꝛ principe: cū ingenti thurcoꝛ manu
obsessam: deinde capta fuit. Inde galli cū venetis p quinꝗ τ quiquaginta annos possidere. postea palea
logoꝛ clarissima familia genuēsiū ope a gallis ademit vsꝗ in annū. 1453. gloriosissime possedit. quo an
         Constantinopolis

42

no Machometes Ottomänus thurcoz impatoz eā cepit diripuit⁊s. Sic nobilissima vrbs in man⁹ infide
lin venit. Ab ei⁹ cōditione.Mcccc. vl'circa. Tátoq⁊ tpe paulo pluri senioz roma steterat. qñ pmo a gothis
capta est Athalaric⁹ eñ anno ab vzbe pdita.Mclxiiii.roma irrupit.at hic ne basilice sctōz effringeret edi
xit. Rabies aūt thurcoz nil sanctū:nil mūdū:i vzbe regia relicjt. sacratissia ei⁹ tēpla machometee spuricie
dedicarūt.Legim⁹ thebanoz res gestas:lacedemonioz ⁊ atheniesiū illustria facta: fuit cozinthioz nō cote
neda respublica.clare oli micene:larissa potes:pluresq⁊ meozabiles vzbes quoz si nūc reqras muros:nec
ruinas inuenias.Nemo solū in q̃ iacuerint queat ostēdere:sola ex tāta ruina vetustatis cōstatinopolis supa
bat:q̃ tm mirabiliū opez:tm armoz:tm lfarū:tm glozie habuit:vt oim ciuitatū damna: hec vzbs sola re
cōpēsare videret.Et licet post diuisuz imperiū siue trāslatū ad frácos sepe cōstātinopolis i man⁹ hostiū ve
nerit:nūcq̃ tm basilice sanctoz dstructe cōbuste:neq⁊ bibliothece cōbuste:neq⁊ despoliata penit⁹ monasteria.Itaq⁊
māsit vsq⁊ i hūc annū vetuste sapie apud ōstātinopolis monumēti.Nemo latinoz satis videri doct⁹ pote
rat:nisi p temp⁹ cōstātinopoli studuisset.Inde nobis plato reddit⁹.inde aristotelis:demostenis:xenophō
tis:thucididis:basilij:dionysij:ozigenis⁊⁊ alioz multa latinis opa(dieb⁹ nr̄is)manifestata sunt.Hūc sub
thurcoz impio sec⁹ eueniet:seuissimoz hoim:bonoz moz atq⁊ litteraz hostiū.Hūc q̃ ⁊ homero ⁊ pindaro
menādro ⁊ oib⁹ illustriozib⁹ poetis secūda moz⁊ erit.Hūc grecoz phoz vltim⁹ patebit interit⁹.Innume
rabiles eñ ex hac celeberrima vzbe in oi scia atq⁊ virtute pclarissimi exiere viri: inter quos cognometo io
hānes crisostom⁹ ipsi⁹ vzbis eps.Atticus eps cui⁹ de virginitate liber extat.gennadi⁹:cassian⁊c̄⁊.Et no
uissime emanuel crisoloras q̃ grecas lf̄as tpe cōstātiesis pcaliij in italia cū ingenti vtilitate retulit.Pcecisus
est aūt nunc fluui⁹ oim doctrinarū.musarū desiccatus fons.Fateoz multis locis apud latinos studia lfarū
esse illustria. vt rome:parisius:bononie:padue:senis:perusij:colonie:vienne:salamātice:oxonie:papie
liptzk:ertfordie.Sed riuuli sunt oēs isti ex grecoz fontib⁹ deriuati. A fonte precide riuū: pcisus arescit.
Nihil aūt sub luna ppetuū.Quomodo aūt impatoz thurcoz machomet⁹ aio voluerat vzbe in medio thur
coz esse sitam:que suo imperio nō pareret:suoq⁊ nomini decus mai⁹ accedere posset:si eā vziem expugna
ret:machinas bellicas admouit. ⁊ insultu magna vi in eā fecit atq⁊ tandē expugnauit:vt h ec ciuitas in po
testatē venerat infideliū spurcissimoz thurcoz hoc infelici anno ⁊ vtriusq⁊ sexus pe rsone cum imperatoze
paleogolo neci dediti fuerant. sub Friderico tercio impatoze oia clarescent.

THE CITY

For almost a thousand years, Constantinople was the greatest city of the western and near-eastern worlds. In fact, for much of that period it was the only city around: Rome and Athens barely survived as smallish towns festering in the ruins of the barbarian invasions; Paris and London were rustic villages; Ctesiphon and Baghdad, briefly rivals of Constantinople in glory, were hardly known in Europe.

This perhaps explains the strange fascination that The City has held for the European (and Muslim) imagination throughout centuries. This was a city with a population hovering around one million, when the next biggest town in Europe barely approached 100,000. It has a market where, for a long time, the volume of trade probably exceeded all of Europe put together. It held regular public games and spectacles in the Hippodrome, at a time when the Greek theater and the Roman arena had fallen into disuse, with neither the opera nor football yet invented. It had a university, when the nearest thing the West could boast was a few monasteries where monks copied manuscripts and tended the goats. It had an extensive social security system, doling out free lunches and Hippodrome tickets to residents, as well as public baths and gymnasia to keep them fit. It had splendid palaces and administrative halls, an overgrown bureaucratic apparatus, and meticulous rules for court ceremonial and official procedure, at a time when the petty kings of Europe lived in dank forts and and got drunk with their boon companions. Much later, when European courts decided to civilize, they would turn to the Byzantine model—the only one then around—for their lessons in royal decorum and palatial glitter, with the compilation of Byzantine court manners by Emperor Constantine VII Porphyrogenitus (913-959) serving as the classic primer on palace etiquette.

The City claimed the most accomplished artists of the time. Many came from around the Empire occasionally to master the latest techniques, and to find the opportunities to exercise their mastery, in architecture and mosaics, in silk weaving and goldsmithry, in carpentry and music. Their work contributed much to the uniqueness of The City. It included The Church, the cathedral of Holy Wisdom—Hagia Sophia—which remained the world's largest man-made enclosed space for a thousand years. It included The Work of Art, now almost forgotten, the fantastic golden tree of the palace garden with its mechanical birds which sang separately and in harmony, of which medieval travelers have left awed descriptions.

Something of the impression that The City made on the mind of an European can be gleaned from Geoffroy de Villehardouin, nobleman of Champagne, a leader and chronicler of the 4th Crusade of 1204:

"All those who had never seen Constantinople before gazed very intently at the city, having never imagined there could be so fine a place in all the world. They noted the high walls and lofty towers encircling it, and its rich palaces and tall churches, of which there were so many that no one would have believed it true if he had not seen it with his own eyes, and viewed the length and breadth of that city which reigns supreme over all others....So many people had crowded on to the battlements that it seemed as if there could be no more left in the rest of the world put together."

The sentiments of a back-country hick first time to town!

...And the ruins: With the exception of Hagia Sophia which survives in some of its splendor, the visitor will find only ruined traces of that ancient glory in modern-day Istanbul. Byzantine Constantinople was wiped out before the Ottoman city once again rose from the ashes of the old site. Having already lost

Preceding page: a medieval vision of Constantinople. Left, the towering dome of the Hagia Sophia, or Holy Wisdom Church.

much of its civic vitality. The City was devastated in 1204 by the motley force of Italians and Frenchmen whose amazement has just been recorded. The Crusaders massacred a good portion of the population, looted almost all artwork and valuables, demolished the palace, and then put the rest of the city to the torch. The splendid quartet of bronze horses which topped the imperial box at the Hippodrome was removed to St. Mark's in Venice, where it incidentally became the model for most Western urban equestrian monuments. The Golden Tree was lost in the melee, and never heard of again.

The last two-and-a-half centuries of Byzantium offer the almost science-fiction aspect of a race of survivors crawling around the ruins of a destroyed civilization. The reconstituted "Empire" of 1261 barely reached beyond the suburbs of Constantinople. Devoid of funds, and with a population reduced to less than a tenth of its former numbers, little could be built, much less rebuilt. Instead, a principal method of raising money in this period seems to have been the sale of whatever could still be unearthed in the city in terms of treasure and artwork. After the Turkish conquest, Mehmet the Conqueror epigrammatized the sad state of the imperial city with the Persian verses of Saadi:

"The spider is curtain-holder in the palace of the Caesars
The owl hoots its night-call on the towers of Afrasiab."

The city recovered under Ottoman rule. But the Ottomans, with that peerless Oriental nonchalance, built solely to solve this or that urban problem, as it pressed itself, or to immortalize this sultan or that pasha, so far as his funds stretched. The ruins of the Byzantine city simply remained, and decayed further in the course of centuries, while swarms of the urban poor carved out a ramshackle existence among the de- **The ruins of the Tekfur Palace.**

bris. Columns and statues that adorned the avenues of Byzantium were used as mortar for the layers of shanties that each generation added on top of the old. The emperors' marble sarcophagi—some of them now displayed at the Archaeological Museum—turned up as doorsteps or washbasins. Colonnaded cisterns were used as thieves dens and weavers workshops. The marble benches of the Hippodrome provided a convenient quarry during the construction of the Blue Mosque. Until the 1930s no street names or numbers existed in the Old City, an impenetrable labyrinth of alleys and dead ends built around the dilapidated walls of some long-gone place or disused aqueduct. To this day, there is no reliable street map of the older part of Istanbul; and the Registry is a lawyer's nightmare, with some property titles going right back to the time of the conquest, and layers of contradictory claims piled on top.

Traces: One of the fascinations of visiting Istanbul is to take a random walk through the squalid maze of the Old City, armed with a volume of one of those 19th-century English gentleman-travelers or their more recent emulators. That garbage-infested massive shell, in some unlikely corner of Zeyrek, amid ancient wooden houses in various stages of collapse, still inhabited, turns out to be the formerly magnificent 12th-century church of the **Pantocrator**. This overgrown yard, with protruding bits of ancient masonry housing a workshop of dubious legal standing, right behind the Blue Mosque in the heart of the city, is part of **Justinian's Great Palace**. The low-lying area encircled by city walls at the far end of the Golden Horn, now a rustic slum with the occasional vegetable patch, used to be **Blachernae**, the imperial residence of the final centuries of Byzantium, of which Villehardouin is at a loss for words to describe the treasures of "gold and silver, table services and precious stones, satin and silk,

Mosaic of Christ and John the Baptist in the St. Sophia.

mantles of squirrel-fur, ermine and miniver, and every choicest thing to be found on this earth."

The remainders of Byzantium in Istanbul—with the exception of Hagia Sophia and the odd piece of brilliant mosaic—are not pretty. But they are rich in philosophical reflection. Wandering through the dusty carcass of old Constantinople, the visitor might even catch a glimpse of the spirit of this city, whose inhabitants hardly even grasp the (perhaps naive) Western faith in progress. Here, buildings and institutions signify, not permanence, but inevitable decay. And faced with the inevitability of decay, it ceases to make sense to invest for the future: one simply endures, building ramshackle and temporary solutions whenever the rotting structure threatens to become untenable.

The city of antiquity: In fact, the cycles of the city's fate extend far before the period of glory, collapse, and rebirth as outlined here. Byzantium was already a thousand years old at its refounding by Constantinople, and the city had seen more than its fair share of fortune and calamity. The city was first established in 658 B.C. as a colony of the Greeks from Megara, near Athens, although the name—which is not Greek—possibly suggests an earlier Thracian origin. It grew to be a wealthy city-state, and played key roles during the Persian Wars, the Delian League, and the Hellenistic era. While the city never reached the prominence of an Athens or Ephesus, its strategic position was such that to permit Polybius, the historian, to comment on the city's extraordinary potential some 570 years before Constantinople.

Byzantium was first sacked by the Iranians of Darius in 490 B.C. Gallic hordes appeared before the city gates in 278 B.C., on their way to their eventual settlement in the region of Ankara, and extorted a payment which ruined city finances for decades to come. Some of them settled on the hill across the har-

Traces of glory in modern rubble.

48

bor, which was thereafter called "Galata". In A.D. 196, Septimius Severus, the Tunisian soldier who had gotten himself crowned Roman Emperor, gave Byzantium its foretaste of the sack of 1204. He then went on to rebuild the city he had razed to the ground, renaming it Colonia Antonina for his son Antonius Caracalla. Germans tried their hand next, but the Visigothic attacks of A.D. 268 failed to breach the city walls. (The English came much later: Warings, a Saxon tribe related to the Angles, having already subdued Russia, attacked Constantinople in 860. They subsequently entered the imperial service as mercenaries, and were settled near the Kumkapi district. The tall, blond, fierce barbarians were much admired by Byzantine women.)

What remained of classical Byzantium was swept away under the grandiose building projects of Constantine. No trace exists now of the **acropolis** on the site of the Topkapi Palace, of the colonnaded **agora** which stood where

the Hagia Sophia Square is now, of the **pre-Roman city walls** which followed the present Babiali Avenue, of the **necropolis** which stretched from the Cemberlitas to the University grounds and the Süleymaniye. Statues and sarcophagi dug up at the necropolis are on display at Hall I of the Archaeological Museum. They indicate a level of civic refinement hardly equaled in "Byzantine" Constantinople, not to mention afterward.

The **Archaeological Museum** is situated in the Topkapi Palace Gardens. It contains a mind-blowing collection of antiquities from Byzantium and other sites around the Turkish Empire. It affords rich opportunities, again, to reflect on the sad regress of civilization from its peaks 2,000 years ago. For instance, there is the lovely *ephebos,* the statue of a young boy relaxing after exercise, with a tired, wistful smile on his face. One imagines him, along with probably a dozen others, adorning a public gymnasium in Tralles (now

The Aqueduct of Valens.

Aydin); the colossal Hercules, ripping a lion, with a very phallic fountain to fill the gap in the loins; the stern and haughty emperors, lining the streets of some obscure town in Asia Minor. One tries to imagine the **Baths of Zeuxippus**, near where the Museum stands now, with 60 bronze statues reputed to have been the finest in the Empire; or the mosaic-paved promenades of the capital, with marble likenesses of actresses and gods and senators, painted in rich color, standing every few paces. Then one returns to a world which has replaced porphyry colonnades with utility polls!

The city that Constantine built: Constantine's decision to have a new permanent capital built for the Roman Empire, around 324, coincides with the start of his thorough reorganization of the administrative structure of the Empire, and his decision to impose Christianity as the new state religion. It ends 150 years of intermittent civil war, during which provincial warlords ruled the Empire from various strongholds while the Senate pretended to function in Rome. (Constantine himself grew up in Diocletian's headquarters in Izmit, east of Istanbul, and assumed the purple in York, England.)

The building of New Rome was thus part of a grandiose project to reshape a world empire. It was also unprecedented as the wholesale and planned creation of a city to serve as the center of, more or less, the world. The scale of the construction lived up to the grandeur of the occasion. A city that equalled Rome in size and architecture was created within six years. The shortage of architects and artisans was solved by setting up schools in the most distant provinces of the Empire to train the most talented youths. And when the artistic talents of the age proved inferior to that of earlier generations, the ancient cities of Greece and Asia were ransacked for their most valuable monuments, their trophies and relics, to add to the glory of the new capital.

The archaeological museum.

Among those looted treasures, one can still see the **Serpentine Column**, which was originally erected in Delphi in 479 B.C. to commemorate the victory of united Greek republics against the Persians at Platea. It was replanted at midpoint on the spine of the **Hippodrome**, where it stands, less the three serpents' heads carrying the golden tripod dedicated to Apollo. (The tripod vanished in 1204; the last remaining snake served for target practice by the 21-year-old Mehmet the Conqueror in 1453.)

Next to it is the **Egyptian Obelisk** which was 1,900 years old when its top third was cut and moved to the present site in the year 390. The marble reliefs at its base carry scenes one was likely to observe then on this spot: race chariots used to turn (and occasionally overturn, with hints of foul play) beyond the rough pillar, formerly sheathed in bronze, that stands further down the spine.

The imperial box was at the opposite end, on the spot now occupied by the bus stop across the Divan Yolu. The benches seated 100,000. A covered promenade circled the top, liberally sprinkled with realistic statues of charioteers and gods and scenes from daily life. One can get a sense of the vastness of the structure, if not of its vanished elegance, by walking down the narrow streets off the south end, where the colossal rump of the Hippodrome juts above a jumble of apartment buildings.

The **Great Palace** was adjacent to the Hippodrome on the east. It extended down to the seashore as a labyrinth of public and private halls, porticoes and pavilions, churches, cloisters and corridors. Nothing but bits of worn masonry stand now, with perhaps only the Kremlin—a copy by a marginal civilization in an inferior age—to convey a picture of what it was once like. In 1933, an enormous expanse of delightful mosaic—probably the floor of an outer hall—was discovered 10 feet below the ground at the market behind the Blue Mosque. The **Mosaic Museum** that is

built around it must take top priority among the sights of Istanbul.

The main avenue of Constantine's city ran westward from the Hagia Sophia and the Hippodrome, exactly following the present Divan Yolu, and branched twice, just as it does now, at Beyazit and at Aksaray. It was porticoed all along, with arcades below, occupied by shops of uniform marble frontage, and terraced promenades above. Spacious plazas punctuated the avenue, the most splendid being the oval **Forum of Constantine**; which inspired Bernini for St. Peter's Square at the Vatican. **The Column of Constantine**—part of which stands as the Cemberlitas, burnt, broken, held by rusty iron rings, rising from the ground like the mast of a sunken ship—marked its center. It was once topped by a colossal statue of Apollo, possibly that of Phidias removed from Athens, doctored to look like Constantine, and the nails of the True Cross substituted for the rays of the Sun-god. It was unveiled

Specimen of pre-Byzantine manhood.

at the dedication of the city on May 11, 330, and fell during a hurricane in 1106.

Replicas of the principal Roman mansions were built along the avenue as part of a deal to attract senatorial families to the new city. One of the most famous was the **Palace of Lausus**, probably situated across the street from the Pudding Shop, which was later converted into a palace hotel for rich visitors. To increase its appeal, it was adorned with some of the greatest works of art of antiquity, including the Venus of Cnidos by Praxiteles, the Samian Hera by Lysippus, and the ivory and gold Zeus by Phidias from Olympia—as well as saints' relics and bits of the rock where Moses parted the waters.

The **university** used to stand precisely where the main gate of the Istanbul University is now, at Beyazit. The freshmen, known as "dupondii", used to be thrown in the fountain by upper-classmen, while the seniors fought duels and played practical jokes on the professors. The student hotel nearby contained a remarkable collection of brass insects by Apollonius of Tyana.

Further west, beyond the great food market at the present Sehzadebasi, Emperor Valens (364-378) completed the **great aqueduct** which still dominates the skyline of the city. It carried water, well until the 19th century, to the countless underground cisterns which still turn up everywhere in the Old City, to the chagrin of property developers. Two of the cisterns, **Yerebatan Sarayi** and **Binbirdirek**, can be visited. Hearing Mozart echo on the waters among the 336 columns of the restored Yerebatan ("the Sunken Palace") far below the din of the city is an experience probably unparalleled in the busy center of a comparable city.

The life of Constantinople: Within a century, the City of Constantine became the most populous city in the world. The city walls, which had scandalized pundits in 325 by their "preposterous" extent, had to be rebuilt during the reign of Theodosius II (408-450) about a mile beyond the original perimeter. The phenomenal growth occurred against a background of the epochal transformation that the founding of The City signaled in the first place. From the loose confederation of semi-independent city-states and client kingdoms that survived into late Antiquity, the Empire was now turning into a culturally and economically centralized monarchy. The stripping of the ancient cities of the Empire to deck out The City was, perhaps, a fitting symbol for the broader revolution that took place at the same time.

People, as a result, flocked to Constantinople. Laborers and artisans came in search of opportunities; veterans of Roman legions sought the anonymity of The City; provincial magnates moved from their increasingly marginal towns nearer the true seat of power, together with their retinues and protégés. "Greeks from all over the empire, hellenized Thracians, western-

ers from Italy and Africa, Latin-speaking Illyrians from the Balkans, Greek-speakers from Asia Minor, as well as others who still spoke one of the ancient tongues of that land, descendants of Hittites and Lydians and Lycians, Aramaic-speaking Syrians, Copts from Egypt, Armenians from the high plateau in the east, Jews, Goths and Herules and Gepids from the Germanic lands to the north; jostled one another in the streets and squares" of Constantinople.

For centuries, The City suffered the natural consequences of mass immigration: overpopulation, urban violence, political turmoil. Ancient economy could never find a satisfactory answer to the problem of employing such concentrated masses. Grand public works temporarily allayed the problem, but inevitably ran against a depleted imperial treasury and overtaxed provinces. To control the dangerous potential of unemployed crowds, a system of benefits was developed on an unprecedented scale. All residents of Constantinople were entitled to free rations of bread, meat, oil and wine, upon presenting a coupon at one of the more than 80 stations around the city. The wheat yield of the Nile basin was allotted to the capital. The resulting alienation of that country has been cited as a reason why that once-rich country went over to the Arabs in the 7th century. It is remarkable to note that the Ottomans maintained exactly the same system of feeding the city population, with Egypt once again serving as the capital's granary after its conquest by the Ottoman Turks in 1516.

Religion and faction: The drama of shaping a new official Creed out of an obscure eastern sect and the myriad local traditions of the Empire unfolded, primarily, in Constantinople: for several centuries it occupied the turbulent energies of its uprooted crowds and the political talents of its faction bosses.

A General Convention was called in Iznik to formulate a definition of the

Traces of Byzantine Art, hidden in an obscure arch.

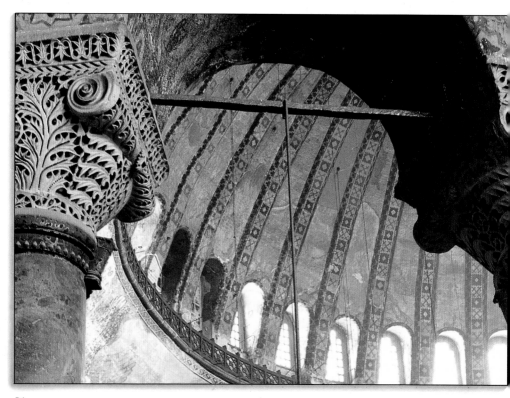

new Creed at the same time as construction began on the City; four of the six subsequent Councils, held to amend the original compromise, took place in the City itself or its suburbs; two moved elsewhere because factional balances within the City made it seem wiser. They combined the features of a constitutional convention and a party congress, including cheering crowds, street fights, and the occasional assassination or lynching. St. Gregory of Nyssa, then a young provincial intellectual from Kayseri, reports with amazement from The City in 381:

"The very workmen and slaves have become profound theologians, and preach in the streets. If you ask anyone for change he tells you how the Son differs from the Father; if you ask the price of a loaf you are told how the Son is inferior to the Father; and if you ask for a bath you hear how the Son is as nothing to the Father."

His friend St. Gregory Nazianzene consolidated the institution of the Patriarchate of Constantinople. For this he used a judicious dose of mass appeal and mob pressure, in a manner strangely reminiscent of the struggles over the people's tribunate in old Rome. Patriarch Paul was exiled and reinstated by clashing street factions no less than five times in 14 years. St. John Chrysostom managed to keep the crowds in a state of perpetual rioting during his tenure at the turn of the 5th century.

Many of the innumerable monasteries and churches that sprung up in The City maintained hostels for the homeless and kitchens for the poor. They provided security, solidarity, shelter, and perhaps employment for the bewildered immigrant; possibly taught him City ways and the Greek language; conceivably saved his son from youthful crisis and crime. In return, they commanded his unconditional loyalty, and harnessed it to the consolidation of their power and the expansion of their resources. Those bonds of loyalty survived through the more settled conditions of later centuries, acquiring an increasingly conservative tone as time went on. Every attempt to tamper with the prerogatives of Orthodox institutions invariably provoked the religious fury of the humble old quarters of the capital.

Remarkably, these traditions were then carried on—in a Muslim guise—to Ottoman times, and to some extent remain alive today. Even some of the localities remained the same: the Church of Holy Apostles, a center of Orthodox sentiment in Byzantium times, was gone; but the Fatih Mosque built on the same spot—and incidentally, incorporating 18 columns of porphyry and verde antique from the former edifice—replaced it as a Mecca of religious zeal in Istanbul.

At the races: Besides religion, the Hippodrome formed the other avenue of public expression, and entertainment, in Constantinople. At first frequently, later on twice a year until the year 1200, a large portion of the city population met there with the imperial family to cheer and shout slogans at the charioteers, to enjoy the music and animal shows and the parades paid for from the city budget. The *vox populi*, often clamorous and explosive, was heard on these occasions. Many magistrates and several emperors lost their offices, and sometimes their lives, on the Hippodrome steps; others built their careers through careful cultivation of organized Hippodrome crowds.

The Blue and Green factions, as well as the several lesser groups, were originally formed to provide charioteers and acrobats for the games. The fanatical solidarity they were able to elicit turned them into political forces to be reckoned with. Their cheerleaders could organize the frenzy of the crowds at the races; their support network in the wards of the city could whip up riots or empty the streets at will; their protection was sometimes essential for finding employment or safely operating a shop. The many Syrians and Armenians in the capital were possibly responsible for the pro-Monophysite sympathies of the Greens during the religious quarrels of the 5th century. The Blue street-gangs which terrorized the city in the 520s, with activists subscribing to the Hun fashion (hair cut short in front and grown long in the back; long moustache and beard; riding breeches), provided a convenient vehicle for the political ambitions of the young Justinian.

The support of the Emperor and his wife Theodora did not prevent the Blues from joining their rivals, in 532, in the great Nika revolt. The riots developed out of a Green demonstration in the Hippodrome. "Shut up you Jews, you heretics!" shouted the exasperated emperor; "Get out you murderer, you ass, you cheating tyrant!" retorted the Greens. Bungled police measures led to a general uprising, during which most of the imperial palace and the original church of Hagia Sophia were destroyed, and a rival emperor crowned. Justinian was saved from panic and an inglorious escape by the contemptous

determination of Theodora. He eventually regained the upper hand after the massacre of some 30,000 in the Hippodrome.

The Nika revolt—along with the massacre of Westerners in 1185, the mutiny of 1622, the rebellion of 1730, the suppression of the janissaries in 1826, and the riot of 1909—was among the most celebrated of the mob scenes that dot the chronicles of the City from the 350s through the 1970s. It captured the imagination of an age that had grown unfamiliar with the life of cities, and helped give a bad name to Byzantine politics, which was probably no more convulsive than, say, Paris, or more corrupt than New York in modern times.

The great church: The construction of a new church that would surpass every other building ever erected to the glory of God, and proclaim forever the greatness of the Empire, was begun within weeks after surpressing the Nika revolt. To the profane mind, the timing hints at

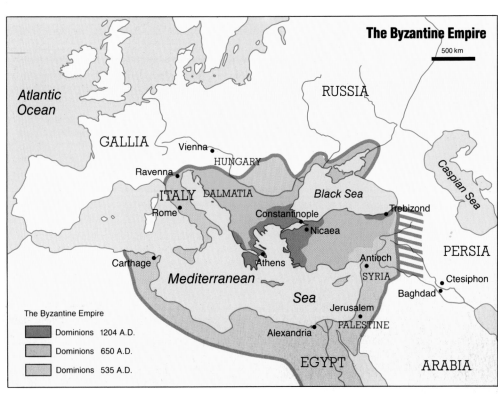

The Byzantine Empire

500 km

Atlantic Ocean

RUSSIA

GALLIA

Vienna

HUNGARY

Ravenna

ITALY DALMATIA

Rome

Black Sea

Constantinople

Trebizond

Nicaea

Caspian Sea

PERSIA

Carthage

Athens

Antioch

SYRIA

Ctesiphon

Mediterranean

Baghdad

Sea

Jerusalem

The Byzantine Empire

Dominions 1204 A.D.

Dominions 650 A.D.

Dominions 535 A.D.

Alexandria

PALESTINE

EGYPT

ARABIA

THE SECRET HISTORY

Basel, the stableboy from Thrace who became the companion of Emperor Michael by manipulating the eunuchs of the court, only to kill his lover in the bath and usurp the purple; Zoe, the spinster-empress who entered matrimonial bliss at age 50 with a bang, marrying three and erasing the mosaic faces of her successively jilted husbands from the walls of the St. Sophia...palace murders, blindings, outrageous torture chambers that would give a Roman pause, and a bureaucracy so self-serving as to deserve a new adjective: *Byzantine,* a word that has entered the languages of the world as a synonym for intrigue, dirty dealings and general corrupt civic behavior, conducted by a tiny elite in a manner which cannot possibly be comprehended by normal mortals.

Webster's, for example, defines the word as "*of, relating to, or characterized by a devious and usually surreptious manner of operation...*"

Clearly, not all Byzantine society was corrupt, but it is with difficulty that the historian searches for those aspects of late classical civilization which were not so described by contemporary historians themselves. A prime example is Procopious, the official historian of the Emperor Justinian, (483-565) under whom Byzantium reached the apogee of its architectural and artistic glory and territorial expansion. But while Procopious was lauding the emperor in public, he also maintained a diary annotating the sleazier aspects of the time. Here is what the (uncensored) Procopius has to say about a certain stage starlet of the day:

"For the time being Theodora was too undeveloped to be capable of sharing a man's bed or having intercourse like a woman; but she acted as a sort of male prostitute to satisfy customers, and slaves at that, who when accompanying their owners to the theater seized their opportunity to divert themselves in this revolting fashion....But as soon as she was old enough, she joined the women on the stage....Often she would go to a party with 10 young men or more, all at the peak of their physical powers and with fornication as their chief object in life, and would lie with all her fellow."

Procopius's fulminations might have just been disappeared as a rather imaginative example of late-Roman pornography but for the fact that the Theodora in question went on to become the mistress of a politician named Peter Sabbatius, known to the world by the name he took when crowned emperor: Justinian the Great.

Whether one chooses to believe Procopius' litany of accusations against Theodora or not, one fact does suggest that the historian was not just taking out his personal spleen on the empress: after sharing the throne with Justinian, the empress had a convent built on the Asiatic shore of the Bosphorus, at the very spot where the Military Academy now stands, for the benefit of her former colleagues in the world's oldest profession.

a policy of mass employment. It may also remind one of that perennial struggle in which the Byzantine State (and its Turkish successor) sought, without ever fully succeeding, to submit religion to its control.

The imperial temple was to accommodate a vast crowd within a cavernous space, and at the same time uplift its sentiments to the majesty of the universal Empire and the universal Church, united in their Sacred Wisdom. The best mathematician of the time, Anthemios of Tralles, was employed for the task. He devised, on the basis of rigorous theory, a design that was unprecedented in architectural history, and in some respects remains unrepeated since. A gigantic and daringly flat dome was placed, by the ingenious use of half-domes and arches, on four freestanding supports, seemingly without effort. This, enhanced by the light effects from high windows, created a stupendous sense of vastness and elevation in the interior. In terms of width, the dome of the Hagia Sohia was first equaled by Michelangelo, exactly a thousand years later, in the (much higher) dome of St. Peter's in Rome. Ottoman architects displayed an obsessive preoccupation with the problems posed by the Hagia Sophia: the many imperial mosques of the classical period can be read as so many attempts to improve on the design of the dome, in the distribution of support to subsidiary domes and arcs, or in the exterior grace of the ensemble.

The external appearance of the Great Church may be somewhat disappointing. It is heavy and squat, especially in comparison to the Ottoman masterpieces around it. The huge buttresses added in 867 to prop up the structure spoil the sense of elevation; the clumsy minarets appended by various sultans contribute a touch of incongruity.

It is in the interior that one can truly appreciate the splendor of the Hagia Sophia, and sense the boundless awe it inspired in medieval travelers. Its effect may be summarized by the reaction of the envoys of Vladimir of Novgorod, sent to Constantinople in search of a creed suitable for adoption in their master's primitive dominions. "We are bound to believe one is more than elsewhere in the presence of God, for the religions of all other countries are eclipsed by a grandeur which we ourselves will never forget." It may have been this recommendation that tipped the balance against Muhammadanism, and gained Russia to Byzantine Christianity.

This episode also underscores the crucial role that the Hagia Sophia played in projecting the image and prestige of imperial Byzantium. Its conversion into a mosque in 1453 had thus a profound significance for the Turks, as a symbol of their conquest and inheritance of the Empire. From the seat of the Byzantine patriarch, the Hagia Sophia was turned into the pulpit of the Turkish grand mufti; until 1916 Ottoman sultans, like Byzantine emperors before them, were consecrated

Preceding page: Byzantine ladies often ran the state from behind the throne, or on it. Left, mosaic of Christ in the Kariye Museum. Right, the apostles at the Kariye Museum.

here. The Turkish Republic, proclaiming the ultimate victory of its early attack on religious institutions, turned the building into a museum in 1935.

Some of the Byzantine mosaics that used to decorate the interior of the church were restored after its conversion into a museum. They are products of later eras, the original mosaics having been destroyed by inconoclasts during the 8th century. The strikingly beautiful trio of **Christ, the Virgin and John the Baptist** dates to the last, brief flowering of Byzantine art in the 1300s, and approaches the quality of the earliest palace mosaics. The composition involving **Empress Zoe** and her husband, on the other hand, is more notable for the fact that the husband in question (Constantine IX, 1042-1055) was the third to occupy this spot, his face replacing portraits of earlier consorts. Constantine reciprocated by elevating his mistress to the throne along with the wife. The happy threesome eventually retired to the reign of Zoe's elderly sister, also named Theodora.

Churches of the back streets: No other Byzantine church resembles the Hagia Sophia in conception or grandeur. The **Kariye** surpasses it in its art treasures; others, lacking either splendor or wealth, compensate by their simple charm and haunted setting. Some 18 secondary churches of the Byzantine origin still stand in the old city. With the exception of **St. Mary of the Mongols** (built 1261) in Fener, where one can still find a tiny congregation of elderly Greeks on an odd Sunday, all were converted into mosques at one time or another. Some remain in use as mosques; others have been placed under public administration but never converted into museums, left to decay in a limbo between desecrated mosque and abandoned restoration site. Except for St. Irene and the Kariye, no tourist crowds spoil their melancholy peace. Most are hard to find in the maze of old city neighborhoods; once found, there is no guarantee that the keeper will be

Old churches down side streets.

on hand, or disposed to unlock the gate. Still, the visitor is very much advised to seek out a few of the off-track churches: if not for the piece of broken inscription and tantalizing mosaic, then at least as a pretext to wander into those parts of ancient Byzantium that one would otherwise so easily miss.

St. Irene, located in the Palace gardens next to the Hagia Sophia, is easy enough to visit. It has been restored as a museum after having served many centuries as palace arsenal. Chamber music concerts are often held now under its bare vaults and arches which enclose a superb acoustic space.

The former church of **Saints Sergius and Bacchus** (Kücük Ayasofya), was built in 527 as a small prototype for the Hagia Sophia—a fact reflected in its Turkish name. Some will find its dilapidated, overgrown backyard more charming than the monumental courtyards of better-kept mosques.

The half-ruined 5th-century monastery of **St. John of Studion** (Imrahor Camii) takes that unkempt charm one step further. Among its ancient tombstones and gnarled trees, one looks for echoes of the dreaded monks who once, in their relentless struggle to maintain orthodoxy against imperial encroachments, made Studion one of the most powerful institutions of later Byzantium. Some Muslim faces from the neighborhood now may supply the looked-for clue into that dark and resentful spirit.

The 12th-century church of the **Pammakaristos** (Fethiye Camii) offers, for the intrepid wanderer who can actually locate it, the finest specimen of late Byzantine architecture in the city, as well as a superb view over the upper Golden Horn. A dozen other churches, both Byzantine and post-conquest (including that of the current Greek Patriarchate) are within walking distance here, a district that kept some of its Byzantine aspect until a hundred years ago.

The swansong of Byzantium: The church of **the Savior-in-the-Country** (Kariye Camii) is also located in this district. It is one of the most celebrated sights of Istanbul and a rival to the Hagia Sophia, if not in architecture, then in the spectacular treasure of mosaics and frescoes that it has managed to preserve. These date from 1315-321, when Theodore Metochites, Lord High Treasurer, had the church restored and partly rebuilt. They are among the greatest masterpieces of the late Byzantine school, whose expressive realism reflected the influence of Italian masters, and which in turn would come back to the West, through El Greco and others, to influence Renaissance styles. The tremendous scene of the **Resurrection** is a case in point. The **portrait of Metochites**, shown wearing an enormous turban while offering a model of the church to Christ, on the other hand, indicates the Turkish influence which held the balance against the Italians during this final period of Byzantium.

One of the (altogether more than 100) wallpaintings in the Kariye depicts **St. David the Dendrite** who spent three years on his almond tree in Salonica. Dendrites, like stylites who preferred to live on columns, were a familiar sight of Byzantine life. The **Column of the Goths**, still intact in the Topkapi gardens, was a particularly popular spot, with one Daniel who occupied it during the 10th century becoming a favorite saint of the Constantinopolitans. Several dendrites lived perched on trees, surrounded by adoring disciples, near the spot on the Bosphorus where, much later, the American College in Rumeli Hisar would offer another form of splendid isolation.

The crumbling walls: From the Kariye, it is only a short walk to **the city walls**, which for a millennium-and-a-half stood next only to the Hagia Sophia in inspiring the awe of visitors to Constantinople. As late as 50 years ago, a writer considered them "one of the greatest sights of Europe." They still do not fail to impress; but choked by the traffic of the peripheral highway and the industrial districts that have grown around it, they seem to be on the verge of finally succumbing, after having proudly withstood countless barbarian waves through the ages.

The walls extend some 11 miles (19 km), enclosing the city within the limits that defined it from the time of Theodosius to about a hundred years ago. Only vestiges remain on the Sea and Golden Horn fronts; but the massive belt with 96 towers on the land side, although cracked and collapsed in places, overgrown with fig-trees, or built-over with ancient and tottering houses, is still the wall that was built 1,500 years ago. One of the best views of it can be had from the fortress-jail of **Yedikule** (an Ottoman addition) near the sea corner. The gypsy quarter between **Vatan Caddesi** and the **Edirne Gate** offers one of the least damaged and picturesque stretches. Further north in a wide bulge lie the scattered remains of the **Blachernae Palace**. The former imperial residence called **Tekfur Sarayi**, lo-

cated at its edge, deserves a visit for its elaborate brick-and-marble facade. It was within this gutted enclosure, then used as a royal menagerie, that the Englishman Fynes Moryson in 1597 became the first European to see the strange creature that Turks called *zürafa*, or "graceful one", which he mispronounced and called "giraffe."

It was also here that Constantine XI, last Ceasar of the Roman Empire, set out for a final, hopeless stand on a May day in 1453. He was last seen charging on foot against Turkish soldiers that poured over the battlements near the Edirne Gate. His Empire had already been reduced to the bare shell of these walls. It had continued to exist for the last hundred years practically at Turkish sufferance. His army consisted of the Genoese, who dominated the city from their colony across the Golden Horn, building the mighty Tower of Galata at a time when the Emperor lacked the funds to repair the leaking roof of his palace, and the Catalans, who pillaged the city and sold its citizens into slavery when not fighting for it. Emperors had flirted with Roman Catholicism since their return to the city after 1204, and finally adopted it in 1438 in a last-ditch attempt to rally European support.

Their disgusted vassals went over to the Turks in droves. The Hagia Sophia, reconsecrated as a Catholic cathedral, was shunned by the Greek population of the city. Public opinion, murmured by the monks of the Studion and voiced by imperial dignitaries, had preferred "the turban of the Turk to the mitre of a cardinal."

Once the days of pillage were over, the abbot of the Studion was consecrated Orthodox Patriarch of Rome by the turbaned Conqueror. The people of Constantinople, whether converted to the dominant creed or content to stay within the sphere delimited for them as Christians, carried with them much of the institutions, habits, and culture of old Byzantium into the newly resplendent Empire.

Left, crumbling city walls, soon to be restored. Right, farmers in the fields before the Edirne Gate.

SURVIVORS

The stately mansions and 19th century rowhouses of the **Fener** district in the old city now provide shelter for the poorest of the immigrants from Southeastern Turkey. The steep, marble-staired streets are crowded with peasant children and colorful clotheslines. The Orthodox **Patriarchate of Constantinople**, once the rival of Rome for the leadership of the Christian world, is tucked away in an unpretentious church on a side street. The ruined **Palace of Dimitrie Cantemir**, Prince of Moldavia and father of the Rumanian national revival in the 18th century, is marked by a darkened inscription in French. The surreal brick-and-granite hulk of the **Greek National School** towers above the hill, doggedly clinging to life with its 5 remaining pupils. This is the district which once housed the wealthiest Greeks of Istanbul, and where dreams of a revived Byzantine Empire remained the currency of political life until the 20's of this century.

The Greeks of the city, who have retained the appellation of "Romans" to the present time, enjoyed both numbers and power under Ottoman rule. Mehmet the Conqueror needed their help in restoring the prosperity of his capital. He resettled a large number of them, not only former Constantinopolitans but colonies from Greece, Cappadocia, and Trebizond as well, in various districts of the city. Between a quarter and a third of the population of Istanbul spoke Greek and professed Orthodox Christianity until the fall of the Ottoman Empire.

The Patriarchate was restored soon after the conquest as an important tool of imperial policy. The Patriarch was granted extensive powers as the leader of the Orthodox "nation", which included Bulgarians, Serbians, Rumanians, Albanians and Georgians as well as Greeks. He presided over the Holy Synod and later the lay "national" assembly; he might levy taxes for his own community and controlled his own police. His Tribunal acted as the final court of appeals in cases arising between Orthodox subjects of the Sultan. (Similar privileges were afterwards granted to the Armenians and Jews.

Commercially emancipated by the abolition of concessions granted to Italians by later Byzantine emperors, the Greeks prospered. Aristocracy of Fener, the "Phanariote" families of Byzantine descent, the Paleologues and Cantacuzenes, the Mavrocordati, Ypsilanti and others, amassed fabulous fortunes and maintained a vigorous political life in the best Byzantine traditions. From 1669 on, the post of the Dragoman of the Porte, in effect the Ottoman Foreign Ministry, belonged to a Greek of the Roumanian principalities. Starting with 1716, governorships were regularly auctioned off to Phanariotes. Their courts became centers of Greek social and intellectual life, and contributed to the revival of the Greek national idea toward the end of the 18th century.

The creation of the small Greek state in 1828, paradoxically, dealt the final blow to dreams of a renewed Eastern Empire. The last, quixotic Greek attempt to regain Constantinople foundered in the Turkish resurgence of 1922. During the first Cyprus crisis of 1964, most of the remaining 100,000 survivors of Byzantium were summarily deported. The few sections of the city which seem to have so far withstood the onslaught of the times (for instance Arnavutköy, Emirgan and Kuzguncuk on the Bosphorus, and the Heybeli Island) owe their remaining charm, by a strange quirk of fate, to the fact that property belonging to the deportees was placed under moratorium, and has stayed in a legal twilight-zone ever since.

Demetrius, Oecumenical Patriarch, inheritor of the throne of St. John Chrysostom, now presides over a dwindling flock of 4000. A Byzantine eagle, its double head representing the temporal and spiritual might of the universal Empire, looks down in forlorn mockery upon the peeling walls of the Patriarchal chapel.

Right, Pope John Paul at the Patriarchate in Fener.

JEAN BRINDESI DEL

KOULOUK NEFERI	KETZELI	ODA BASCHI	KOULOUK BARIAKTARI
Janissaire de Corps de Garde.	Officier payeur du 25ᵉ batⁿ	Chef de Chambrée.	Sous-Offᵉ de Corps de Garde

OTTOMAN ISTANBUL

The Empire on the borders of Europe: Within the century following the conquest of Constantinople, the Ottoman state grew into the most formidable superpower of the old world. Its territories extended farther than the Eastern Roman Empire at the peak of its power. A thousand years after Justinian, the petty kingdoms of Europe once again cowered before the danger of being swallowed by an empire ruled from the shores of Bosphorus. At the fall of Byzantium, the Sultan invited what he called "governors of Rome and Frankistan" to submit to his will and become his vassals.

The ultimatum was driven home as country after country fell like so many dominoes: Greece, Serbia and Albania were taken by 1468; the Rumanian principalities submitted at the turn of the century; Croatia and most of Hungary became Ottoman dominions in 1526. Eastward, the elimination of the remaining Turkish and Greek states of Anatolia was followed by the conquest, in one fell swoop, of Syria, Palestine, and Egypt in 1516-17.

Nothing came out of the first siege of Vienna in 1528, but Turkish cavalry put the fear of God in the heart of German princes by their raids into Bavaria and Bohemia and following years. Ottoman privateers controlled the north coast of Africa, and almost squeezed the Spanish and the Venetians out of the Mediterranean.

The Sultans put their military muscle to diplomatic use as well. For a while they even pursued an alliance with France against the Hispano-Austrian empire of Charles V. It must be recognized, however, that they failed to cash in their armed strength to become a true regional superpower; to translate their power *against* European states into a power *among* and *over* them; to convert fear into loyalty and menace into influ-

ence. This had much to do with the difference of religion; in part it was also due perhaps to the cultural barriers, that is to say the mutual ignorance, that separated Muslim Turks from Christian Europe. As a result, a concentration of power that Europe had not witnessed on its borders since the 540s and would not witness again until 1804 or 1945, remained something marginal and alien to its history. What else "might have been" is best expressed by a remarkable document that Pope Pius II addressed to Mehmet II shortly after the Conquest:

"Be converted to Christianity," wrote the Pontiff, "and accept the faith of the gospel. Once you have done this there will be no prince on the whole earth to outdo you in fame or equal you in power. We shall appoint you emperor of the Greeks and the Orient, and what you have now obtained by violence and, hold unjustly, will be yours by right. Many will submit to you voluntarily, appear before your judgement seat, and pay taxes to you.... The Roman

Church will embrace you in the same love as other kings, and all the more so accordingly as your position is higher."

The proposal was never a terribly realistic one, but it is tantalizing to imagine the possible consequences of a restored East-West Roman Empire that its acceptance would have undoubtedly meant!

Europe strikes back: As it was, no accommodation was ever reached, and the Ottoman Empire was locked in a perpetual and damaging cycle of warfare against European states throughout the centuries of its rise and decline.

For a while—some would say until the disaster of Lepanto in 1571, or perhaps until as early as 1528 or as late as the second failure at the gates of Vienna in 1683—the balance seemed to favor the Ottomans. But by that time Europe had already undergone the great economic and cultural transformations that would soon launch it on the path toward dominating the globe. Eventually the tide turned, and the Turkish wave began

to recede after 1683 as spectacularly as it had earlier expanded. Provinces were lost; sea power was relinquished; and by sometime during the first quarter of the 19th century the empire came to the point of utter collapse. That it survived another 100 years was strictly due to the exigencies of European power politics. England and Russia took turns (to be replaced eventually by Germany) to prop up and forcefeed the terminal "sick man on the Bosphorus" so as to prevent each other from grabbing his legacy.

Ottoman elites from the Sultan downward adapted themselves to new realities, and took on the role of manipulating one or the other European power, pleading that the empire "deserved" to be preserved by Europe, striving to prove themselves worthy of belonging to Europe. For a brief and fascinating interlude culminating with the Allied occupation of 1918-1922, the capital, if not the sullen provinces, seemed to have at last become an inte-

The Ottoman Empire

The Ottoman Empire

- Dominions in 1323 A.D.
- Dominions in 1451 A.D.
- Farthest extent of Ottoman power (c. 1600)
- Turkish Republic

gral part of Europe—succeeding in debility what it failed to achieve through strength.

Turkish attitudes to the outside world are still shaped by this history of conquest and failure to dominate, defeat, capitulatory zeal, and perceived betrayal. Culturally, the country has much in common with the Muslim societies of Asia. But one is surprised to find here an almost complete ignorance and indifference with regard to the Eastern leg of this so-called bridge between continents, and instead a preoccupation with the West that borders on the obsessive. Lurking just below the surface of the unfailing Turkish friendliness, one may discern the undercurrents of pride and regret, fascination and resentment, emulation and envy toward the elusive adversary/master/friend that has been the West.

In quest of unity: Was the failure simply a matter of the overwhelming progress of the West, or did the Ottoman system somehow contribute to its own decay? Why were Turks unable to keep, if not their apparent superiority, then at least a degree of parity with the West? The questions keep forcing themselves on the visitor, as he/she compares the "third-world" reality of today's city with the unmistakable signs of a past of wealth and confident power at every step and turn.

Prior to the capital of Istanbul, the Ottoman state was still an offshoot of the semi-nomadic band of Turkish raiders who originally started it at the end of the 13th century. They had been settled by the Seljuk rulers of Anatolia in the borderlands near Bursa. They took advantage of the chaotic state of Byzantine provinces following the return of the emperors to Constantinople after the disaster of 1204 to expand their sphere of domination in northwest Anatolia and Thrace. Turkish adventurers, Muslim religious fraternities and disgruntled Greek noblemen joined their bandwagon, lured by the opportunities of chivalry and conquest. Each confederate led his own troops into

battle, and received provinces and fortresses in return. The sultan was not much more than a first among companions: he lived simply, often without a fixed residence, and ruled by consensus. And his reign was marked by recurrent internal feuds and wars of succession that brought the dynasty more than once to the brink of disintegration.

With the conquest of Byzantium, Mehmet II inherited a great empire with its millennial prestige and traditions. It gave him and his successors—Beyazid II (1481-1512), Selim the Grim (1515-1520), and Süleyman the Magnificent (1520-1566) the opportunity to establish a lasting order over vast territories following centuries of feudal chaos. During their age of glory, the four great sultans undertook to create one of the most thoroughly centralized ruling machines in history.

The total state and its capital: A striking feature of the imperial order was its hostility to any form of established power and privilege beside that of the

Engraving of Süleyman the Magnificent.

state. This—in marked contrast to Europe—checked the emergence of a hereditary nobility. It also gave the empire an extraordinarily egalitarian aspect. The sultan appeared, above all, as the protector of his subjects, to a remarkable extent regardless of status, wealth, or creed, against the encroachments of the mighty and the entrenched. His annals record an incredible preoccupation, not so much with war, as with the day-to-day administration of the minutest aspects of the life of his people.

They dealt with justice: in keeping with both Turkish and Byzantine traditions, the sultan was regarded as ultimately responsible for "the poorest widow and the weakest orphan" in his empire.

The palace regulated the economy in a meticulous and authoritarian manner, with priority given to the protection of the consumer as opposed to producer and merchant. Prices, manufacturing methods, shipping procedures were set down by law to the infinitesimal detail. The monarch took a direct interest in the quality of yogurt and sherbet sold in the market, the ingredients that went into candles, the standard temperature of hamams, and the hazard posed by chickens in flourmills.

The grand vezir, and often the sultan himself in disguise, personally inspected the markets, searching for irregularities of production distribution, of quality and price.

This single-minded concern with central control required a civil service of huge dimensions. When that grew unwieldy, further layers were added to control, inspect, and reinspect the bureaucracy. Everything was recorded. Ottoman archives are one of the greatest achievements of this civilization: all property, all actual and potential sources of income in every part of the empire were inventoried. Taxes to feed the system were laid down on this basis from the capital. The sultan's treasury strived to gather all, and redistribute all,

Left, miniature of Turkish conquests and right, Sultan observes acrobat.

according to single-voiced imperial policy.

Istanbul, the seat of the huge control machinery, once again grew in leaps and bounds, in a way strikingly similar to its growth after 325 and with similar consequences. Troops and scribes with their retinues were followed by the merchants and artisans who catered to their needs, then by immigrants of all descriptions who flocked to the capital to participate in its glory and its opportunities. Muslim Turks and Arabs, Albanians, Bosnians and Tatars were joined by Christian Greeks and Armenians who accounted for almost a third of the population, and Jewish refugees from Spain who made up 10%. The population went up to 70,000 during the reign of the Conqueror, and reached 500,000 toward 1550. At the end of the 16th century, Istanbul was once again the largest city in the world with 700,000 souls.

Imperial arts: Ottoman culture reflects admirably the spirit of the bureaucratic and egalitarian empire. Absent were a vigorous nobility with competing courts, independent and powerful social institutions, or a proud, aggressive middle class: so also independent and original works of philosophy, of social and religious theory, or political speculation. Literature—with a few exceptions—is, frankly, barren.

Illustrative arts, already constrained by the Islamic uneasiness with regard to human representations, was further hampered by the fact that the sole potential patron/buyer of art was the imperial palace. Ottoman miniatures, while interesting and often lovely, never reach the exquisite refinement of their Persian models.

Calligraphy, on the other hand, is altogether worthy of a society that took its writing and registering seriously. Three museums in Istanbul—the permanent display at Topkapi Palace, Ibrahim Paşa Museum by the Hippodrome, and the Museum of Turkish and Islamic Arts near Süleymaniye—con-

Left, miniature of Sultan Süleyman, and right, miniature of Harem women in bath.

tain splendid collections of Ottoman art. Their greatest treasures are neither divine representations, or paintings of noble or ordinary life, but…imperial edicts done to the perfection of calligrapher's art! One has to see them to realize that the artist's brilliance can be expressed as finely in a well-drafted property deed or tax report as in any Biblical scene that conventional Western art in the same period chose as its medium.

Theater, in the absence of a privileged class to enjoy and support high drama, developed in the direction of popular entertainment. The traditional Karagöz shadow-play reached levels of bawdiness that would make Shakespeare blush. But the supreme form of Ottoman theater should perhaps be sought in the ceremonial display of imperial pomp that sultans regularly put up to the delight of commoner and dignitary alike. The procession of the sultan to the mosque on Fridays, the public festivities held at the Hippodrome for weeks at an end at the circumcision of princes, the majestic ceremonies performed on imperial births and accessions and the reception of ambassadors have been recorded among the most memorable features of Ottoman culture by both locals and visitors. A brilliant account is left by de Busbecq, envoy of Francis I at the court of Süleyman the Magnificent:

"Around the sultan stood officers of high rank, troops of the imperial guard, the janissaries…an immense crowd of turbans with innumerable layers of the whitest silk, the brilliant costumes of every form and color, and the shine of gold, silver, silk, and satin all around. Words cannot convey a true idea of this strange spectacle. I have never seen anything so beautiful.... The janissaries, lined up apart from the other troops, were so motionless and silent that at first I thought them to be statues, until they at once inclined their heads in response to my salutation."

Decorative arts, especially those

Ottoman city as seen by a European artist.

CONSTANTINOPOLITANÆ VRBIS EFFIGIES AD VIVUM EXPRESSA,

CONSTA

connected with the Palace, reached a level of great mastery. Chief among them was the art of glazed tiles (çini), originally acquired from China and perfected at the imperial workshops in Iznik. The best can be admired in Topkapi Palace and some of the mosques, notably that of Rüstem Paşa, and constitute one of the highlights of a visit to Istanbul.

Civic architecture was also split between an exquisite showpiece of the Topkapi complex and the shops and homes of simple folks—mostly of wood, and no longer standing—with few "noble houses" and private monuments to fill the gap in between. The only field that offered the opportunities for a relative artistic freedom was that of religious architecture. It was in the countless mosques and the associated tombs and seminaries that the Ottoman architect found an outlet for his genius. The spectacular results deserve to be treated in a separate section.

Servants of the sultan: The center-piece of the imperial system were the *kapikulu*, the "servants of the Porte"—imperial slaves trained for the highest military and administrative posts of the realm. Reflecting the Ottoman distrust of any basis of privilege or power independent of the sultan, they were recruited neither from a hereditary class, nor from the ranks of the Islamic institutions or the companions of the early sultans. They owed their sole allegiance, and often their life, to the sultan: they were his creatures. Technically, they could neither hold property under ordinary law, nor enjoy the protection of ordinary courts. Some amassed fabulous fortunes; others held sway over continents: but it took only the displeasure of the sultan for them to lose all—power, property, and often life as well.

The most important military component of the *kapikulu* was the elite corps of janissaries, or "new troops". Janissaries were—at least initially—levied as young boys from Christian families subject to the sultan; raised as Muslims;

encouraged to abandon all ties with their past; then recruited into a praetorian career. They were known for their fanatical esprit de corps, and equally fierce loyalty to the sultan—in any case so long as he kept them in good humor and in good coin.

The brightest among janissaries-to-be, as well as promising slave boys captured by pirates or sent from the provinces, were selected for training at the schools of Inner Court (*Enderun*) and Outer Court (*Birun*) at Topkapi Palace. Most ministers, governors, and army commanders rose from their ranks through rigorous criteria of merit, much remarked by European visitors of the time.

Few were ethnic Turks; fewer came from backgrounds of any prominence. Ibrahim, the greatest of Süleyman's grand vezirs, was a janissary of Greek origin: his palace beside the Hippodrome, now converted into a fantastic museum of Turkish arts, gives a hint of the might he came to enjoy. Sokollu

Mehmet, who in effect ruled the empire under three successive sultans, was a Bosnian peasant. Others were Georgians and Russians, Arabs and Ethiopians, even the occasional Italian and Frenchman. Many are known simply as yet another Mehmet or Abdullah: no family names, no titles to indicate origin or background—the almost anonymous servants of the sultan who rose through merit, and were discarded once they rose far enough.

Dynastic degeneration: The sultans' determination to eradicate all sources of privilege beside their own acquired a terrifying, and eventually self-destructive aspect when applied, logically, to the dynasty itself. Chastened by the dynastic squabbles of his ancestors, Mehmet II instituted the rule whereby all surviving brothers of a sultan were executed at his accession. Mehmet III, for one, had to dispose of 19 brothers in this fashion. When this produced fratricidal wars among desperate princes under each of the succeeding three

Artist's view of the entrance to the Topkapi.

reigns, the further measure was taken to keep all heirs to the throne under lock and key in a gilded cage within the Topkapi Palace harem. The splendidly tiled and glazed suite that once held Ottoman heirs is now open to visit. Osman III (1754-57) passed 50 years here in the company of odalisques and deaf-mutes, and when he emerged he had all but lost the power of speech. Süleyman II (1687-91) was buried for 39 years copying and illuminating the Quran. Throughout his brief subsequent reign he begged continually to be restored to the peace of his prison. Selim III (1789-1807) came out after 15 years with what can only be termed a seething hostility toward the institutions of the state he was supposed to uphold.

Potentially as worrisome as brothers were in-laws, who might one day claim their share of power, or at least dignity, as imperial forebears and cousins. With the exception of one or two, therefore, no sultan bothered to get formally married, or dallied with any woman whose status in life might require formal treatment. Hürrem (known to Europeans as Roxelane), who exercised supreme power during the dotage of her husband Süleyman the Magnificent and the debauchery of her son Selim the Drunk (1566-78), was a Russian slave brought at the market. Selim acquired his beloved Nurbanu, a Jewish girl, by the same means. Kösem Mahpeyker, who built the New Mosque at Eminönü under the reigns of a husband (Ahmet I, 1603-17) and two sons (Murat IV, 1623-40, and Ibrahim, 1640-48), was the orphan of a Greek village priest. Naksidil, who gave birth to Mahmud II (1808-39), was in fact—probably— Aimee de Rivery, a French creole of Martinique who was carried away by Algerian pirates. Her graceful mausoleum adorns the courtyard of the Fatih mosque.

Death of an empire: One enthusiastic American author states that "human history has never known a political institution that for so long was so thoroughly dominated by government." For the span of one brilliant century, this characterization comes close to the truth. Then, the oppressive logic of the all-encompassing state begins to collapse under its own weight. The bias toward the consumer end up stifling innovation and investment. The systematic leveling of society extinguishes provincial magnates and civic notables, and with them all vestiges of economic and cultural vitality in the provinces. The traveler in Ottoman provinces is struck by the absence of any significant work of architecture (outside the capital) from the 1550s to the 1830s, while the pre-Ottoman period of chaos is one of rich building activity. Istanbul continues to flourish through the early 17th century, but cannot maintain its splendor for long as the provinces decay. The lifeblood of the empire seems to recede in ever-closing circles from the provinces to the capital, then to the citadel of the Topkapi palace, then finally to the inner sanctuary of the harem.

The young Sultan Ahmet.

THE PALACE OF THE SULTANS

For almost 400 years Topkapi Palace was the stage for the rise and subsequent decay of the Ottoman Empire. It was from within these walls that powerful armies were sent into Europe and Asia, where great and despicable sultans ruled, and others were imprisoned, driven mad, or slain—an expanse of buildings that housed one of the world's most absolute monarchies. Today, the corridors and paths are empty of the people who inhabited them, but the buildings remain, redolent of history, a museum containing the finest treasures and foulest memories of the Ottomans.

Located at the confluence of the Bosphorus, Golden Horn, and the Sea of Marmara, covering the first of the seven hills of Old Istanbul, the palace is hard to beat in terms of beauty of situation. The grounds extend down to the sea. Some of the most beautiful pavilions once used to line the shore before they were razed to build the railroad line in the 1840s. The extensive outer gardens are now shared by a military garrison and the rather sordid municipal **Park of Gülhane**. But the main compound sprawling at the top of the hill remains one of the most extraordinary sights of Istanbul, and possibly of the world.

Construction was begun by Mehmet the Conqueror, at the site where the acropolis of the pre-Roman city once stood. But the harem and the full-time living quarters of the sultan were not moved here until some 80 years later during the reign of Süleyman and the ascendancy of Roxelana. The buildings that actually date to Mehmet's time are only the **Treasury** section and the charming **Tile Pavilion** (Çinili Kösk) located in the outer gardens and accessible by the Gülhane park entrance. Other buildings were added in haphazard fashion over the centuries to fit the needs, the fancy, and the fashion of the times. The **Harem** in its present form belongs mostly to the reign of Murat III (1574-95), with additions by Mehmet IV (1648-87) and Osman III (1754-57). The finest buildings in outer courts are the contributions of Murat IV (1623-40) and Ahmet III (1703-30). The wholly incongruous **Mecidiye Pavilion** dates to the time of Abdülmecid (1839-61).

The walled-in compound is organized roughly around four successive courtyards, each more exclusive and sacrosanct than the last. It grew in the spirit of the Kremlin or the Heavenly City of Peking, as a town-within-a-town that housed the private quarters of the monarch as well as the halls and offices of state, the barracks of pretorian guards, and the residences of royal relatives and retired servants. No less than 5000 people lived and worked in Topkapi, not to mention the peacocks, giraffes and panthers that once roamed its extensive grounds.

Courtyards, treasures and kiosks: Bab-i Humayun (the Imperial Gate, located near the Hagia Sophia and next to the ornate marble fountain built in 1728 by Ahmet III), **Bab-us Selam** (Gate of Peace), and **Bab-us Saade** (Gate of Felicity) are the entrances to the first three courtyards of Topkapi, respectively. Each had a specifically defined function in the elaborate court ceremonial. (**Bab-i Ali**—the Sublime Porte—which was once a synonym for the Ottoman government, is opposite the Gülhane Park entrance on Alay Köskü street. It used to be the gate of the Grand Vezir's compound.)

The outer courtyard was once (before it was converted to a bus parking lot) a meeting and exercise grounds for the Janissary corps. The sultan's hunting masters, halberdiers, guards, and protocol officers also had their offices here. The palace proper began (as the museum begins now) at **Bab-us Selam**, which Süleyman the Magnificent modeled after the Central European castles he saw during his Hungarian campaigns. **The second courtyard** behind it was where ceremonial processions and state banquets were held, and top officers of the state could be petitioned. The Sultan's council met four times a week for 400 years at **Kubbealti** ("Hall under the Dome") which stands to the left. The sultan never attended these meetings, but could observe proceedings through a secret gallery; Vezirs who drew his ire were intercepted at Bab-us Selam to have their heads displayed later at the **Executioner's Fountain**.

Nicer objects are now displayed at the former kitchens, stalls, office rows etc, that line the second and third courtyards. Beside collections of imperial carriages, weapons, and costumes, they include one of the world's most impressive collections of

Ming and Ch'ing dynasty porcelains, and an extraordinary selection of Turkish and Persian calligraphy and miniatures on permanent loan from other museums. The best-known display, though, is the **Imperial Treasury**. The wealth of precious stones and jewelry is fully in the spirit of Ebenezer Scrooge, but the artistry in some cases is of surpassing beauty. Note, for example, the pearl-studded **throne** presented by Nadir Shah of Persia. The famed **Topkapi dagger** was intended as a return gift, but remained undelivered by Nadir's untimely overthrow. The giant **Kaşikçi diamond**, named after the spoonmaker who sold it for a few pen-

nies, was probably discovered by him in the debris of the Palace of Blachernae.

The third courtyard housed the *Enderun*, the school of Sultan's servants who rarely left the premises except to take high offices of the state. They were overseen by the White Eunuchs, castrated Caucasian slaves whose gelded chief was often the second most powerful man of the realm. The sultan held his Friday audience at the decorated **Hall** which stands near the entrance of the courtyard. The **Mosque of the White Eunuchs** is now used, together with the **Library of Ahmet III** adjacent to it, to house the Topkapi collection of some 20,000 manuscripts.

The **Chambers of the Holy Relics** contain the paraphernalia that once served as the ultimate ideological justification of the Ottoman state. Until the end of the Ottomans, the sacred relics were revealed with appropriate ceremony only once a year, on the "Night of Power" in the month of Ramadan, to the Sultan and the Grand Mufti alone. The only chance others got to see them was when **the Prophet's mantle, banner and swords** were hauled out on the occasion of a Holy War. The relics now on display include, in addition to these, some 60 **strands of the Holy Beard**—many kept in jeweled boxes of exquisite workmanship,—a **Holy Tooth**, a **Holy Footprint**, and several **letters** attributed to Muhammad. For the more profanely inclined, the tileworks of the Chambers— easily the most impressive in the palace compound—provide sufficient grounds to make the pilgrimage along with a yearly 1.5 million awed believers.

The fourth courtyard is a raised terrace that was a private area for the sultan and his (male) companions. It holds six freestanding kiosks or pavilions. The **Revan and Bağdad Kiosks**, built in the 1630s to commemorate victories of Murat IV, are arguably the two most exquisite corners of Topkapi. The intricately tiled **Circumcision Hall** and the baldachined marble **terrace** built for royal dinners were contributed by Ibrahim (1640-48).

The Harem: "They entered the Harem, those women of unearthly beauty, languor and grace, those rarest of human flowers.

They passed within that blank and mocking wall, they flitted from room to room, and yet on earth none of them is even a shadow now." In the Harem, several hundred select beauties languished and intrigued for the attentions of the sultan, crown princes awaited the fateful day when they would either ascend the throne or die, black eunuchs nursed the rage of impuissant love. Few who went in ever came out again; few of the royal daughters and discarded concubines (often presented to the harems of favorite pashas), or the rare doctors and repairmen who made a call ever broke their vow of silence. Life in the Harem was shrouded in

Their master, rising through the ranks, could enjoy even greater power than his white counterpart who was reserved for outer-court duty. The other power-holder in the Harem, the queen-mother, lived in the **Valide Sultan's Suite**, which is strategically located between the apartments of the Sultan and his ranking concubines. It was here that Kösem Mahpeyker ruled the empire through the reigns of two sons, and was strangled in 1648 by the orders of a daughter-in-law. Also here, Selim II was murdered in 1808, while the future Mahmut II escaped death by hiding in a cupboard. (He abandoned Topkapi for good as soon as he ascended the

total mystery for centuries, and the compound was first fully opened to visitors in the 60s. Even now, less than a tenth of its 400 rooms are included in the standard tour.

The Harem can only be toured in groups which start according to a posted schedule at the former utility entrance at the second courtyard. One first enters through the **quarters of the black eunuches**—Sudanese slaves who governed the sultan's household.

Left, outside the Harem. Above, inside one of the baths of the Harem.

throne.)

The sultan entertained his ladies in the grand **Hünkar Sofasi** (Imperial Hall), while musicians made discreet music on the mezzanine. Nearby, the crown prince lived in sequestered luxury in the **Veliaht Dairesi**, known as the **Golden Cage**. Built in Murat III's reign (1574-95), the quality of its stained-glass windows and tile and mother-of-pearl decorations almost compensate for the unhappy reality of its function. The dining room of Ahmet III, called the **Fruit Room** because of its wallpaintings, is the only part of the Harem that can arguably surpass the Cage in sumptuousness of decor.

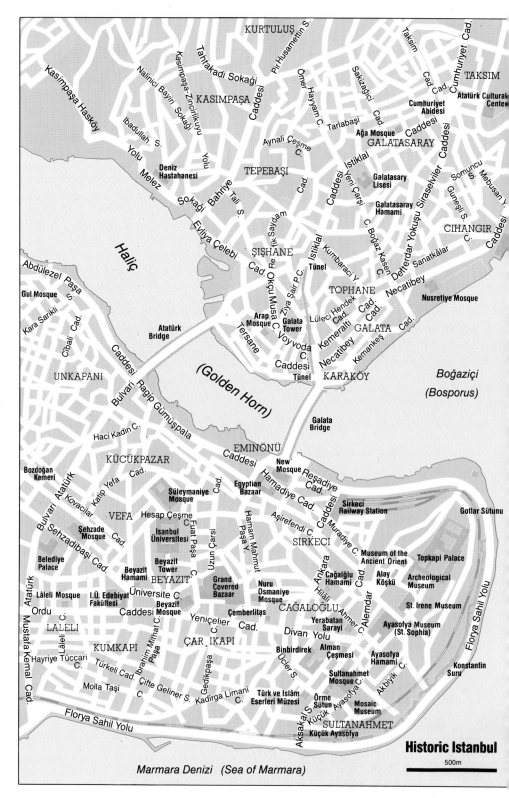

Historic Istanbul

500m

Marmara Denizi (Sea of Marmara)

MOSQUES AND MINARETS

For nearly 500 years of empire, the Ottoman Turks ruled much of the known world from their capital city astride the Bosphorus, and the mosques, minarets and *medreses* of Istanbul still remain the enduring testament of the power and glory of those centuries. The branch of fine arts in which the Ottomans excelled was architecture, and they used their gifts as civil and military engineers to bring building of sacred structures to new heights and profoundly influence not only Muslim architecture throughout the Middle East and Asia, but also Christian architecture in Europe, from which Ottoman architecture had itself borrowed.

Long before the conquest of Constantinople, the Ottomans knew of the great church, **Hagia Sophia**, and its awesome dome. One of the first acts of Sultan Mehmet the Conqueror after capturing Constantinople was to visit Hagia Sophia, which he converted into the chief mosque of his new Islamic city forthwith. It is as if the tremendous impression the vast dome floating overhead made on the Conqueror were repeated in every generation of Ottomans, for Ottoman mosque architecture after the conquest of Constantinople is preoccupied with the problem of creating a huge central covered space.

The Fatih Mosque: Mehmet II had his own mosque built in the district named Fatih ("Conqueror") after him, and the **Fatih Cami** and the surrounding complex of religious schools and other charitable foundations are dramatically situated on high ground specially raised on an elaborate system of vaults. The present mosque dates from the 18th century, however, for the original 15th-century buildings were destroyed in an earthquake in 1766. The mosque one sees today is not a copy of the original Fatih mosque, but it was built on the old foundations, from which it is possible to tell that the original mosque had a dome with a diameter of 85 feet (26 meters), making it the largest Ottoman dome until the construction of Süleyman the Magnificent's mosque one hundred years later. Art historians have speculated and squabbled about the form of the original mosque, but suffice it to note that the Conqueror himself was not pleased, for the unfortunate architect, Atik Sinan (not to be confused with the later and greater Sinan) first had his hands cut off, because the mosque was not as high as Hagia Sophia, and was executed a year after the mosque's completion. The **medreses** (religious schools) on each side of the mosque were the pinnacle of higher religious and legal education in the empire. Eight of them were preparatory, while the other eight were for the advanced study of Islamic jurisprudence, Quranic analysis and rhetoric. Mehmet II and his wife Gülbahar are buried in tombs next to the mosque.

A classical minaret—a spire to the heavens and a call to prayer.

The earliest surviving imperial mosque complex in the city is therefore that of **Beyazid II**, built in 1501-2 and located by the University of Istanbul and the **Covered Bazaar**. The mosque is quite an oasis of calm in the crowded and busy part of the city. Next to it is the pleasant, always bustling **Cinar Alti Cafe**, ("under the plane tree") few of whose throngs of customers pass through to the mosque's lovely, tranquil courtyard. The architect, one Yakupshah Bin Sultanshah, designed a mosque roofed by a large central dome supported by two semi-domes, much influenced by the Hagia Sophia, but on a smaller, somewhat stolid scale. The two aisles extending to the right and left of the exceptionally beautiful and commanding entrance are an unusual feature, not to be repeated. Beyazid II, who was known for his piety, was supposed to be something of a reactionary after his father's open-minded and eclectic ways. Ironically, next to his tomb behind the mosque lies Koca Resit Paşa, one of the 19th-century reformers of the Ottoman empire.

Overlooking the Golden Horn in a neighborhood little frequented by tourists is the comparatively modest mosque of **Sultan Yavuz Selim** (the Grim). No doubt Selim had little time to spare for the arts and culture after his stupendously quick conquest of the Arab lands. Yet it was in the first year of Selim's reign that the man who was to dominate the golden age of Ottoman architecture was conscripted into the Janissary service.

Sinan: The great architect Sinan was born the son of Christian peasants near the town of Kayseri in Central Anatolia—whether Greek or Armenian is still a question. He was in his early twenties in 1512 when the Janissary officials came to his village to levy the *devşirme*, or "harvest of boys", and he was taken from home to become a slave of the state. After his education and compulsory conversion to Islam, Sinan was not selected for the elite palace

The domes of Sultan Ahmet.

service of officials, but became a member of the Janissary fighting corps and rose through the ranks, gaining a sound knowledge of military engineering until in 1539 he was appointed Chief Architect.

Sinan's first commission, oddly enough, was not for his sultan, Süleyman I, but for Haseki Hürrem, known as Roxelane in the west, the Russian girl who had so captivated the Sultan that he had broken all the imperial traditions and married her. For Haseki Hürrem, Sinan built a smallish complex in Aksaray, near where the women's slave market used to be, with a special hospital for women.

It was a personal tragedy in the life of the Sultan which occasioned Sinan's first really important royal commission. Returning triumphant from campaign in 1543, Süleyman was stricken to learn of the death from smallpox of his favorite son, Prince Mehmet. He ordered a great mosque be built to the memory of the prince, and the result was the **Şehzade Cami**, or "Prince's Mosque" across from the municipality building in Saraçhane—near the Aqueduct of Valens. In 1548, when Şehzade was completed, there were only three other imperial Ottoman mosques in Istanbul, and Şehzade, Sinan's first large scale mosque, surely impressed the populace with its size and magnificence. Looking back at the end of his long life, Sinan himself called the Şehzade the "work of an apprentice", and others have criticized the building too. At Şehzade one sees Sinan's first attempt to deal with the idea of unifying and centralizing the interior space beneath a great dome, supported on four sides by semi-domes. Critics say the effect within is heavy and stilted, that the massive supporting piers are too apparent and find fault with the lovely exterior stone decoration, unique among Sinan's buildings. In the mosque garden is Prince Mehmet's tomb, its inside covered with lovely **An ablution** tiles showing spring gardens to symbol- **fountain.** ize the peak of youth from which death

plucked the unlucky prince.

It was not until the latter part of his reign that Süleyman the Magnificent gave orders for work to begin on another imperial mosque in his own name, the **Süleymaniye**. A site was chosen on the Third Hill of the city's seven hills, in the former gardens of the Old Palace, which had been almost vacated by the court. Elaborate foundations and vaults were laid, and limestone in vast quantities was quarried in Bakırköy, on the Marmara shore. In addition to a mosque, the Sultan ordered four major colleges to be built to extend and supercede the teaching of religious law at the colleges at Fatih Mosque, as well as a soup kitchen, hospital asylum, bath and caravansary. Another two specialized colleges taught *hadith*, or the pious traditions of the Prophet, and another taught medicine. These colleges were the highest ranking in the empire, and graduates could expect to hold the premier legal and religious positions.

Building work lasted seven years.

For expenses, Sinan had at his disposal the Sultan's fifth of the booty from the conquest of Phodes, 34 years of accumulated revenues from the Dodecanese and the entire income of the wealthy province of Egypt during the years of construction.

The magnificent complex of Süleymaniye was completed in 1557. Most important of all the imperial mosques of Istanbul, the great building broods massively over the city. A superb view over the complex may be had from the gardens above it at the very back of Istanbul University. There one may admire the great dome and piercing minarets, set amid the smaller domes of subsidiary buildings cascading down the hill, the whole silhouetted against the waters of the Golden Horn.

The interior of the mosque is as vast and overwhelming as one would expect. A dome 85 feet (26 meters) in diameter and 174 feet (53 meters) high, in approximate proportions of one to two (compared with Hagia Sophia's of 34 meters diameter and 56 meters high) crowns the lofty space, supported at two sides by semi-domes and on the other two by a huge arch whose tympanum is filled with windows. On the dome, the master calligrapher Çerkes (Circassian) Hasan Çelebi inscribed the Quranic verse "*Nur,*" or "Light:"

"God is the light of the heavens and the earth

the likeness of his light is as a niche wherein is a lamp

(the lamp in a glass,

the glass as it were a glittering star)

kindled from a Blessed Tree

an olive that is neither of the East nor the West

where oil well nigh would shine, even if no fire touched it;

Light upon light

(God guides to his Light whom he will)"

Above the Iznik tiles of the *mihrab,* or niche denoting the *qibla,* or direction of Mecca, the luminous stained glass of the windows is by Sarhos Ibrahim (the

The Şehzadebaşi— Sinan's first major commission.

drunk). In Süleyman's day a choir of some 250 *muezzins* climbed to chant the call to prayer from the ten galleries of the four minarets. So great was the renown of the Süleymaniye that the 18th-century English architect Nicholas Hawksmoor even planned to build a replica of it in Oxford in the place of the Radcliffe Camera.

A year after the mosque was completed, Haseki Hürrem died. Her tomb is by the small graveyard against the mihrab wall. Iznik tiles of blossoming plum and cherry trees cover the outside of the tomb, and a few yards away is the grander, imperial tomb of Süleyman the Magnificent, the Lawgiver, as the Turks call him. Below the east wall of the complex is Sinan's own modest tomb. A fountain he endowed stands at the bottom of the garden of his residence used while supervising the construction of the mosque.

Putting up a new dome the old way.

Great notables of the empire also commissioned mosques from Sinan. Among his most important patrons were Süleyman's daughter Mihrimah and her husband the Grand Vizier Rustem Paşa. A child of the *devşirme*, like Sinan, Rustem was the son of a Croat swineherd. A squat and ugly man, he was popularly known as the "Louse of Fortune". Nonetheless he was a financial wizard who successfully lined his own pockets as he guided the empire. So great was his personal fortune that at his death he left some 5,000 kaftans and ceremonial robes, to say nothing of lands and jewels. It is said that he even made money by selling off discarded fruits and vegetables from the imperial gardens and pocketing the proceeds. However ill-gotten his gains may have been, to them we owe some fine buildings. Mihrimah's first commission was the **Iskele Cami** (Port Mosque) opposite the ferry station in Üsküdar, built in 1547-8. The **Rustem Paşa Mosque** built in 1561, in the busy, cluttered market area a little beyond the Spice Bazaar should not be missed. Sinan

brilliantly adapted the mosque's design to the oddly shaped site in a crowded, commercial district. Mosque and courtyard are on the upper story above warehouses and shops. Narrow staircases lead to the small courtyard. Some battered but charming Iznik tiles are on the outside walls of the mosque, a foretaste of the interior. For every inch of the mosque inside, seemingly, is covered in panels of Iznik tiles. Row upon row of flowers, arabesques and swirling abstract designs greet the enchanted eye. This is one of the most sumptuous and ornate Ottoman mosque interiors, worthy of the millionaire patron, but in stark contrast to the large congregation of poor workers who pray today.

In 1562, the widowed Mihrimah again put Sinan to work. This time she wanted a full scale mosque and foundation built by the Edirne Gate on the Sixth Hill, the highest point in the city. The resulting **Mihrimah Cami** is one of the most unusual, abstract mosques in the history of Ottoman architecture.

The square interior is covered by a soaring dome of 66 feet (20 meters) in diameter and 122 feet (37 meters) in height. Light floods the mosque through many windows, which fill the tympana of the arches, strongly emphasizing the mosque's structure outside, to an almost baroque degrees, and creating a sense of unlimited airy space inside.

Another fine mosque, a miniature masterpiece, was built in 1571 by Sinan for Sokollu Mehmet Paşa, the son of a Bosnian village priest who was Grand Vizier in the closing years of Süleyman's reign. **Sokollu Mehmet Paşa Cami** is situated below the At Meydani, conveniently close to his palace, which was later demolished to make room for the Sultan Ahmet mosque. In this exquisite jewel of a building, form, light and color balance and enhance one another to delight the senses. Six pillars in a hexagon support the dome, and the walls are decorated with floral Iznik tiles and calligraphic

European engraving of St. Sophia interior during Muslim prayers.

88

tiles proclaiming the 99 Names of God. The genius of this mosque is that the tiles are not just brilliant sheets of surface decoration as at Rustem Pasa, but are unerringly placed to emphasize and highlight the structure. The conical hood of the *minbar* (pulpit) is covered by fine Iznik tiles, and several small pieces of the sacred black stone of the Ka'aba in Mecca are set into the *mihrab.*

One of Sinan's last works was the distinctive little white mosque on the Asian shore of the Marmara at Üsküdar which he built for Şemsi Ahmet Paşa in 1580, who succeeded Sokollu Mehmet Paşa after the latter's assassination. Şemsi Ahmet Paşa, a descendent of the noble Turkish families of Isfendiyaroglu and Candarli, was a witty and corrupt figure, a sort of Ottoman lobbyist. His **Şemsi Ahmet Paşa Cami** is built right at the water's edge with the pasa's tomb opening off the diminutive, domed prayer hall of the mosque, an unusual feature.

Sinan died in 1588. He was in his nineties and had been Chief Architect for some 50 years. It has only been possible to mention a select few of his vast oeuvre. He was responsible for at least 120 buildings in Istanbul and hundreds more in the provinces. More than any other single man, he is responsible for the Ottoman, Islamic appearance of Istanbul.

Sinan was succeeded as Chief Architect by his pupil Davut Aḡa, who was commissioned in 1597 to build the **Yeni Valide Cami**, (The New Queen Mother's Mosque, usually just called the New Mosque or the Yeni Camii) whose gray bulk looms over the bustling commercial district of Eminönü at the foot of the Galata Bridge. In those days the quarter was a smelly slum inhabited by Jews who had to be paid to move. From the start, the mosque project was dogged by difficulties. The treasurer embezzled the funds and had to be replaced, water seeped into the underground bridges, and the architect himself, Davut Aḡa, was executed for

heresy in 1599. Work came to a complete stop when the Sultan died and his mother, Valide Safiye, no longer had access to funds to continue the mosque, which remained an abandoned construction zone for over 50 years until another Queen Mother, Valide Sultan Turhan Hatice, decided to complete the building. In plan the Yeni Camii resembles Şehzade, with its square room canopied by a central dome and four semi-domes. Inside the walls are covered by pretty blue- and- white tiles. Attached to the mosque is a rather extensive imperial suite, reached by an unusual ramp outside.

Each of its two minarets have three serefiyes, or galleries, from which six *muezzins* used to climb to give the call to prayer five times a day. During the Muslim holy month of fasting, Ramadan, the galleries are lit to announce the *iftar*, or time to break fast. A string of lights forming pious epithets called the *mahya*—formerly gas lanterns, but now electric bulbs—were and are hung

Some are not so serious about their prayers.

between the two minarets in accordance with an imperial decree issued in 1723, which made the *mahya* obligatory for all mosques with more than one minaret. The Yeni Camii is one of the few Istanbul mosques which still upholds the tradition.

Perhaps the best loved and most famous of all mosques in Istanbul is the **Sultan Ahmet Cami**, known to many as "The Blue Mosque" because of the tilework inside. Building began in 1609 under the supervision of the architect Mehmet Ağa, to be completed in 1617. Last of the royal classical mosques of Istanbul, and the only one with six minarets, the Sultan Ahmet Mosque achieves grace and monumentality outside. Despite the 20,000 Iznik tiles on the walls inside, however, the interior is dark and the four pillars supporting the dome unpleasingly intrusive and massive.

The **Nuruosmaniye Cami** complex, situated at the main north entrance of the Grand Bazaar, was begun under

Mahmut I and completed in 1755 by Osman III and is the first and perhaps most striking of the baroque style mosques in the city. Sultan Mahmut, we are told, really wished for a completely European style building, but the clergy objected, and the Nuruosmaniye, with its reworking of traditional Ottoman forms, was the compromise result. One break with tradition is the courtyard's horseshoe shape, instead of the conventional rectangle. In typically baroque fashion the structural elements are heavily accentuated and ornamented. Some of the other baroque mosques of Istanbul are the **Ayazma Cami** (Holy Spring Mosque) built in 1760-61 by Mustafa II in Üsküdar, and the **Laleli Cami**, also built by Mustafa III in 1759-63 in the quarter between Beyazit and Aksaray.

Lastly, no section on Istanbul's Islamic monuments would be complete without a mention of her most sacred shrine, the great **Mosque of Eyüp**, at the end of the Golden Horn. Eyüp (Job) was the standard bearer of Muhammad and the last surviving of the *Ansar*, or Companions of the Prophet. When the Arabs first besieged Constantinople (674-8) they took the aged Eyüp along for his holiness' sake. He died during the campaign and was buried somewhere outside the city.

The story goes that his long lost (actually known and mentioned by several travelers in Byzantine time) tomb was miraculously discovered by Sultan Mehmet the Conqueror who raised a religious complex on the site in 1458. The Conqueror's original foundation was in ruins by the 18th century and Sultan Selim III had a new building erected in 1798. In Eyüp, new sultans were girded with the Sword of Osman, the founder of the Ottoman family, and to be buried in the extensive graveyard beyond the complex is still counted a privilege. The faithful still crowd the shrine to make their prayers to the buried Companion of the Prophet and to sustain the great Islamic tradition of this fair city of Istanbul.

Crowds in front of the Yeni Camii, or New Mosque. Right, the Green Door to Islam.

GHOSTS AND GOBLINS

Although cemeteries are often thought of as gloomy places which sadden us, they need not be so. The cemeteries and individual tombs of Istanbul, besides containing interesting architectural features, are open air "museums", steeped in history and provide social commentaries that give insight into the incredibly diverse, multi-cultural legacy of the city.

There are over 100 cemeteries in Istanbul. A good beginning point for a tour is **Eyüp**, a

Aziyade contains autobiographical elements in an innocent romance between a naval officer and a young maiden who have clandestine meetings in the cemetery of Eyüp. The setting, as described, is refreshing and joyful rather than somber; it reflects Loti's view of physical instinct as a challenge to inexorable death.

The tea house is still open today and one can enjoy a tea or coffee or puff on a *nargile* (waterpipe) provided by the house. The cosy

huge burial ground which winds its way up the hills on the western shore of the Golden Horn outside the city walls.

Folk tradition claims that writer Pierre Loti (1850-1923) was a habitué of the tea house which is nestled in the plane trees and cypresses at the pinnacle of Eyüp cemetery.

Loti's writings are distinguished by romanticism and exotic word paintings which give extensive background on the social customs of the last days of the Ottoman Empire. Although they are paeans to love and life, at their core lies despair at the passing of sensual pleasure. His first novel

interior, with kilim covered divans and brass tables, remains unchanged since the days when Loti was said to have poured over his manuscript in the early morning or sat chatting with his friends in the mellow glow of the late afternoon.

The lower levels of the cemetery have tombs closely clustered in walled gardens with poetic names such as "The Valley of the Nightingale". The older graves consist of two upright gravestones—the one at the foot end shorter—and a stone slab over the grave in which the deceased would lie facing Mecca. The grave itself should be of ample size to allow the departed one to sit up respectfully when quizzed in the hereafter about his religious beliefs by the angels Munkar and Nakir.

In Ottoman times, the headstones of the graves were decorated with turbans, the variety and number of folds indicating the social rank of the deceased and his position i.e., whether he had been a pasa, dervish or eunuch, etc. If a turban were placed a little to one side of the gravestone, it indicated death was due to decapitation.

Other headstones are humorous and inspiring testaments to those who joyously pursued life's pleasures until the end. For instance, on the elaborate tombstone with the relief of an almond, cypress and peach tree is the lament, "I've planted these trees so that people might know my fate. I loved an almond-eyed, cypress maiden and bade farewell to this beautiful world without savoring her peaches." Or what can create a more vivid image than the following epitaph, "A great pity to good-hearted Ismail Efendi, whose death caused great sadness among his friends. Having caught the illness of love at the age of seventy, he took the bit between his teeth and dashed full gallop to paradise."

But Eyüp is by no means the only cemetery of note. **Karaca Ahmet** in Üsküdar is said to be the largest Islamic cemetery in the world. Among the many ornate rows of graves, near the central crossroads is a large mausoleum with six columns and a cupola where the beloved horse of Sultan Mahmut I (1730-54) is buried (his hoof prints are seen in the stone slab).

The Muslim cemetery at **Rumeli Hisari** is in an excellent location on a hill overlooking the Bosphorus on the way to Bosphorus University. One most unusual grave, which lies off the main road, is that of Rona Altinay, a young stewardess who died in an airline disaster. Her family had her tomb marked by a detailed miniature plane crashing into the stone slab, a tiny recreation of the original tragedy.

Individual *türbes* (tombs) of "saints", usually called *Baba* (father) or *Dede* (grandfather), are to be found throughout the city and are visited by the faithful who often leave flowers or small presents as symbolic offerings. Poorer pilgrims leave a piece of their clothing as an intimate reminder of their personality. They believe that the holy man in paradise will be reminded of them every time the rag blows in the wind and will answer their prayers. Traditional families often take their newborn children there and put them under the saint's care whereupon the children are obliged to make periodic visits to the shrine throughout their lives.

Most of these saints are considered to have general curative powers. Telli Baba, the most famous, is supposed to have communicated with the Prophet Joshua, and his casque is always decorated with gold and silver ribbons worn traditionally by brides. **Oruç Baba**, in Topkapi, is currently very popular. During Ramadan, many of the faithful go to his tomb to break their fast while making a wish.

Other saints have their specialities as well. **Horoz Dede** (Grandfather Rooster), buried in **Unkapani**, received his nickname during the siege of Constantinople when he made the rounds each morning and crowed loudly to wake the troops. He was killed in the final battle and was buried after the city fell, with Mehmet the Conqueror among the mourners. The grave is still venerated and is often visited by women, because for some strange reason he is said to help them find husbands.

Those wishing to find work should go to see **Tezveren Dede** in **Divanyolu**. If you have lost something, go visit **Abdurrahmani Sami**, who lost his head in battle while a standard bearer of the Arab Sultan Eyüp. His casket, covered in velvet of the traditionally holy color emerald green, is on display in a small building next to the Yeşil Konak Hotel.

Left, a cozy corner among the gravestones.

LIVING ISLAM

It is the little things that one notices first: the cab driver, turning the ignition to his car, the bellboy as he lifts your luggage, the elevator operator, as he pushes the button to the third floor, whispering:

Bismillahirahmanirrahim

"In the name of God,
the Compassionate, the Merciful..."

The signs and tokens are everywhere— not the women in kerchiefs or the men with

child bearing and finally, death, the life of a Muslim in Istanbul is intimately wrapped in the metaphysical landscape of Islam.

Cars, buses, trucks and homes are decorated with religious stickers in either the old and revered Arabic script or in modern Turkish transliteration, all exclaiming simple but salient principles:

La illah il allah

"There is no God but the one God"

neatly trimmed beards and skull-caps (although these are common enough, too), but the decals on car bumpers, warding off the Evil Eye; worry beads in the hand of an older man, unconsciously reciting the 99 attributes of God as he waits for a bus; the middle aged woman who collects scraps of newspapers in Arabic or Farsi off the street, believing anything and everything written in the original language of the Quran—even an advertisement for cigarettes—to be holy writ and thus deserving preservation.

This is a very deeply religious society indeed, and piety is not far from the surface. From birth, through circumcision, marriage,

Mashallah

"What God Wills"

And then, the most basic but exquisitely reverent invocation, the syllables that make up the name of the Prophet:

"Mu-ham-mad"

Every child is supposed to be conceived in an act that began with the *bismillah*, and only given a name after the father or another male relative whispers the *Tekbir*, or declaration of the Greatness of God, the *Ezan*, or call to prayer and the *Fatiha*, or opening chapter of the Quran, which is also the Muslim creed of faith:

La illah il allah

wa Muhammad Rasul Allah
"There is no God but the God,
And Muhammad is His Prophet"
Simple, direct and compelling. And once declared, there is no going back; one has embraced more than a religion; one has embraced an entire way of life.

There is no room for separation of religion from the world in Islam. Any and all conflict between the moral and material needs of

Law, and one *will* submit to it, from cradle to the grave.

Circumcision: Although Muslims maintain that all children are born Muslim and that non-Muslims are lead from the True Path by their parents, the first real act of fulfilling God's will is the mandatory circumcision of all male believers.

Circumcisions are conducted amid great pomp and ceremony in a semi-public serv-

human existence is likewise denied. Islamic teaching contends that man is born pure and that evil is neither essential nor original: individual perfection is possible in this world and need not be postponed until the suppression of bodily desires is achieved. As long as he submits to Divine Law as expressed in the Quran and in the *Hadith*, or traditions of the Prophet, one is free to shape one's own destiny. But the Divine Law is *the*

Preceding page: The ubiquitous "crying boy"—an official symbol of Islam, with older believer. Left, through any glass, a very religious society. Above, women at prayer—in their separate part of the mosque.

ice, either in a grand hotel or in one of the scores of "circumcision houses" that dot the city. "Graduates" of any given house tend to cleave together in a sort of loose fraternity; and it is not altogether uncommon table talk for two grown men to discuss who their *sünnetçi* was. The most famous of the *sünnetçi's*, Kemal Özkan, has set records circumcisizing up to 2,000 boys in a day.

Hospitals, under anesthetics and beneath the scalpel of a trained surgeon, are the least desirable venue for a circumcision, and reflects badly on one later in life.

So deeply embedded is the ceremony—a passage not only into religion but also into manhood—that normally sober newspapers run headlines on recent converts from other faiths, with the contented new Muslim—be he originally from Germany or Japan—photographed on his circumcision bed.

Ramadan: By the time they reach puberty, most children have learned at least a few rudimentary *surahs* from the Quran, and the basics of the *namaz*, or prayer ritual to be repeated five times a day, starting with ritual ablution. By the age of seven—and mandatory for all but the feeble or sick—is the *oruç*, or fast during the Muslim holy month of Ramadan. The rigorous fast, from dawn until dusk—when even the saliva in one's

throughout the previous year place skull-caps on their heads or, if female, wrap themselves in white scarfs and attend service at mosques which they will be unlikely to visit again for another 12 lunar months.

At the end of the fast, children wander door-to-door collecting candles from friends and relatives, much along the lines of Halloween, albiet without the ghosts; there were no ghosts in Istanbul until English seamen brought the notion of haunted houses, incubi and sucubi with them for entertainment, and even today, although Turks understand the concept of other-worldly souls, the stories themselves are

mouth should not be swallowed—attracts the participation of large sections of the population, even those who have no visible interest or even respect for religion during the other eleven months of the year. The holiest of nights during Ramadan (the *Leilat al Kadir*, or "Night of Power" during which, according to Muslim tradition, the Quran first descended, pure, eternal and unadultured from heaven to the Prophet Muhammad) can only be compared to the Christians' Christmas or Passover among Jews. It is a night when prayers are worth those of "A thousand other nights," a night when ostensibly lay Muslims who have not prayed once

boring and totally lacking social or intellectual reverberation.

The period between the *Seker Bayram*, or Sugar Feast, ending Ramadan, and the *Kurban Bayram* at the end of the Hajj, or the month of Pilgrimage to Mecca, is regarded as inauspicious for marriage, a belief which accounts for the numerous weddings during Ramadan itself. Marriage, too, though legally conducted before a civil magistrate in accordance with the reforms of the 1920s which declared Turkey to be a secular republic, is virtually meaningless unless accompanied by the traditional Islamic *imam nikahi* performed by a Muslim cleric. There are, in fact, far more Islamic unions than legally binding secular marriages, resulting in periodic mass-marriages to legitimize children who are technically bastards.

Kurban Bayram: The Muslim Holy Month of Hajj derives from the pre-Islamic tradition in Arabic wherein all fueds, wars and conflicts were forgotten so that all might come to worship their respective dieties at the Ka'aba in Mecca. Islam maintained the same tradition and decreed as a duty for all able-bodied believers a pilgrimage to Mecca in the course of their lifetime. Modern jet travel has lessened the rigors of the journey, and made it accessible to more, and certain neighborhoods in Istanbul—notably Fatih and Umraniye, literally empty as the pious depart to fulfill their duty.

For those who remain, the *Kurban Bayram*, or Feast of the Sacrifice (according to Islamic tradition, it was Ishmael, and not Isaac, who was spared on the altar) is arguably the holiest feast day of the year. Not only in the more conservative quarters, but even in the brothel districts of the city, the streets are literally awash in blood and offal as hundreds of thousands of sacrificial sheep, camels and cows are ritually slaughtered with the meat distributed to the poor as alms.

The *Kurban Bayram*, however, is not the only occasion for the ritual slaughter of animals to acquire a blessing. When moving into a new house or apartment, it is not uncommon to slaughter an animal over the doorstep; the same holds true for shops and even newly purchased automobiles. As part of the Eyüp Mosque complex, the local religious foundation maintains an abattoir for athletes and sundry passersby to select their sheep from the stock on hand, pay for it according to its weight, and lift their hands toward heaven as the ritual butcher slits the animal's throat over a bloody drain (taking care to leave enough to anoint the pious purchaser). The meat of the slaughtered animal is then donated to the poor.

Contradictions: Ever since Atatürk declared Turkey a secular republic oriented toward the Christian West rather than the Muslim East, Turkey, and especially Istanbul, has had a peculiarities. Here is a Muslim nation that takes its day of rest on Sunday but where Friday mosques are so full that worshippers spill out on to the street, a nation that has provided itself with sufficient excuses for drinking alcohol, but still ostensibly refrains from pork.

Still, vestiges of popular belief live on: groups of young men (and some women) now meet clandestinely to perform the *sema*, or whirling ceremony, in the privacy of their homes, the erstwhile dervish monasteries having been given over to touristic "dis-

plays" of the holy rite.

More significantly, a certain Adnan Hodja, who had collected a following in university circles before being shuttled off to an insane asylum and conveniently labelled a schizophrenic, continues to enjoy popular support despite—or perhaps because of—his travails.

The former film star Leyla Sayar had turned into a wandering prophetess who can blow on knots and create holy water, while actors and whole football teams make regular pilgrimages to Eyüp Cemetery to pray at the *hacet*, or "need window" for the fulfillment of their wishes.

Left, lads on their way to the circumcision ceremony. Above, everything goes better with coke.

TURKISH BATH

What do Franz Liszt, Edward VIII, Kaiser Wilhelm and Florence Nightingale have in common? Each spent a few hours relishing the healing and cleansing delights of the 300 year old Cagaloglu Hamami in Istanbul.

Only about a hundred years ago, as a social and recreational center, a *hamam* or the public bath, was an indispensible part of Istanbulites daily life. Because "cleanliness" is a basic part of Muslim life, Turks took to Byzantine public baths with enthusiasm and enriched them architecturally and culturally. Up until the 1920s, hamams were owned by *"vakifs"* (or pious foundations.) Built as part of mosque complexes, they were open to the public and free of charge. Donations were welcomed as they helped to maintain the building and provide for the personnel.

Most hamams were built as duplexes, consisting of two separate units, one for men and another for women. Inside the building the usual plan is a domed dressing room, the *camekan*, which leads to a relatively small *sogukluk*, or cold section, which opens into the *hararet*, the hot room.

The 16th century was dubbed the golden age of the Ottoman empire and perhaps of Turkish architecture. This was the time of Süleyman the Magnificient (1494-1566) and his world renowned architect Mimar Sinan (1489-1588) who built 40 hamams in addition to 135 mosques and scores of medreses, palaces, caravansaries, aqueducts, tombs, and public kitchens in Istanbul alone. Although not many of these survived, several impressive hamams can still be found in the city.

Istanbulites believed that hamams were in fact an ethereal medicine, which cured both the body and the soul. A few hours in the hamam helped to free the body of toxins, opened up the pores, cleaned the skin, cured diarrhea, scabies, high fever, rheumatism, chronic depression and impotence.

It is perhaps this last claim which wrongly (if not unfairly) associates Turkish baths with sex. As public institutions, hamams were always regulated very strictly. Under whatever pretext or excuse, a man entering a woman's hamam (or woman entering a man's hamam) was punishable with death.

In fact, everything about the hamam was strictly controlled. Bath attendants, *tellaks*, had detailed rules of conduct. They could not, for example, even imply that they expected a tip, if the person they waited on was poor or a traveler. While helping a customer bathe, the attendants had to wear a towel over their neck to avoid perspiration dropping on the customer. Their towels and *pestemals* (waist cloth, compulsory for both men and women) were scrupulously clean, violation being punishable by 1000 blows with a club!

Not that any self respecting Istanbulite would use the towels or waist cloths provided by the establishment. Personal hamam kits consisting of towels (two large and two small), a *kese* (bath glove made of coarse cloth, used to rub away dead skin), a *sabun bezi* (washcloth), a *sabunluk* (soap dish), a *tas* (water bowl), a pair *nalins* (clogs), and of course the *pestemal* (waist cloth) were the fashion of the day and as one would expect, reflected the status of the customer. Copper soap dishes and bowls were the rule, but silver and even gold were not unknown.

Today, Istanbul boasts several historic hamams as well as scores of more obscure neighborhood baths which are often just as good if not better than the "touristic" ones. The most popular, however, are the Galatasaray Hamami, (located near the Greek Consulate in the Galatasaray/Beyoglu section of Istanbul) first built as the palace baths in 1481, now restored to pristine condition, and the Cagaloglu Hamami (situated in the Sultanahmet area) with a "menu" conveniently written in English, German, French, Dutch and even Japanese.

Right, a classic Turkish Bath, or Hamam.

A VANISHING GRACE

La Belle Epoque: The history of Istanbul is in general divided into three major parts: the Ottoman period follows the Byzantine and leads up to that of the Republic proclaimed in 1923. Yet, there exists also a secondary period which has been called, rightly or wrongly, *la belle epoque*, and which deserves to be recalled on its own right. This is the time when, for a fleeting historical moment, Istanbul missed becoming a European metropolis through its cosmopolitan and multicolored aspect which earned it the name *Darsaadet*: the Port of Felicity.

From the beginning of the 19th century, many Europeans, including writers and poets as well as merchants and diplomats, came to see for themselves the mystical capital of the Orient. Constantinople lured with its Byzantine past and Ottoman present; the call of history and art combined with the curiosity evoked by minarets, cemeteries, and the promenades on the banks of the Bosphorus. Modern times added to this already irresistible mixture and attractions of a city half-way between the East and the West, where *savoir vivre*, adventure and love were added to the exoticism of a distant culture.

Toward the middle of the century, the real social and economic center of the city shifted to **Pera**, called Beyoğlu by Turks, the region along the axis that extended from **Galata Tower** to **Taksim Square**. The district across the Golden Horn (*pera*, in fact, meant "the opposite side" in Greek) had always been a town apart, a place where foreigners lived, a foothold of the West in Istanbul. It was first colonized by Galatians—i.e. Gauls—in pre-Roman times; in the 13th century, the Genoese rebuilt it as a fortified trading colony while Byzantium looked on helplessly. The conservative orthodoxy of either Byzantium or Islam never penetrated it

far. Until late into the present century, in fact, few Muslims ever lived there. Native minorities—Greeks, Armenians, and Jews—moved in mainly after the 1830s, as shopkeepers, clerks and professionals. Apart from them and foreign diplomats and political exiles, the true inhabitants of the district at the time were the Levantines.

Levantines, descendents of Westerners settled in Istanbul or offspring of their marriages with members of the minorities, formed a distinct social layer and rapidly acquired the character of a Constantinopolitan "nobility". The policies of Westernization adopted by the sultans since early 19th century served them well. They excelled not only in commerce and finance but, following the imperial reform of 1839 which made it possible for non-Muslims to serve in government posts, in every stage of the administrative hierarchy as well.

Elegant life at Pera: Daily life at Pera changed rhythm as a result. In 1854 an informal municipality was set up and boulevards and streets were named—among them, *"Rue de Venise"* and *"Passage d'Europe"*. A year later, the arrival of gas lighting on the main avenues facilitated nightlife in the district. One by one, the *"Grande Rue de Pera"*—today's **Istiklal Caddesi**—then the streets that opened on to it were lined with luxurious private mansions. As the area became the commercial center of the city where hundreds of stores catered to all the possible needs of a visitor, *"Wagons lits"* chose to open its office here. Elegant hotels followed suit, including **Grand Hotel de Londres, Hotel Royal, Hotel d'Angleterre,** then **Pera Palace Hotel** which remains as the sole witness of the age today. **Café du Luxembourg,** located at the street level of the Grand Hotel, regularly received a sampling of the cream of Istanbul's high society: each afternoon, toward five o'clock, prominent ladies and young *beys* made their customary appearance at its tables. The **Café-Restaurant de Paris,**

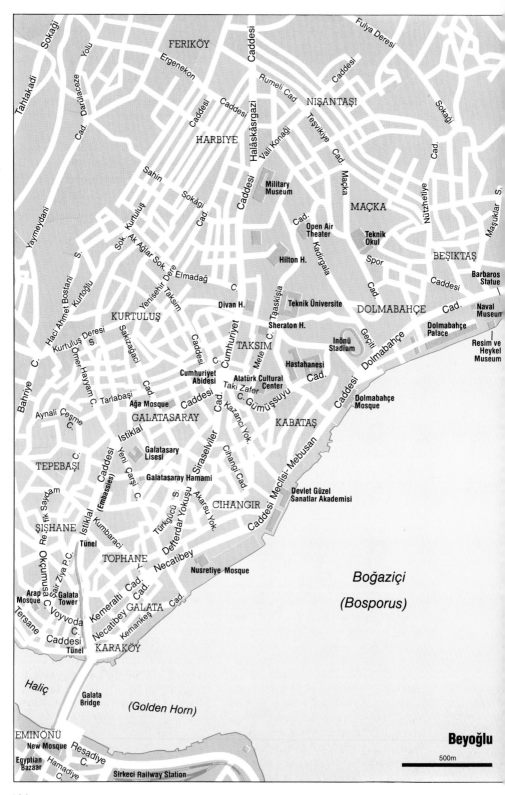

Beyoğlu

500m

on the other hand, was frequented by theater circles, being within a stone's throw of both **Theatre Verdi** and **Nouveau Theatre Francais**. Further south, between Galatasaray and the Tünel, **Brasserie Dimitri, Brasserie Viennoise,** and the cafe-chantants **Eldorado** and **Concordia**, among others, enlivened social life. *Patisserie Lebon,* later replaced on the same premises by the *Marquise*, remained in perennial fashion. Though Marquise is now out of business, the allegories of the Four Seasons done in tiles on its walls can still be admired at the site located at the corner of Kumbaraci Street.

Nightlife reached its full bloom toward the end of the century. Entertainment, which was limited in traditional Istanbul to activities at the imperial palace (and to the folk arts of the humbler classes), acquired a new life when foreigners began to organize soirees attended by the ladies and gentlemen of the city. The best were held at the magnificent ballroom of Pera Palace, where the orchestra of Monsieur Nava delighted dancing couples around 1900 with *Viens Poupoule, Polka des Anglais* and *Valse Amoureuse*. Opera conquered Constantinople in 1847, shortly after Donizetti arrived at the imperial palace to instruct the young Abdülmecid I in Western music. The company of Naum Efendi, a Catholic Arab, staged the operas of Bellini, Meyerbeer and Berlioz sometimes even before they appeared in Paris. Theater in the European sense arrived around the same time. Shakespeare played in French some years before Armenian, then finally Turkish, were adopted as stage languages in response to swelling audiences.

The majestic decors of two theaters, **Alcazar** (at #179 on the avenue) and **Alhamra** (near the church of St. Anthony), convey today an aura of the epoch—though both have now turned into sleazy cinemas that show sex films.

Places and traces: Over the summer, most inhabitants—including shops, restaurants, and embassies—deserted Pera for the cooler shores of Bosphorus or Princes' Islands. For the rest of the year, life centered on the **Grande Rue**.

The **Tünel** facilitated the descent into the Turkish city, down the steep hill of Galata, avoiding the unsavory district below Galata Tower. This oldest—and also shortest—public subway in Europe, built by the French in 1875, continues to carry passengers between the foot of Galata Bridge and the southern end of Istiklal Caddesi.

Emerging from the Tünel, **Passage du Tunnel** is the first of many privately owned shopping arcades in Pera which still reveal their architectural grace through the accumulated grime of a century. They include the **Syrian Passage** (#346 on Istiklal) built in 1908 by a former governor of Syria; the splendid **Cité de Pera**, now converted into the colorful tavern-alley of Çiçek Pasaji; the **Aleppo Passage** (#138); the **Emek Pasaji** (#124) which earlier housed the exclusive club of Cercle d'Orient; and the **Cité Roumelie** (#88),

Sultan Abdülmecid—determined to make Istanbul another Versailles or Berlin.

built by Ragip Paşa, palace chamberlain, who was one of the small number of Turks who trickled in at the turn of the 20th century. The best among the survivors, arguably, is the statue-lined **Passage de l'Europe** (Aynali Pasaj) which connects Meşrutiyet Caddesi and the fish market at Galatasaray. The great stores which once furnished the best and the latest of Europe—**Pygamalion, Carlmann, Bazaars de Paris et des Provinces, Bonne Marché**—no longer exist. A few like **Mayer** and **Lazzaro Franco** remain as nostalgic reminders of a different age. Angelidis' Havana Bazaar is gone. So are the studios of Photographie Berggren, though their original prints go for a fortune at London antiquarians.

The private residences and townhouses also reflect the wealth and refinement of the belle epoque. The incomparable art nouveau residence near the Tünel used to belong to the Dutchman Botter, private tailor to Abdülhamid II. **Misir Apartmanti**

(#311) and **Appartements du Louvre** (#146) deserve to be noted. In and around them lived Runzler, the ordnance officer of King Othon of Greece before he abandoned the throne; the German Bruchs who opened the first beerhouse in the city; the Kellner brothers who made carriages for the czar and the king of Spain; Madame Trophe, maker of hats; Lewis Mizzi, publisher of the *Levant Herald*; Basil Zacharoff before he became the world's richest arms merchant; one Giuseppe Garibaldi who gave French lessons, and one Franz Liszt who gave a few concerts during his stay in 1847 at **Nuruziya Street** #13. Flaubert spent a few months, seeking, and finding, passionate love. Young von Moltke delighted in the cosmopolitan atmosphere so lacking in the provincial backwater that was then Berlin.

After the Bolshevik Revolution, it was the turn of refugee Russian aristocrats to add a new dimension to the district. Destitute princes and princesses were known to sing in cabarets and run restaurants in the 1920s, at the twilight of old Pera. One such restaurant, the **Regence**, continues to serve on the narrow alley across St. Anthony's. And such delicacies as *borshcht*, *kievsky*, and *strogonoff*, which appear on the menus of all classy restaurants in Istanbul echo an episode in the history of the city.

The discreet charm of colonialism: The transformation of Constantinople differed in one crucial respect from that undergone, for instance, by London and Paris in the same period. The European metropoles had very rapidly changed their visage through industrialization. A large working class formed the principal part of their population. The capital of the East, on the other hand, continued to be, as it had always been, a center of commerce. Long-distance trade which had suffered badly during the decline of the Empire revived impressively following the Reform Decrees of 1839 and 1854 which liberalized the legal framework affecting commerce.

Grand staircase at the Beylerbey Palace.

**Inside the
ornate
Dolmabahce
Palace.**

Those who benefitted from it, though, were almost exclusively European firms, through their Levantine associates and the Christian and Jewish communities. As they expanded their enterprises across the extent of the Empire, the commercial center of the capital shifted from the old Bazaar district to Galata and Pera. The great foreign and multinational banks—Credit Lyonnais, Ottoman Imperial, Bank of Salonica—had their offices along the Grande Rue. The illustrious bankers Corpi, Lebet, Camondo and Zarifi (Greeks and Levantines) held court there: between themselves, they mortgaged the Imperial treasury several times over. The stock exchange was set up in Galata: daily rates were reported in journals published in Pera in several European languages. Government bonds were issued through the Galata market to European buyers. The Ottoman debt grew until the treasury went bankrupt in the 1880s, and was placed under the receivership of international commissions. The Regie Ottomance and the Public Debts Committee acted as the de facto financial administration of the empire during the decades preceding World War I.

Commercial expansion was accompanied by its educational counterpart. Englishmen and Americans, Jesuits and Lazarists, Jews and Armenians opened up their own educational centers, some of which continue to excel as the leading schools of modern Turkey. The Turkish government joined the trend by establishing in 1868 the **Imperial Lycée of Galatasaray**, modeled on French public schools, with instructions conducted in French. Its monumental cast-iron portals opening on a tree-lined courtyard, flanked by two fountains of sculpted marble, still dominate **Galatasaray Square** at midpoint on Istiklal Caddesi. Its graduates furnished the old empire—as they continue to furnish the republic—with prime ministers, diplomats, writers, and journalists, while the (no longer

existing) British High School for Girls on Rue de Pologne furnished the wives. Further up, on narrow Meselik Street near Taksim, the neo-classical facades of **Zapion** and **Esayan**, the Greek and Armenian girls' colleges, faced each other, as they still do in a losing struggle for survival. **Notre-Dame de Sion**, located in nearby Harbiye among what used to be suburban fields, was run by Catholic sisters then as it is now. **Robert College** and its sister institution, the American College for Girls, on the other hand, preferred the splendid landscapes of their perfectly reproduced Anglo-Saxon campuses out on the hills of Bosphorus to the cramped hub of Pera.

A stroll through Europe: The principal institutions of Pera, though, were undoubtedly the embassies of the Great Powers. These were reduced to the status of consulates when the capital moved to Ankara, they still fascinate the stroller with their reproductions of the palatial architecture, style, atmos-phere of their respective countries.

The **French Embassy**, off the avenue behind St. Anthony's was the earliest one to be built—appropriately so, as France under Francois I was the first European country to be befriended by the Ottomans. The present building was erected in 1831 after a fire destroyed the original 16th-century palace, though the **Chapel of St. Louis** dates to 1581, a pretty example of French Renaissance architecture.

Very close to Maison de France is **Palazzo di Venezia**, which became the Italian consulate after the unification of Italy. The present building dates from 1695. The little square which the Palazzo faces is a perfect corner of Italy, with the Italian Consulate, the Italian Lycee, and Hotel Italia surrounding it. (The hotel has recently changed its name, and apparently its owner.) Also nearby, to the left on a very narrow alley that climbs up to Istiklal Caddesi, is the old **Spanish Embassy**, with a chapel dedicated to

Istiklal Caddesi today.

110

Our Lady of the Seven Sorrows. Originally built in 1670, the present structure is a 1871 reconstruction.

The **British Embassy**, built in 1845 by Sir Charles Barry who was also the architect of the Houses of Parliament in London, is in Tepebasi, that is to say on the avenue that runs parallel to Istiklal on the west. Though Sir Charles adopted a more Italianate style with the building, the garden is typically English. This Italian influence seems to be a tribute paid to the earliest "foreigners" of this city by the nations which got more important before the Sublime Porte at later times—so the **Dutch** and **Russian Embassies**, both on the avenue, built in the 1840s by the Swiss-Italian Fossati brothers who also undertook the first great renovation of the Hagia Sophia in modern times. The old Russian Embassy, on the other hand, located on the narrow back-street facing the upper entrance of the Tünel, and divided up into shops, ateliers and rental rooms, has a more genuinely Russian look.

The **Swedish Embassy** is also near the Tünel. Its central location reflects the fact that the Swedes (and the Poles) were important allies of the Ottoman Empire for a long time due to their common enmity toward Russia. The former Corpi family residence, later converted into the **US Embassy**, is tucked away on Meşrutiyet Caddesi next to Pera Palace. The **Embassy of Germany**, another latecomer to the diplomatic scene, is also slightly off the center of action, on Ayazpaşa (İnönü) Caddesi going down from Taksim.

Churches: Quite a few churches were built to satisfy the spiritual needs of the Pera community. The two largest Roman Catholic temples are both on Istiklal, and both belong to the Franciscans. **St. Mary Draperis** dates to 1904, although the original church on the site went back to 1584. It is possibly the only Catholic church in the world whose inscription commemorates a Muslim Monarch, ie. Abdülhamid. Italianate **St. Anthony of Padua** is also

a late building, dating from 1914. In recent years it has become fashionable among a section of the Turkish intelligentsia to attend Christmas service here after customary visits to nearby taverns—a subterranean influence, perhaps, of the fact that Concordia, the best night-club of Pera, once stood where the church is now.

Two other important Catholic churches are found not far from the area. **Sts. Peter and Paul**, a Dominican church, is in Galata, on the descent from the Tower toward the sea. Originally of the 15th century, it was rebuilt by the Fossati brothers in 1853. Gravestones in its attractive courtyard indicate that the numerous Maltese community of Istanbul adopted it in mid-19th century. Another Catholic church, **Saint Espirit**, is located within the Notre Dame de Sion School in Harbiye, and dates to 1846. A majestic statue of Pope Benedict XIII dominates its courtyard. The largest Protestant church is the **British Crimea memorial**, on Serdari

Ekrem street, behind the Swedish Embassy in Tünel. Built between 1858 and 1868 by C.E. Street, who also designed the London Law Courts, it is currently unused.

Visually the most striking religious monument in Pera, though, is the Greek orthodox church of the **Holy Trinity** towering above Taksim square behind a facade of ramshackle shops. Its distinctly western neo-Gothic architecture dates from 1880. Another Greek church, **Panaghia**, on a narrow cul de sac off Galatasaray was built in 1804. Nearby, reached through the Galatasaray fish market is the largest Armenian church in town, **Surp Yerrortuyan**, another Holy Trinity, that dates from 1838. It is interesting to note that 32 of the 34 Armenian churches in Istanbul, and a similar proportion of the more numerous Greek ones, were built in their present form during the 19th century, more precisely, during the years 1826 and 1895.

Jewish monuments, while not less numerous, are less notable—perhaps because the large Jewish community of Istanbul traditionally avoided making itself conspicuous. Modern **Neve Shalom**, the largest synagogue in the city, is on Büyük Hendek Street, immediately to the west of Galata Tower. The Ashkenazi synagogue and the chief rabbinate of Turkey are nearby.

Where is the Turk?: As noted before, Moslem Turks kept aloof from Pera until about the turn of the 20th century. It was only during the final brief period between the Young Turk revolution of 1908 and the post-war Allied occupation of 1918-22 that Pera, or more accurately the new districts on its northern extension—Nişantaş and Şişli—became a center of gravity for the "westernized" Turkish elite of the Empire.

In Pera itself, there are only three properly "Turkish" buildings of note. All predate the Grand Epoque of the district. **Ağa Cami**, located on Istiklal Street, and until recently the only mosque far and wide, goes back to the 16th century, though most details date from more recent renovations. **Galatasaray Hamami**, on a side street near the Lycee, is, with the sumptuous marble interiors, built in the 1570s, one of the best Turkish baths in the city. By far the most interesting of the three, though, is the former **Mevlevihane Hani** of Galata, off Tünel square, now converted into a museum of Ottoman music. This used to be a *tekke* of the Whirling Dervishes, the distant Muslim counterpart to a monastery, where Muslims devoted themselves to the contemplation and celebration of the deity. In the peaceful courtyard beside the charming *tekke* (rebuilt in 1796), there are the tombs of past devotees, including that of Humbaraci Ahmad Pasa (1675-1747). The Pasa, who introduced modern artillery into the Ottoman army, was originally named Count Claude Alexander De Bonneval, as his man Süleyman Ağa was named Viscount de Latour—a fitting symbol of the fascinating historical paradox that was Pera.

Femmes turques chez eux.

Left, Pera girls at the turn of the century. Right, Le Belle Epoque—an age gone by.

ORIENT EXPRESS

The whistle blows, the locomotive ejects a blast of 19th-century steam, and the passengers crowd to the art-decor windows to watch as the minaret-spiked sky of the City of the Sultans comes into view. The Orient Express—that legendary train whose mystic and luxury attracted an elite clientele of crowned and deposed royalty, maharajahs, moguls, *femmes fatales* and spies both of fact and fiction, is underway again, and the only thing missing is an unsolved murder or the ghost of Mata Hari.

By most accounts, the inaugural journey of the original Orient Express in 1883 was by no means as memorable as the legend the train subsequently inspired.

Put together by the Belgian entrepreneur Georges Nagelmakers under the sponsorship of King Leopold II, the first train consisted of the engine, two sleeping cars, a diner, and a baggage wagon. The train, as it happened, never made it to the Ottoman capital, and passengers were obliged to complete their journey via coach and boat.

The through-link by rail to old Istanbul was completed in 1888, when one Baron Hirsch, a contractor from Austria, was paid by the kilometer of track to finish the job. Remnants of the good baron's work can still be seen today, weaving like a mountain trail through the perfectly flat landscape of eastern Thrace—a lasting monument to the first con-job associated with the Orient Express.

Service of the original Paris-Istanbul route continued up to World War I, and after the hiatus of the war years, resumed with a vengeance in the 1920s. It was during this period that the train earned its reputation for intrigue, when it seemed decidedly bad form *not* to conclude a shady deal in the smoking lounge or plot an assassination when the engine plunged into a tunnel in the ever scheming Balkans.

What fact did not offer, fiction soon provided, and numerous literary creations began stalking the handsome wagons. Graham Greene's first successful novel, *Stamboul Train*, took place entirely aboard the Orient Express or on the station platforms along the way, and there are few English language readers who are not familiar with Agatha Christie's *Murder on the Orient Express*.

Characters—both real and imaginary—inevitably checked into the Pera Palas or the Park Hotel; the latter, especially during World War II, was indeed a veritable nest of spies. Those fond of such Eric Ambler thrillers such as *Journey into Fear* and *The Light of Day* as well as the exquisite *Coffin for Demitrius* will have to look for their Colonel Hakki's elsewhere, however: the wrecker ball has insured that the Park's famous bar is dry, and that espionage in Istanbul must be conducted in less evocative venues like the Hilton, Sheraton or Etap chain.

The Orient Express, too, suffered in the modern era: following the advent of commercial airlines, the classic art decor pullmans and the heavy oak diners were absorbed piecemeal into other lines in Europe or removed into railway graveyards to gather dust, the old steam-powered engine having long been declared obsolete. Finally, in 1977, the last few decrepit wagons in active service were retired from the tracks to be put on the auction block. The Queen of Trains and the Midwife to Mystery was no more.

Today, as a result of the nostalgia craze in travel, several "Orient Express" trips are available, but only one—the Nostalgic Orient Express—maintains original cars pulled by an original steam engine, plying the original route between the Gar de l'Est in Paris and the Sirkeci Train Station in Istanbul, with the 100th anniversary held in 1988.

The price tag for the five day trip insures that only dyed-in-the-wool train enthusiasts or the idle scions of wealthy families will be on board—just the sort of people to attract an Ambleresque confidence man or a modern day Mata Hari.

Right, book cover to Old Stamboul.

STAMBOUL

RECOLLECTIONS OF EASTERN LIFE

BY

PREZIOSI

1858

THE ONCE AND FUTURE CITY

But if Frenchmen were "turning Turk" and whirling as dervishes, a more profound conversion to European ways was occurring among the educated classes of 19th-century Turkish society of Istanbul.

Starting with the period of reform under Mahmud II, more and more young Turks were sent abroad for study, especially that related to the military arts. Inevitably, a taste of the social and technological progress in the lands of the traditional enemy made a great impression on those sent abroad in the sultan's service. In the words of the post Ziya Paşa:

"I passed through the lands of the infidels, and saw cities and mansions
I wandered through the realm of Islam, and saw nothing but ruins."

In 1876, the reformers deposed the increasingly autocratic Sultan Abdülaziz, and had his successor, Sultan Abdülhamid, establish the first elected parliamentary government in the history of the Ottoman Empire, or indeed, the Islamic world. But the parliament only met twice before being dissolved in 1878. It was not to meet again until 1908, when the Young Turk movement, spear-headed by the Committee for Union and Progress, overthrew Abdülhamid who had defied all efforts to turn him into a figurehead ruler for 30 despotic years.

But the days of democratic rapture were short-lived. Responding to threats perceived and real, the CUP triumvirate of Enver, Cemal and Talat soon took over the government at the expense of the other anti-Hamadian alliance partners and ruled alone as crisis after crisis rolled over the tottering empire. First, Italy invaded the distant and indefensible Ottoman province of Libya. Then in 1912, the First Balkan War broke out,

The Ministr of War— now Istanbul University.

with the Bulgarian army advancing to the fields of today's Yeşilköy Airport. The city was only saved from siege and conquest when dissensions broke out between the Balkan allies over who might claim Constantinople (and in effect, the legacy of the Byzantine empire) as their own.

The Balkan wars—and the deteriorated state of the city—were amply covered by such cub-reporters as the young Ernest Hemingway (who loathed Istanbul) and the doyen of war correspondents, G. Ward Price, who was not much fond of the city either. He warned potential visitors:

"...never set foot on shore, for the sordidness and squalor of that city's ancient streets and the incongruous modernity which is gaining ground in its more prosperous districts destroy the romance and seduction of what was once the capital of the Eastern Roman Empire."

World War I: In 1914 the Ottoman state was dragged into World War I on the side of the Central Powers as a junior partner. The Empire, long known as the "Sick Man of Europe", was quickly targeted as the weak-link in the German/Austro-Hungarian alliance. Within months of the commencement of the war, British and French warships attempted to force the Dardenelles and steam up to the capital to knock Turkey out of the war and open a sea lane to Czarist Russia. The government in Istanbul had already packed its bags to flee to the depths of Anatolia when word came through that the battleships had been stopped, and that the land battle at Gallipoli was safely in stalemate. With the exception of a British submarine which managed to run the mine fields and nets along the Dardenelles, surfacing in Istanbul Harbor to cause momentary panic, Istanbul was spared direct assault for the course of the war.

The end of the Ottomans: Following the armistice at Mudros in 1918, an allied fleet sailed past the silent guns of Gallipoli and anchored in Istanbul harbor, and a military government of occupation established.

Other portentous events followed fast on one another. In May, 1919, a Greek army landed in the Aegean port city of Smyrna—now Izmir—to implement the "Grand Idea" of restoring Greek control over the lands of classical civilization—including, ultimately, Istanbul. Within days, Mustafa Kemal, the hero of the Gallipoli defence and later known to the world as Atatürk, slipped out of Istanbul to start organizing the nationalists resistance in Anatolia against the Greeks, Armenians, French, Italians, and finally the Sultan himself.

The process of emerging from centuries long tradition of fealty to the Ottoman dynasty was difficult to break, and one of Kemal's first resolutions was to separate the temporal power from the religious power vested in the sultan. The newly formed Grand National Assembly in Ankara—the farm-town that served as the headquarters for the

Symbol of the New Turkey— Mustafa Kemal Atatürk.

nationalists in their war of liberation—thus declared that while the Ottoman house retained the right to the Caliphate, or religious leadership, of the nation, the Sultanate, representing temporal power, was banished from the land. On November 17th, 1922, Sultan Vahideddin VI slipped out a side door of the Yildiz Palace to board a British warship which would spirit him to Malta and eternal exile. His cousin, Abdülmecid, was elected Caliph the next day, an office he was to hold only so long as Kemal found the outward symbols of religion useful.

When the new Caliph started gathering support in Istanbul as the last and most cogent symbol of continuity between past glory and the uncertain future under the nationalists in Ankara, he was deposed as quickly as he had been elected, and banned along with all other descendents of the House of Osman. Within days of the Caliph's departure on March 3, 1924, the remaining kiosks, pavilions and palaces along the shores of the Bosphorus were sacked by mobs acting in the spirit of the October Revolution in Russia, and with Ankara's tacit approval.

In autumn of the same year, more symbols of Ottomanism were brought low: the imperial banner above the **Sublime Porte** was removed, while the **Grand Vizierate** was converted into the office of the provincial governor appointed by Ankara. Significantly, the **Ministry of War** in Beyazit was converted into today's **Istanbul University**, while the symbol of Imperial fiscal decadence—the **Ottoman Debt Administration** building in Cağaloğlu—was turned into the **Boys' Lycee of Istanbul**.

And there were heavier psychological blows to follow: in 1924, the **Topkapi Palace**, the nerve center of Ottoman Turkey for centuries, was opened to the public as a museum, with the last of the black eunuchs and concubines evicted to fend for themselves in a totally alien world. More radical still

Rural migrants in the Big Town.

was the conversion of the **St. Sophia Mosque** into a museum. The Byzantine cathedral, converted into the imperial mosque immediately after the conquest of the city in 1453, was the very symbol of Ottoman Islam, and its reduction in status to a "mere" museum spoke volumes about Ankara's attitude toward both the Ottoman past as well as the Islamic religion itself.

The Provincial City: The nationalist antipathy toward Istanbul did not stop at the symbols of the former royal family, however. Although nearly 40 percent of the city's population of 600,000 in 1927 was non-Muslim, a language campaign, replete with the equivalent of "Red Guards" to enforce it, was initiated under the banner of "Citizen, Speak Turkish!", and over 30 French and Italian language schools were closed, in keeping with efforts to impose a monolithic identity on a multi-ethnic fabric. The city was far too cosmopolitan for the new "Turkish" nation, which meant to find its "authen-

tic" traditions not in the salons of Pera, but in the coffee houses of the hinterland. Kemal himself underlined this bias by avoiding Istanbul on his frequent trips around the country.

The most salient examples of decline during this period are the once exquisite *yali's* and kiosks along the Bosphorus. One gets a sense of what once was in such restorations as the **Yildiz Palace** up Barbaros Bulvari in Besiktas, now turned into a culture and arts center, or the **Pembe Köşk** and **Mavi Köşk** in Yildiz Park which have been restored along with their gardens, and give a taste of late Ottoman private architecture. There were many, many more such dwellings along the shores of the upper Bosphorus more reminiscent of bygone-Byzantium of the 6th century than the house of a prince or notable less than 100 years ago: a trace of wall protruding from weeds outside **Bebek**, an unpainted wreck of a fine building in **Rumeli Hisar**, and a coal loading station outside **Ortaköy** are all that remain

Laundry in the ruins of Old Constantinople.

of the residences of the lesser princes of the house of Osman. The **Cirağan Palace** on the waterside near Yildiz, is a good example of the fate of a fine building: burned in the 1920s, it remained a shell flanking a public swimming pool until 1986, when work started to restore it as a luxury hotel.

World War II: If the 1930s are celebrated by foreign writers for the journeys of the Orient Express, the 1940s saw one of the city's gloomiest eras, when—with the exception of a few spies and con-men stalking victims in the better bars, the city had become a virtual ghost-town.

The center of the spy action was the **Pera Palace** (which still attracts diviners and seance-leaders to the "Agatha Christie Room", and the **Park Hotel**, now sadly destroyed, but formerly the venue for singing duels between the British and the German delegations when they were not occupied making "preventive purchasing deals"—buying up every scrap of cloth which could possibly be used for bandages (the bales were sold by weight and usually contained a good amount of scrap-metal in the middle) or tons of hail-damaged wheat.

The depopulation of the city was aided by the gouging new tax law, which allowed local officials to set exorbitant capital levies on the minorities amounting to over ten times that paid by Muslims or resident foreigners. Corruption abounded, with vindictive officials arbitrarily deciding who should pay what amount, with defaulters shipped out to hard-labor camps in the east. The policy, abandoned in 1944, effectively brought legal business to a standsill, as honest brokers were thrown into jail while bribers and blackmarketeers went free. Even more old and established Istanbul families were either forced to leave or chose to abandon the city, with old houses given over to tenements and decay.

Although formally allied with Britain and France in World War II, Turkey

Art Deco and crass ads, side-by side.

remained neutral in the conflict, and even tilted toward the Nazi side after the German invasion of Russia—the traditional enemy of the Turks. German submarines and supply ships allegedly used the Bosphorus as a route into the Black Sea. The same channel served as an exit for German dead from the Crimea, and a peculiar place to visit is the **German War Memorial Cemetery** on the grounds of the German Consulate's summer residence in Tarabya on the upper Bosphorus. The cemetery was officially dedicated as a German war memorial in 1982.

Post-war boom: Pro-forma declaration of war on Germany in 1945 insured American protection from Soviet threats as well as American assistance in rebuilding the economy. Istanbul rapidly became the growth city in the country as banks, business and industry moved in.

Initial efforts to provide a modern urban infrastructure were soon abandoned, and within the short span of a decade, the city had grown from a Charleston, South Carolina to a Gary, Indiana. The **Golden Horn**, formerly the pristine private lake of the sultans, was soon converted into the local equivalent of Lake Erie due to the indiscriminate dumping of industrial wastes. The shoreline of the Sea of Marmara, especially around **Kuruçeşme** and **Florya** on the European side and **Moda** on the Asian side of the city soon became places where only the brave might bathe.

Gecekondu: The newly established industries in the city soon attracted hundreds of thousands of unskilled and semi-skilled workers from the vast Anatolian hinterland. From less than a million in 1950, the city's population rose to over three million by 1970, and six million by the mid-1980s.

Festering rings of squatters shacks (*Gecekondu*, meaning literally "Put up at night") soon sprung up near the ancient land walls as well as the new industrial areas around **Kasimpaşa** and **Eyüp** on the Golden Horn, and spread

like mushrooms over every piece of unclaimed land in the city. Periodic amnesties designed to garner votes before elections encouraged the trend of converting the city's green areas into eye-sore slums, enveloping what remaining charm the city had. Areas of Greek settlement such as **Arnavutköy** on the Bosphorus or **Tarlabaşi** near Taksim were particularly hard hit following the expulsion of over 200,000 Greek nationals in the wake of the Cyprus crisis of 1964.

Neighborhoods, more often than not, were composed of homogeneous migrants from one area, so that **Zeytinburnu** in Asia had collected a nearly exclusive Alevi Kurdish population from the east who were embued with leftist tendencies, whereas **Gaziosmanpaşa**—the sprawling eye-sore along the airport road—became the abode of the ultra-conservative Sunni Muslim migrants from Yugoslavia and Bulgaria.

"Luxury" apartment complexes,

New owner—a contrast in style and taste.

meanwhile, were being slapped up by land speculators and contractors for the nouveau riche in the place of traditional Ottoman homes—*yali*'s on the Bosphorus in such suburbs as **Yeniköy** and **Kanlica** or traditional courtyard houses in the **Beyazit** area. This insured that what little remained of the city's architectural heritage was doomed to vanish under the weight of construction run amok. The fulfillment of Ward Price's observation of "sordidness, squalor and incongruous modernity" made half a century before was at hand.

Urban polarization had political ramifications as well. Whole slum areas became "liberated" zones controlled by extreme leftists or rightist militants, where the newspaper which one carried or the type of beard or moustache one wore identified one as a friend or foe. The residents of **Fatih** and **Eyüp** on the European side of the city yearned for an Islamic-style government, while neighborhoods in the Asia suburb of Üsküdar were controlled by extreme rightist sentiment.

On September 12, 1980, the military in Ankara staged a coup, imposing a total curfew on Istanbul and much of the country while thousands of suspected militants were rounded up, including the former leftist mayor of the city. In late 1982, the midnight to dawn curfew was lifted, and nightlife slowly began to return to the sobered city, with martial law finally being lifted in 1986, two years after municipal elections were held.

The Big Apple: Today, anarchy in the city is restricted to traffic; from 2,000 private vehicles in 1950, there are more than 400,000 today, engaged in daily grid-lock during rush hours. Traffic on the first Bosphorus Bridge is so heavy that for the first time, the straits have become a real obstacle between the two halves of the city, with residents of either side remaining in their respective worlds with little communication with the other.

More to the point, the massive immigration of rural Turks over the past two decades has forever changed the complexion of the city, dividing it into two groups—one that yearns for the Istanbul of the elusive, pristine (and probably imaginary) past, and the other that continues to view the city as the Turkish equivalent of the "Big Apple". where with sweat, hard work, a little luck and maybe the help of a relative, one can get ahead.

The first attitude is best summed up by the condescending phrase trotted out by the scions of old families (or those arrived a generation ago from the provinces who assume similar regal airs) directed toward the second group: "Mehmet the Conqueror captured the city in 1453, but the Turks only took over in 1983."

But for the newly arrived rustic from the hinterland, working in a leather factory to support his seven children while his wife works as a maid, Istanbul remains the city where dreams can be fulfilled, and where the traffic clogged streets are still paved with gold.

Left, a typical Gecekondu neighborhood. Right, the shell of the Çirağan Palace, with public swimming pool.

TALE OF TWO CITIES

Throughout the 1980s, the fate of the city has seemed to rest increasingly in the hands of two colorful, intense and visionary men, both of whom have captured the imagination of all those who care about Istanbul. Their respective visions of the city, however, are at such odds that as of this writing, the two "Mister Istanbuls" are not on speaking terms with one another.

Çelik Gülersoy, the aristocratic executive

bos there. The Malta Pavillion in Yildiz Park and the White and Yellow pavillions in Emirgan Park, too, are quiet respites from the city, as is the recently restored Hidiv Kasri overlooking the Bosphorus from its extensive grounds outside of Kanlica on the Asian shore. The structure once served as the summer residence of the Ottoman governor of Egypt, but had fallen into an incredible state of dilapidation before being "saved" by

director of the Turkish Touring and Automobile Association, has devoted most of his life and much of his personal fortune to acquiring the rights to battered old buildings and parks, restoring them to their original pristine condition, and then opening the establishments to the public at large.

A tour of the Touring Association's establishments is often enough a complete tour of the city itself. Camlica, the small mountain on the Asian side of the Bosphorus topped by the radio and television relay towers, provides an exquisite overview of the city and is a favorite place for young newlyweds, many having first met in one of the pleasant gaze-

Gülersoy and converted into a deluxe ten room hotel. Like all of Gülersoy's projects, the before-and-after pictures of the Hidiv Kasri stand in amazing contrast to one another.

The flagship of Gülersoy's empire (he prefers to call his restorations "pearls on a necklace") is the Yesil Ev, or "Green House" on Sultan Ahmet Square— the former residence of an eminent citizen of Istanbul whose fate is reflected in the state of his house before Gülersoy arrived to turn the burnt and shattered boards into a thing of beauty. Nearby is Sogukeçesme Street, consisting of a row of houses which are now open as upmarket pensions. The row also houses Gülersoy's private library—a veritable treasure of books, engravings and memorabilia on Istanbul. At the end of the charming street is the "*Saraç Taverna*," or Byzantine Tavern, a fabulous underground restaurant with wandering musicians built into the depths of one of the city's many cisterns.

Currently, the Touring Association is building its first establishment from the ground up near the Kariye Museum, where it already maintains a pleasant tea house for visitors. The owners of a row of quaint houses nearby have also been provided with paint and restoration advice in a further effort to preserve traces of the Istanbul that once was.

But if Gülersoy represents Istanbul's genteel past, the present is dominated by the aggressive personality of Bedrettin Dalan, a man who has arguably done more to change the physiogomy of the city than anyone else since the Turkish conquest of Constantinople by Mehmet the Conqueror in 1453 or maybe even its founding by Constantine the Great in 432.

Dalan, an engineer from Urfa in the southeast of the country, in many ways represents the antithesis of Gülersoy's elitism. Elected mayor in 1984 thanks to a massive outpouring of votes from the urban poor, he immediately set to work making himself the best known "Istanbulite" in the city, possibly the country, and maybe even abroad.

The cornerstone of Dalan's publicity campaign was (and is) the much heralded project to clean up the Gold Horn, the sliver of water leading from the Bosphorus up into the heart of historic Istanbul. Formerly the private lake of the sultans, and much celebrated in song and poem, the waterway had become a virtual sewer, and a place to be

avoided at all possible costs.

Benefitting from a new law governing the country's municipalities which allowed local governments direct control over locally collected revenues, as well from a cowed public still inured to martial law, Dalan declared that within the term of his administration the Golden Horn would be made "as blue as my eyes."

The Golden Horn project is in fact but one

part of a massive sewage system overhaul for the city, but the most dramatic scenes were to be found along its polluted banks, with the mayor himself mounting a bulldozer to smash into the first line of illegal housing and expropriated factory buildings in the area. The only buildings spared were those of proven historical value—if then. In the waterway itself, a lone dolphin was spotted, and in a highly publicized event, the rowing teams of Cambridge and Oxford arrived to race across the waters without having to plug their noses. Dalan himself vowed to swim in the Horn by mid-1988.

Although the Golden Horn clean-up

Left, Sogukçesme Street rowhouses, restored from the ruins. Above, Mr. Istanbul, the restorer, Çelik Gülersoy.

campaign has been the most publicized of the mayor's projects, it is by no-means the only one on the drawing board.

Urban transport—in Istanbul's case, both on sea and land—has also been addressed as top priority by the mayor, and several large hydrofoils have been added to the Bosphorus ferry network to facilitate commuting between the European and Asian shores of the city. Istanbul's buses, meanwhile—in a cheap but incredibly effective move—had their exhaust pipes placed on top, thus removing the immediate blast of smoke from pedestrians standing nearby.

Dalan also began to experiment with the

traffic flow itself, and for months, one could never be certain whether the one-way street one had used in the morning was still running in the same direction that night. Successful and irritating by turns, the new traffic plan for Istanbul seemed innocuous enough until the mayor decided that certain sections of the city had to be razed in the interests of better vehicle flow.

The first and most publicized neighborhood to disappear was Tarlabasi in Beyoglu, where the middle class of Levantine Istanbul had once lived in the quaint, 19th-century Mediterranean-style row houses. Çelik Gülersoy, for one, pointed out that the area

could have been made into a string of pension hotels along the line of his Sogukçesme Street, and that the architecture of the area was unique in Turkey. Dalan replied that 100 year-old buildings, inhabited by drunks and whores, could not be called "historic" in a city whose history stretched back 1500 years, and the bulldozers moved in to the dismay of nostalgists and conservationists alike.

Possibly to assuage the ruffled feathers of those who opposed the destruction of Tarlabasi, Dalan has gone out of his way to encourage the restoration of other buildings, chief among which are the newly restored Tayara Apartments, now managed by Ramada Hotels after an exquisite restoration, and the Ciragan Palace, also scheduled to open as a "historic" hotel after being left vacant for over 50 years.

Bigger projects, too, are in the works. If half of them are realized, the city and its current skyline will be unrecognizable in ten years. Chief among the new projects with some hope of realization is a third Bosphorus Bridge, which will contain a rail-line for another big-ticket project—an underground metro. Plans for tube crossing beneath the Bosphorus have temporarily been shelved due to a lack of cash.

Critics of Dalan, such as Gülersoy, maintain that the mayor is effectively—and maybe deliberately—destroying the city, and that soon Istanbul will have about as much character as, say, Ankara.

Dalan, for his part, says that without the creation of proper infrastructure that responds to the reality of the city of seven million, the present will swamp the past, and leave no room for the future at all.

Both men, happily, have their own group of vocal supporters. And, although it is doubtful that either will concede the point to the other, the peculiar creative tension between the two visionaries seems to insure that Istanbul will remain a unique city, with its feet rooted in the past while walking boldly towards the future.

Left, Mr. Istanbul, the bulldozer, Mayor Bedrettin Dalan. Right, hold on to the past, or run toward the future?

THE LIVING CITY

A bird's eye view: The best way to get a comprehensive view of the confusing maze of Istanbul is, no doubt, to hire a helicopter. **Sancakair** or **Nesu** would be glad to oblige. In fact, the hopeless congestion of city traffic has made such flights of fancy so popular in recent years that some are afraid the city's traffic problem will soon reproduce itself in the skies. But, assuming your budget is not as loose as some of the Istanbul's rich, there are several other points which offer relatively unobstructed panoramas of the city, and much more cheaply, too.

The view from **Galata Bridge** is, of course, the classic Kodak point. For a different angle, you can try the top of **Çamlica Hill** on the Asian side. The delightful turn-of-the century cafe/tea garden rebuilt there by the ubiquitous Mr. Gülersoy adds the place an aura of Renoir's or Proust's Paris. Closer to the heart of the city, the 14th-century **Galata Tower** permits a stupendous overview of the city for those who do not suffer from height sickness. Avoid by all means the ridiculous night-club and the pricey restaurant, and stick to the open terrace that surrounds the phallic cap of the Genoese tower.

If you insist on wining or dining with the city under your feet, keep in mind that you are likely to get a marvelous vista if you go up high enough in just about any part of central Istanbul. Besides the roof bars/restaurants of the **Hilton, Sheraton** and **Etap Marmara**, two outstanding spots recommend themselves; the restaurant of **Bilsak** near Taksim (Soğanci Sokak, Siraselviler), and the bar of the **Journalists' Association** in Cağaloğlu (across from the Iranian Consulate). Although the latter is theoretically members-only, keep in mind the golden rule that in Istanbul no rule ever overrides the "human factor", and few would ever

have the heart to say "no" to a nice foreigner.

Contemplating the city from the region of the birds, you may note that Istanbul does not have a single center, but rather a series of nodes strung along a long backbone. The vertebra starts at **Fatih** and **Aksaray** in the middle of the old city, goes east along the central axis of the peninsula, curves north and crosses over via Galata Bridge, somehow negotiates the steep Galata hill, follows the avenue along old Pera (Beyoğlu) to Taksim, then goes on the Nişantaşi, Şişli, Mecidiyeköy, Etiler and Levent. A branch follows the coast from Karaköy, through Tophane and Dolmabahce, to Beşiktaş. On the Asian side, the main axis leads off from Kadiköy and Moda, following Bağdat Caddesi to Göztepe, Erenköy and Bostanci. Some 70 percent of businesses in the city and almost all of the bigger ones are found along these lines. It is one of the unresolved mysteries of life that the sections north of Şişli and

east of Kadiköy are never included on standard maps of Istanbul, even though, if anywhere, these are where the pulse of the modern city beats the strongest.

Traditions, mysteries, politics: Faith is middle-lower-middle class, conservative, very "Turkish". Older women wear the scarf and off-color long coats—so do some of the young and educated who have "rediscovered" Islam. (Distinguish the black *çarşaf*, which is hard-core Muslim defiant, the grey *başörtüsü* knotted under the chin, just old-fashioned conservative; and the loose *türban* held by a pin under the chin, which is born-again and highly political. As of 1986, women wearing the *türban* are not allowed into the university.) Men are petty bureaucrats or shopkeepers. The myriad shops are sober, inexpensive, basic, although the consumption-mania of the 80s have now made some inroads in nearby Aksaray, and even Benetton have recently opened a franchise of their jazzy teenager boutiques. This is "down-town" for the sprawling poor neighborhoods of the Old City—poorer as you go outward, the poorest near the city walls and along the shores of the Golden Horn.

You may find many Istanbulites who have spent a lifetime on "the other side", as in Sisli or Etiler, including those with an intimate knowledge of the Sahara and the Andes, to be altogether clueless about these parts of the city: a vague rememberance of having once been in Fatih many years ago, and no, never even heard of **Fethiye, Draman,** or **Çarşamba.** In recent years, with the clearing of the intractable mess along the southern shore of the Horn, it has become mildly fashionable to make trips to such neighborhoods as **Fener** and **Balat;** and you may overhear folks in Taksim getting truly excited about their latest "discoveries" in the old city, in a tone that reminds of Stanley discovering the natives.

Next to Fatih is Saraçhane-Şehzade-başi, dominated by the **Aqueduct of**

Some signs are easier to read than others.

Valens (370), **Şehzade Mosque** (1548), and the **City Hall** (1960s). Having been as dead as the aqueduct for decades, the City Hall has come back to life with a vengeance since 1984 under the active government of Metropolitan Mayor Dalan, alias the Bulldozer. The municipal decentralization of the same year has produced such eccentric figures as Mayor Kola of Beşiktaş with his pro-consumer antics, and Mayor Emin Sungur of Şişli with his anti-smoking campaigns, and overall has had a wonderfully tonic effect on the life of the city.

At the same time as decentralization, and possibly affected by it, has been the return of city voters to a more traditional "conservative" line after a decade of social-democratic dominance. By and large, the newer working-class regions in the outskirts, as well as the better-off and educated middle class remain on the left, while the right is solidly entrenched in the Bazaar and the old city as it has been since Byzantine times. The wild new **Monument of Sultan Mehmet** (on flying horse) near the the City Hall is a token of the recent conservative surge, since the Conqueror of Constantinople has become, by some quirk of fate, a symbol of Islamic-nationalistic conservatism. His recently proliferating monuments carry a subtle rebuke against Atatürk, whose statues normally adorn every inch of public space in Turkey. Speaking of Atatürk, you must keep in mind that *all* Turks revere the founder of their Republic—except that conservatives abhor him for his anti-Islamic policies, liberals detest him for his one-party regime, and leftists dislike him for being the official symbol of the state. Beware, and smile politely if you get drawn into a discussion.

While on the topic of statues, one might as well mention that the only really fine public statue in Istanbul is the equestrian **monument of Ismet Inönü** (done by Belling in 1940 while Inönü was president) which stands in a

And some are the same the world over.

little park in front of his erstwhile house in Maçka, above Dolmabahce. The site has a superb view over the harbor.

Refugees, hotels, cafes: The axis between Aksaray and Beyazit have in recent years become the main gathering point of the "other" tourists of Istanbul: Iranian refugees, Arab tourists, Polish and Yugoslav blue-jeans hunters. The hotel district on **LaleliCaddesi**(parallel to the main avenue on the south) has been fully taken over by them, replacing an earlier population of Istanbul University students. The Hogarthian late-night market that operates there is definitely worth a visit. Haggard Iranians hang out at street corners, selling the art treasures of Persia and other, less savory, merchandise, desperately friendly toward anyone who holds out a glimmer of hope for a western visa. Arab families make a spectacle of themselves, oblivious to the unconcealed contempt of the natives. (Turks, who are otherwise remarkably devoid of ethnic prejudices, regard their south-ern neighbors in the same light as Kansas farmers do theirs across the Rio Grande.) Cutthroat Poles exchange Bohemia crystals for leather jackets, wearing a dozen layers of them to the airport at the end of their day-trip to Turkey. Serbian and Arabic (and recently, Greek) replace English and German as the lingua franca of international commerce.

The new **Ramada Hotel,** offering a posh atmosphere in a fantastically renovated turn-of-the-century housing estate, is likely to add a new "gentrified" dimension to the area.

The pseudo-Anglo-Indian monumental arch of **Istanbul University** in Beyazit dates from the 1860s, and once served as the entranceway to the Ottoman Ministry of War. The modern university was set up here in 1933 under the guidance of refugee academics—liberals, Jews, Catholics—from Hitler's Germany, including some of the world's best in their fields. Whatever academic worth it retained through

When it snows, the city stops.

the turmoil of the 70s was finally extirpated under political pressure in the 80s. **Bosphorus University,** the former American College above Bebek, nationalized in 1971, maintains its higher standards.

The best cafes in any city are found near student hangouts, and Istanbul is no exception. The open-air "**kahve**"under the ancient plane tree behind Beyazit Mosque, tucked between the university and the second-hand book market, is one of the most popular, though huge **Marmara Kiraathanesi** across the avenue is possibly more "authentic". B.U. students and nostalgic former graduates form the clientele at three particularly lovely spots on the Bosphorus, **Ali Dayi**'s in Rumelihisari, the **cafe** behind the mosque in Bebek, and the one at the village square in **Ortaköy.** As just about everybody speaks reasonable English here (and is compulsive about bridge and backgammon), these might be among your best bets for meeting

sensible people in Istanbul. Just barge in, and ask somebody sufficiently nice-looking the time, how to catch the boat, or how to play a tricky 6-spade contract! And while on the topic, did you know that bridge was invented in Istanbul by English officers stationed here during the Crimean War, and that its name refers to the Galata Bridge which the gentlemen had to cross for their weekly pastime?

Speaking of cafes, one should not forget to mention absolutely quaint **Erenler Kahvesi** located within a kilim market in the courtyard of 18th century Çorlulu Ali Paşa Medresesi, on Divanyolu past Beyazit. Hookah-smoking, a custom that had gone out of fashion in Istanbul before tourist interest revived it in recent years, can be practiced here as in two other historic sites: **Erzurumlu** teahouse, under Galata Bridge with a magnificent habor view, and **Pierre Loti,** nicely redone on Eyüp hill (not the fake of the same name on Divanyolu).

Not every place is too crowded— the Emirgan Park.

Tourists, journalists, criminals: Tourists of the first world variety take over past a magic line at the eastern edge of Beyazit Square, and literally swarm at **Sultan Ahmet.** Germans predominate, followed by the British and the rest. The young and carefree find accommodations in the area; others stay elsewhere in the city but gravitate here during most of the day. The famous **Lale Pudding Shop** at Divanyolu #6, while no longer the fabled halfway point to Katmandu of 60s hippie lore, still serves as a meeting and eating point for hitchhikers, fortune seekers and traveling companions. Their notice board has become a venerable institution of Istanbul tourism.

The maze of alleyways and dead ends north of Divanyolu, extending down to the seashore, houses the old market district, including, but not limited to, the **Grand Covered Bazaar.** Most of the city's commerce in gold and jewelry, rugs, cheap and wholesale textiles, kitchen and tableware, spices, chemi-

cals, foreign currency, furs, pets, copperware, and contraband takes place here. **Cagaloğlu**, the area immediately before Sultan Ahmet, houses the headquarters of seven of Turkey's nine major daily newspapers, and much of its publishing, printing and wholesale stationery trade. Conveniently for reporters, law courts and Police HQ are located nearby.

The district, of course, is deserted at night except for the odd tourist wondering where to find "Istanbul by night", and especially the lower areas around **Sirkeci** and **Eminönü** can get somewhat eerie. Don't worry too much, as the crime rate in Istanbul is per capita less than a fifth of New York, and although violent crimes are slightly higher than in Europe, they are almost always crimes of passion or vengeance, so they don't concern outsiders. Armed robbery and random violence are just about unknown, and petty thievery occurs within reasonable limits. Would-be tourist swindlers are often feeble-hearted young amateurs whom an experienced traveler would have fun counter-swindling if so disposed. You may even end up becoming good friends with them if you play your part with gusto.

Commuters, crowds, wanderers: Having a population of almost a million during the day and being virtually deserted at night, of course, means spectacular rush hours. The harborfront stretch between Eminönü and Sirkeci is the nerve center of Istanbul's rather inadequate public transport system, and so turns into a full-scale battleground twice a day involving infantry battles, tank charges, navy manoeuvers and guerrilla skirmishes. It is fun to watch, with billowing black smoke from boats and a red sun setting behind the giant mosques adding truly dramatic color. If you *have* to participate, take the ferryboat whenever possible. Buses are frequent, and are recommended (at rush hour) for those who desperately yearn for the warm human touch. Vehicle traffic is too often hope-

Left, Sakip Sabanci—possibly the richest man in Turkey. Right, a new face job on one of the ubiquitous banks in town.

The metropolitan police of Istanbul are counted among the world's most effective police forces, despite low salaries, lack of facilities, and an uncommon lack of respect for them among the citizenry.

Wearing a somewhat darker version of the old German *feldgrau*, the Istanbul police have proven their usefulness under a wide range of circumstances. They are stunningly effective in solving all sorts of crime, scor-

than an indication of the neighborhood's desire for a responsible and contented constabulary.

If emergency strikes, police assistance is a mere phone call away. (One must, of course, have available a token—*jeton*—and one is well-advised to carry at least one for emergencies). Don't forget that the numbers change—166 66 66, 366 66 66, or 566 66 66, depending on which quarter you are calling

ing banner successes against drug dealers, black-marketeers and organized crime (yes, there is a Turkish Mafia). Their most evident failure is one which threatens Istanbul's citizenry most gravely and most often: traffic.

The average policeman earns the equivalent of less than $1,000 a year, and it is difficult for the devoted force to replenish its ranks with fresh bodies. Its problems in manning the various posts and patrols are chronic. Accordingly, the tolerant tourist will recognize the locals' practice of contributing beer and pocket money, even leather jackets, boots and stationery, as less another manifestation of third world peccadillos

from. If a crisis of lesser dimensions occurs, one may contact the *Emniyet Müdürlüğü*, or Security Police, headquarters (telephone 528 51 73) and ask for "*Yabancilar Polisi*," the section charged with care and feeding of foreigners.

There is no such thing in Turkey as the "tourist police," although some, usually in civvies, claiming to be such appear before the unwitting traveler on Istanbul's streets from time to time. Reporting such assaults on Western gullibility can, however, mean hours in the bowels of the Turkish bureaucracy, answering interminable questions, swearing depositions taken on antiquated typewriters, and suffering lengthy examination of record books to identify your suspect among hundreds of dark, mustachioed mug shots. Best not to bother.

Beware the "Envelope Men": The so-called "gypsy district" of **Hacihüsrev** is famous for a distinctive local craft—picking pockets, swindling, and an extraordinary menu of rip-offs. The police concede the district its success. The most usual method of the quarter's aspiring artisans is to pick your wallet or even the contents of your well-sealed handbag while crushing against you in a crowded place—a bus, movie theater, or just on the street. But such common pickpockets are simply unqualified apprentices to the true craftspeople.

Kids start young here. A favorite of the street urchins is the cardboard trick. In this ruse, the unsuspecting benefactor is approached by a gaggle of doe-eyed youngsters, proferring a large piece of flat cardboard as if to gather alms from the better-off. The patron declines, but may not escape; he is assaulted by the prodding of the bizarre object which, he notices upon close inspection, is uniquely unsuited to its putative purpose of gathering coin. As his viscera are poked with the cardboard he may be prompted to loose a note or two. In the meantime, the handy youngsters have plumbed the depths of his pockets, safely under the visual cover of the cardboard.

High art it is indeed when one pours murky water on you from a high window, then rushes down offering profuse apologies, forcing you to take off your coat for immediate cleaning. Of course, in your concern to forgive the poor devil you forget all about your wallet. (He hasn't.) A Passerby spits particles of chewed newspaper on you and, apologizing profusely, brushes you down while taking even better care of the money in your pocket. Also beware of what Turks call "Oh my father-ism." The stranger who embraces you with high-pitched squeals of delight, only to apologize for having mistaken you for someone else has probably made no error in locating—and lifting—your valuables.

Even these ruses, though, are eclipsed in the penumbra of that formidable master, Osman the Pheasant. This patron saint of the

neighborhood is credited with a lifetime of flim-flammery, including having "sold" the Galata Tower, the Bosphorus Bridge, a red-and-white city bus, and a large share of public real estate to boot.

Finally, when you pass a beggar, keep in mind old Fagin from Dickens' *Oliver Twist*. In reality, many beggars are much better off than yourself, and, taking up their platforms of cardboard or wooden sleds on skates, may go home to a life of comfort and ease replete with villas and cars. These are the artists who arouse the envy of many a veteran thespian; their stage is the world and its unwitting players the generous and the gullible.

Left, beware the Envelope Man! Above, some police are friendlier than others.

SAILING WITHIN BYZANTIUM

The old-style *dolmus* is an odd sight, a car of often nostalgic vintage being stopped by passengers along its fixed route like a bus. It will take five, six or even more people, depending on the weather, the greed of the bullying driver and benevolence of the passengers, who, previously complete strangers, stop it like a shared taxicab, yet pay their fares like a bus or tramcar. The *dolmus* is more expensive than public transport, how-

ever, although still cheaper than a cab.

Born out of World War II fuel shortages, the *dolmus* is a feature of Turkey, and particularly Istanbul, its birthplace. Migrating Turks have carried the *dolmus* concept into many Middle Eastern areas and even to New York, where Turkish-origin cab drivers can be seen with their passengers, stopping for an extra fare! Sadly, however, the old-style Istanbul *dolmus* is fast disappearing with the prosperity of modern times, although it survives in many parts of the old city. Imagine the pleasure of traveling in a 1939 Mercedes' Benz, a 1946 Packard, in 1948 De Sotos and 1952 Buicks and Plymouths—the

types of *dolmus* cars often found in Istanbul. Now up-to-date, purpose-built mini-buses are gradually replacing these much-loved juice-guzzlers.

Nevertheless, even a ride in a modern *dolmus* remains an experience. Hail one in the street, pass your fare to the driver, and you'll be in a cabin decorated with the stickers of your driver's particular artistic choice. The radio is guarantee to be blasting Turkish music which is not quite Western, not quite oriental, but which has become such a feature of a *dolmus* ride that it's known as "*dolmus* music".

But a *dolmus* seems too adventurous, try the New York-style "Yellow Cabs"— although the visitor must be content with Turkish-made Fiats and Renaults, or even the odd-looking and stubborn Anadol, a fiberglass-bodied first attempt by Turkey to enter the automotive market in the late 1960s. Taxi meter fares seem cheap to foreigners, and the passage can be quite rapid, especially with taxi-drivers' common disregard of traffic regulations!

Train buffs should experience the very cheap, although crowded and somewhat unhygienic suburban lines from Sirkeci Station to the European coast, or from Haydarpasa Station to Gebze on the way to Izmit. Prepare, though, for all sorts of demands on your wallet. You could be offered ballpoint pens, aspirins, neckties, glasscutters, anthologies of Nasreddin Hodja, copies of the Quran and even ladies' panties, all very cheap. Beggars will tell you they've just come out of the hospital and haven't the money to get home. For the last 20 years, a beggar woman has been riding between Yedikule (Seven Towers) and the slum district of Zeytinburnu, collecting money from brotherly Muslims by saying her husband is about to have a serious operation in the hospital!

Such people can be found also in the excellent shuttle ships that cross the Bosphorus between the continents of Asia and Europe, about 25 minutes each way.

OFF LIMITS

Tarabya is a charming village resort with a marina at the Black Sea end of the Bosphorus. You may notice the particularly nice 19th-century buildings offering superb views—but don't try to get in. They are strictly reserved for the military! Most places offering excellent panorama, services and facilities, in fact, turn out to be reserved by Turkish officialdom. Many are officers' clubs, others turn out to be reserved by different ministries for their officials and civil servants. They are run with gusto for members and guests, and are incredibly cheap, perhaps as a sort of reward for those who elect to spend their lives in the vacuum of state bureaucracy. A meal in such establishments often costs less than a beer in a regular bar.

Especially at the northern end of the Bosphorus, there are areas of huge emptiness, surrounded by barbed wire, which are not for the sightseer. These are military zones, and not to be approached, at all.

In the city, on the other hand, many nice places fall into a different sphere of exclusivity. They become private clubs— the **Moda Sea Club**, the anachronistically named **Lausanne Club**, the **Levent Club** for the nouveau riche, or that reminder of distinguished Ottoman days, the **Cercle d'Orient**. There, the creme de la creme of Istanbul society congregates. These are the people never seen on the street, who go to their offices at 11:30 a.m. and relax at their clubs at noon; industrialists, leading academics, scrap-metal dealers and bankers, there with their wives to see and be seen, gamble, drink and support local schools with lavish donations. Strangely, perhaps, these street-shy creatures seem to delight in appearing in the weekend editions of the more color-splashed press to a degree unheard of in society pages elsewhere. No one seems to notice or care that one $10,000 bouquet of roses at a wedding looks much like another.

Left, a familiar face aboard Big Red. Above, a reject from an elitist club.

lessly clogged, so calling a chauffeured limousine (**Carey-Vip** at 141-6514, or **Inter Limousine** at 150-2423) doesn't help a lot. The traffic problem has much to do with the fact that the half-a-million cars now in circulation are to a large extent limited to a few main arteries, side streets being often too steep, too irregular, too narrow for cars. Subway, pondered, planned, and postponed for the past 30 years, is of course the only real solution, but the extremely uneven structure of the city along with the hopelessly tangled layers of history that lie underground make it prohibitively expensive. So the city takes the easy way out, and cuts a new swath through the urban jungle to make room for cars whenever gridlock seems imminent.

Try walking. Strolling along the **Galata Bridge** is one of the basic pleasures of Istanbul, and millions engage in it daily. Watching the human torrent crisscrossing the bridge will yield two interesting observations, viz., that the male/female ratio is 7-to-1, and that exactly 87 percent of the grown men wear moustaches (figures tested by your author). As to the first, no, Turks don't discard baby daughters. A walk through the poorer residential neighborhoods during work hours will reveal the other half, a female overpopulation that can get positively titillating if you don't mind the sexism. Things are more balanced in places like Nişantaşi and Etiler. By and large, the legal status of women in Turkey is similar to the West, and in the mid to upper strata of society women participate in public life rather successfully. There are proportionally many more female lawyers, judges, and doctors for example than in Anglo-Saxon countries (though few corporation managers, and almost no waitresses). As for the rest of the population, perhaps the key insight into many aspects of Turkish society is that it is based on an extremely solid, close-knit, and conservative family structure that conditions the roles and behavior of individuals through every stage of their lives—at times oppressively.

With regard to moustaches, let it be reminded that at least in Istanbul they carried a very plebeian stigma until the late 60s, and became fashionable only during the political turmoils of the following decade. Even now, most true-blood Istanbulites don't wear them unless they have leftist sympathies, or wear distinctive varieties *a la* Nietszche or Gustav Adolph. The social and sexual significance of moustache for the masculine majority, on the other hand, can be deduced from the fact that waiters, soldiers, and policemen are required to shave them, in an act of symbolic castration, as a sign of due respect and obedience. As for the rare beard, it signifies that the wearer is, or likes to be seen as, one of three things: a Muslim fundamentalist, an "intellectual", or a wino.

Speaking of intellectuals, it must be pointed out that they have been the principal proponents of "westernization" in this country, which is probably why the whole enterprise has never really gotten off the ground. *Entel's* can often be seen pondering on this failure over quantities of alcohol at specific establishments mentioned elsewhere in this book. As for winos: *berduş* is the Istanbul equivalent of the Parisian *clochard*, and *köprüalti çocuḡu* ("underbridge kid") the kind of Oliver Twist. Galata Bridge has always been their favorite dwelling. Neither variety is very numerous: one of the often unexpected realities of Istanbul is that, while you see a lot of poverty around, true down-and-out misery is much rarer here than in Frankfurt or Paris, not to even mention New York, which comes closer to Bombay and Rio in this respect.

Shippers, brokers, players: **Karaköy** was originally *Karaiköy*, named after the community of Karaite Jews who lived here for many centuries before they are swamped out by Sephardim from Spain in 1492.(The *Karaite* cemetery in Hasköy—opposite Fener, on the north shore of the Golden Horn—is one

Left, despite a non-smoking campaign, the nation puffs on.

of the wholly unknown little surprises of Istanbul.) The western part of today's Karaköy is covered by the bustling hardware-trade district of **Perşembepazari**—hard to believe maybe, but a delightfully colorful area that deserves a stroll through—while the east is dominated by the **Port of Istanbul,** with customs houses, shipping companies, insurance firms, and stout 19th-century banks to complete the ambience. Captains and overseas merchants eat at **Liman Lokantasi,** situated directly above the cruise ship quay and Marine Bank headquarters, and one of the culinary peaks of the city despite its somewhat musty appearance. The altogether unbelievable **brothel district** is located—naturally—not far from the port, on the steep hillside that leads up to Galata Tower.

The coastal avenue to the east and north was created in the 1950s at the expense of the series of dynastic residences that used to line the coast all the way to Dolmabahce. Few royal traces remain; instead you get an endless row of trading company offices. A newcomer to the area is the fledgling **Istanbul Stock Exchange.** It was set up in 1986 (more accurately, revived after being technically dead for over 60 years) as a crucial component of the government's economic modernization program, with the goal to divert savings from the time-honored traditional favorites of gold and real estate. It was so successful in doing this that the market index went up 15-fold in less than a year, creating a stampede worthy of Charlie Chaplin's gold rush. Then it crashed royally in August 1987. There is still money to be made, though, and especially if you manage to find a good inside tipper it is definitely a more exciting place to try to finance your stay in Istanbul (or lose your shirt) than the gambling casinos of the big hotels.

Speaking of excitement, however, few places can beat the atmosphere of **Dolmabahce** (Inönü) **football**

Conserving energy resources, down by the docks.

stadium further up the coast. Get this straight: football guides the hearts and minds of average Istanbulites far more deeply than by any other institution or phenomenon you have seen so far, including religion, politics, or tradition. During major games (on Sundays and sometimes Saturdays in season, July-August being off-season) life comes to a full stop around the city, and the tumult in the stadium—often outside it as well—is worthy of Justinian's Hippodrome. The Blue and Green factions have been replaced by Fenerbahçe, Galatasaray and Beşiktaş, the three Istanbul teams that often dominate national leagues. The loyalties they elicit are never short of fanatical, and the easiest way to earn the friendship and respect of a normal Istanbulite is to figure out the team he supports, and then to show oneself sympathetic, or at least knowledgeable, about it. Even the most devious rug merchant is known to fall for this ruse. Keep an eye out for flags—blue/yellow striped for Fener,

red/yellow for G'saray, black/white checkers for BJK. Say you were impressed by their game in Europe last year; then demand a reduction on that lovely rug.

Sports in Istanbul means football, and just about nothing else. The only other spectator sport that is remotely popular is horseracing, and for that you have to go to **Veliefendi Hippodrome** near the airport. (Enthusiasts may find interest in the fact that the forefathers of all English thoroughbreds, Godolphin, Darley, and Byerly the Turk, were Istanbulites sent as a gift to King James.) Car and go-cart races are held in the Asian suburb of **Tuzla,** and have recently become popular among the socialites of Bağdat Caddesi. Unless you relish inhaling diesel exhaust and sulphur fumes, the only place you can freely jog is **Belgrade forest** far away in the north, where the first and only full-fledged golf course of Istanbul is also scheduled to be operative in 1990.

Besides football, Dolmabahce offers

Küçükçiftlik Gardens, with a year-round pleasure park and periodic visiting circuses, and the ornate palace of the last sultans, with a recently installed mock-Buckingham guard of honor guarding the nonexistent monarchy—or possibly the tour groups inside. Further up, Beşiktaş is a colorful, mostly residential district that curiously reminds one of Brooklyn in relation to New York. Like the latter, it used to be a separate town until about 100 years ago. The main shopping street and the grand produce market are among the liveliest (and least expensive) in the city: a stroll there during the Saturday shopping spree is probably as close as you could get to the "authentic" colors of lower-middle class Istanbul.

Memories, escapes, dreams: To get from Karaköy to Beyoglu proper, formerly known as Pera, you can take the historic Tünel or you may tackle the almost-vertical Yüksekkaldirim/Galip Dede street through the former Jewish district of Istanbul are to be found along the upper part of this climb, including Librairie de Pera at Galip Dede #22 which is the city's foremost authority on rare and out-of-print books. The area is also the place to wander around if you are looking for musical instruments, old records, or stamps.

Old Pera has come down a long way since the genteel days of the turn of the century, and now bears a distinct resemblance to New York's West 42nd Street. There are signs, though, that its decline into sleaze-city may have hit bottom in the 70s, and now there is a movement to revive the place. Istiklal Caddesi may soon be turned into a pedestrian mall once the ghastly 6-lane road that was recently cut along historic Tarlabasi Caddesi is completed.

The nightclubs, pavyon's and girlie bars that dominate side streets in the district may not necessarily appeal to all tastes, but the jam-packed beer alley of Çiçek Paşaji is sufficiently wholesome—if not exactly fit for kids—to be a must item on your "Istanbul by night"

agenda. Watch gypsy performers, sex-goddesses of bygone decades, inebriated businessmen and lovesick youths mingle in an alcohol-induced haze. Keep an eye out for Ms. Anahit, the queen-size accordionist who can sing in a dozen languages in a croak that may become tolerable after a few pitchers of beer. The area behind the Pasaj is the equally colorful fish and produce market of Galatasaray, which also hides some of the best hard-drinking taverns of Istanbul, including the excellent Hasir Sütte, the German delicatessen run by a Bulgar, maintains here the venerable tradition supplying such un-Turkish specialties as pork, snails, frog legs, and the like.

Ask the owner, one Mr. Eldik (perfectly friendly and fluent in Turkish, Bulgarian, German, French and English) to direct you to his pig farm just outside the city.

Innocent-looking Yeşilçam street nearby is the Turkish Hollywood, the dream alley where most film studios,

Left, in a city of spectators, everybody goes to the games. Right, but even lady body-builders are making headway.

producers' offices, and model agencies are located. Having been one of the world's most prolific manufacturers of kitsch since the 30s, Yeşilcam is reputed to have recently gone high-quality under directors like Atif Yilmaz—an assessment that some may find slightly exaggerated. Of the many cinemas in the area only **Emek** shows decent films (mostly foreign). For a fuller selection you have to move on to the Osmanbey-Şişli district, where cinemas like **Gazi**, **Site**, and **Kent** usually screen the latest American hits in their original versions.

Beside entertainment, the other main activity along Istiklal Caddesi is fashion, although Beyoğlu has long lost its lead in this field to the more fashionable Nişantaşi-Osmanbey region. One major exception that has remained is **Vakko**, Istanbul's equivalent of Saks Fifth Avenue and Galeries Lafayette. The six-storey department store offers primarily top quality women's clothing (their hand-printed scarves deserve special note), as well as an excellent cafeteria and art gallery. Their casual wear section is called Vakkorama and is located next to the Etap on Taksim Square.

Pretension, alienation, power: Sprawling, shapeless **Taksim Square** and vicinity is where you find the top international hotels (**Sheraton, Hilton, Pullman Etap;** with Hyatt soon to join them) and the modern aluminum cage of the Opera, officially known as **Atatürk Cultural Center.** Here they occasionally stage mockeries of Verdi, or make strange noises which the program would like to attribute to an innocent Mozart of Beethoven. The Center was inaugurated in 1970 after exactly 23 years in construction, but burned down completely the next year, possibly because somebody in the audience could not stand the quality of the performances. (The fire occurred during a performance of Arthur Miller's The Crucible, just at the moment when John Smith thundered about fire and brim-

Lest we forget the military tradition.

stone. The performance of Kerim Afsar, the actor, was, in fact, superb.)

Being the largest public space in the city, Taksim Square was once used for the most spectacular political rallies in the history of Turkish democracy, culminating with May Day 1977 when a crowd of half a million got involved in a melee which left dozens dead. **Siraselviler** and **Cihangir** districts nearby have become the focal point of a radicalism of altogether different sort involving environmentalists, feminists, and homosexual activists.

The environmental movement has coalesced lately around the big fuss created over the construction of Gökova power plant , and the threatened extinction of giant sea turtles in the south . Feminism has acquired a bit of respectability with the smashing success of *Woman Without Name*, a novel by Ms. Duygu Asena who is also editor of the popular monthly *Kadinca*. The pink persuasion, normally a matter of extreme forms of public disapproval,

has also acquired more balanced publicity recently in part as a result of the extraordinary proliferation of transvestite and transsexual prostitution (very visible along the Siraselviler-Taksim-Harbiye axis) in the 80s, which raised some disturbing questions regarding the latent preferences of Turkish macho men. Disciples of Sappho have been less prominent, but **Pub Astoria** in Osmanbey (#265 on the avenue) is said to have a large proportion of them among its upmarket clientele.

The Radical Party of Mr. Ibrahim Eren (contact through **Bilsak** or **Pub Yeşil**) tries to bring the various marginal movements under an umbrella. Needless to say, the cultural divide mentioned earlier in this chapter works both ways, and attitudes that are regarded as acceptable or harmless around Taksim get about as much comprehension in Fatih as Martian invaders.

It is Fatih that has the votes, but if the theory which holds that the true center

Marching during funeral for leftist leader.

of a modern city is where major airline companies congregate—then **Elma-dag**, the section of Cumhuriyet Caddesi that leads north from Taksim, is downtown Istanbul. Along with the airlines go major travel agencies, rent-a-car companies, etc. The all-too-familiar golden arches put up an appearance, too, although this is probably the only place in the world where **McDonalds** has acquired the status of a fancy "in" eatery among the young and pecunious. Then again, the transformation of Western commonplaces into status symbols is one of the hallmarks of this part—at least—of Istanbul. Discotheques are a case in point, and Adidas or Puma sneakers represent the ultimate sign of social distinction among the teen-crowd of Nişantaşi. Fine specimens of the latter may be seen mingling with their mates, or with dad's business guests, at the numerous night spots along airline-row—a nice and comparatively low-key one of which is **Swiss Pub** at #14. The gourmet restaurant of **Divan Hotel** may be a little too-exclusive even for Adidas kids, but the downstairs **pastry shop** is a sweet-tooth's paradise regardless of age or class, as well as being an ideal place to date the secretaries of area companies.

Harbiye is where Cumhuriyet Caddesi forks into **Halaskargazi** (left) and **Valikonaği** (right). It is named after the **army academy** whose grim facade you see on the right. A majority of Turkish army officers graduate from here, after having first studied at military lycees where they get recruited at the age of 12. The norm, in a faithful continuation of janissary traditions, is complete institutional self-sufficiency with little civilian contact. The *"orduevi"* in each city provides a full-fledged social center—hotel, shopping arcade, and recreational facilities—from which civilians are excluded. **Istanbul Orduevi,** next door to Harbiye, is the tallest building in town. The next tallest are two American-built hotels, Sheraton and Etap (formerly Intercontinental), followed

Some use walls for art.

by headquarters of the Istanbul Chamber of Commerce in Beyoğlu—an apt reflection, perhaps, of a certain pecking order.

Class, style, riches: Nişantaşi and Şişli (also Bagdat Caddesi on the Asian side) are where most non-rustics of Istanbul live: the sidewalk male/female ratio is quite balanced, and the moustache rate among men can get as low as 45 percent. You can observe here the occasional remnant of an old Istanbul upper class—ancient ladies in fur, enduring the degenerate age with an expression of utter disgust—but to find the contemporary filthy-rich you have to go on to Etiler, or to places like Bebek, Emirgan or Yeniköy on the Bosphorus. Nearer here, **Maçka** (due south of Nişantaşi, overlooking the big park and a superlative panorama) is also a neighborhood for the kind of people who can afford $5000 residential rents. Nişantaşi-Şişli is mainly inhabited by a well-off middle class, consisting of medium businessmen, company managers, professionals—people of the 10 to 30,000-dollar annual income bracket. They are numerous and visible enough to noticeably differentiate Istanbul from the hardcore third-world look with its stark rich/poor gap, and strong enough to sustain a rather sophisticated shopping life in this part of the city.

Some 1000 department stores, boutiques, and specialty shops line **Rumeli** and **Halaskargazi** avenues. Ever since going into exports in earnest in the 80s Turkish textile designers have steadily improved to West European standards, and the time has perhaps arrived when shopping for clothes on Rumeli Caddesi can be as valid a reason for visiting Istanbul as gawking at the walls of Hagia Sophia. A good place to start is **Yargici**, at the corner of Rumeli and Valikonaği, which offers the best in modern semi-casual wear. **Mudo** still dominates casual styles; **Titiz** is somewhat highbrow; **Kip** usually has the best selection of men's shirts; **Derimod** offers the classiest leatherware; and

And others use walls for target practice.

Beymen is the acknowledged pinnacle of the male image in Turkey. You can look for unexpected bargains on **Sair Nigar Sokak,** the back street next to Rumeli on the north, which is lined with workshops and the wholesale outlets. Ignore the "wholesale only" signs—a foreigner is always nicer to deal with than the wolves who do wholesale buying—but don't forget that you are no longer in the Bazaar, so bargaining is not likely to be very effective.

For really fancy stuff you have to go the opposite direction, toward the back streets of Maçka and **Teşvikiye.** **Zeynep Tunuslu** has taken the fashion world by storm with her striking designs at the boutique that carries her name in Topagaci—if not also with her airplane flying and body-building. **Ipek Kramer** at Abdi Ipekçi street #7/2 deserves a visit to observe the ultimate in silkwear and lingerie designed by the inimitable Ms. Kramer, even when your wallet is not fat enough to buy them. Mr. Kramer runs a fashion-

able coiffeur at the same address, although the top name 'in town in hairstyling is undoubtedly **Muammer**, two blocks further down. (The street, by the way, memorializes the prominent journalist of Jewish extraction whose assassination in broad daylight in 1980 at the corner of Karakol street here was the lowest point of the political chaos of the period. Mehmet Ali Ağca, the man who shot him, later moved on to the world stage with bigger and better assignments.)

Widening horizons: Halaskargazi Caddesi used to be lined with stately mansions surrounded by gardens until it was transformed into a concrete canyon almost overnight in the 60s. The graceful **Bulgarian Exarchate,** the religious center of the 1000-strong Bulgarian Orthodox community in Istanbul, stands as a lone reminder of the past—and a challenge and insult to the appetite of property developers. The year 1965 is in fact a date that may have been as fateful in the urban history of

Snap shots on the street.

Istanbul as 324 or 1453: the law that made it possible to own apartment flats independently was passed that year, making it easy for the middle class to own real estate, and so—aided also by the wave of immigration that started around the same time—causing property values to skyrocket. Owners of old-fashioned single-unit housing capitulated almost to the man (rather the woman, since most real estate in the city is traditionally owned by women). Financially it made a lot of sense to exchange an albatross, even when it might be an architectural masterpiece, with the two or three apartment flats that a developer—often a quick-buck artist from the Black Sea region—offered in return. So the city was transformed to an extent that would have made Constantine proud, and the Istanbul you now see is one of the newest cities in the world in addition to being one of the oldest. That the whole madness happened at a time when municipal government was half dead was a misfortune that has resulted in a town-planner's nightmare, with no zoning to speak of, and hardly any green areas left to relax the eye.

Fake-classical **Şişli Mosque** used to mark the precise outer limit of the city until the 60s, with woods and meadows beyond where bourgeois families of Şişli would make Sunday outings to buy fresh "village" eggs. You will have hard time believing any of this, of course, as the **Mecidiyeköy-Gayrettepe-Zincirlikuyu** axis has now become one of the main business centers of the city where the headquarters of almost all major corporations of Turkey are located. Main units of the **Koç** and **Sabanci** groups, great conglomerates whose interests range across every aspect of industry, banking, and trade, and whose control over the Turkish economy is said to rival that of the government, are here. So are **Enka** and **STFA**, top names in construction industry in the 70s and 80s, respectively; **Eczacibaşi**, the chemicals, giant; and **Alarko**, the Jewish-

owned investment group. Despite the magnitude of their resources, most of them remain one-main (or one-family) affairs that depend on government contracts and/or protection for their survival. You may run into some of those responsible at the restaurant and nightclub row at **Etiler**.

The planned construction of a second peripheral freeway in conjunction with the new Bosphorus Bridge will probably give a yet further push to the northward expansion of Istanbul. The hills of **Ayazağa** and **Maslak** have already become the choicest development land in the city. **Levent**, which was created in the 60s as the first and only American-style residential suburb of Istanbul, is now being transformed rapidly into a business district. By the time you get around to visiting Istanbul, the modern center of the city may have decisively shifted as far as here, and it is a matter of just a decade or two before the Grand Bazaar gets moved to the sandy beaches of the Black Sea coast.

Waiting for line.

A GARLAND OF VILLAGES

As late as in the 1960s, one author would describe Istanbul as a "big collection of villages". The typical urban hub centered around a quaint square, flanked by the local mosque (or church or synagogue) and a market street of rickety shops shaded by ancient plane trees and creeping vines, surrounded by a maze of residences. This structure not only imparted distinctly human proportions to the urban environment. Each village being a community in microcosm, complete with its prominent rich houses, shopkeepers and poor-man's back alleys, it also gave the city a markedly different look than the much more broadly (regionally) segregated Western cities.

Under the onslaught of mass immigration and development, predictably, much of this structure has been swept away. What remains of it is often the old village name which now designates an arbitrary city block—several hundreds of them within the Old City alone—and Istanbulites' habit of specifying an address simply by the name of the neighborhood. The villages of Istanbul survive in something like their original charm in the outskirts, notably along the shores of the Bosphorus. A trip along that enchanted waterway is thus, above all, a selection of the delights of the little communities that line its shores.

Bosphorus villages existed since time immemorial as semi-rural settlements, inhabited during Ottoman times mainly by the Christian and Jewish minorities, that supplied the capital's fresh produce and fish. Arnavutköy was popularly known for its aromatic strawberries; Çengelköy specialized in sweet cucumbers; while the Jewish gardeners of Kuruçeşme held the market in artichokes.

Then, first in the halcyon days of the 1720s, and again more decisively to-ward the middle of that century, it became fashionable for the Ottoman high society to retire to the shores of Bosphorus for summer residence. A special style of architecture evolved for this wood-built waterfront mansions, distinguished by an elegant simplicity of form, graceful cascades of eaves and balconies, and—after the mid-19th century—intricate ornamentation: they were called *yali*, with inland versions called *köşk* or *konak*. Sultans built their own lavish *yalis*, then moved their permanent residence to the new Dolmabahce Palace in 1853. During the reigns of Abdülmecid (1839-61) and Abdülaziz (1861-76), half a dozen baroque/neo-classical palaces, several bright mosques, imposing official halls and innumerable kiosks and gazebos improved the visual grace of the Bosphorus under the direction of the Balyan family of imperial architects. The life of the capital increasingly seemed to converge on the Bosphorus. Bosphorus became associated with a

particular end-of-the-century lifestyle, perhaps somewhat illusory, of gentle refinement and cultivation, combining idealized European manners and an imagined Oriental tranquility—an ivory *köşk* that grew the more gracious the more the economy collapsed and the empire disintegrated around it.

Reality has returned to the Bosphorus, first with the apartment blocks of the wealthy of a less esthetically inclined age, then with the proletarian shanties that have claimed their share of the once-wooded hills. Nevertheless, enough traces of a bygone beauty remain to make a Bosphorus tour a most worthwhile experience on a visit to Istanbul. The best way is undoubtedly to take the ferryboat that leaves **Sirkeci** (downtown) at cryptic hours to ply a leisurely shuttle between villages, and to stop at any one of them that captures the fancy. One cautionary note: the reality that has descended upon the Bosphorus in latter times tends to become rather acute on summer weekends, so weekdays should be preferred if at all possible.

Palace of the last Sultans: As the boat leaves behind the unforgettable sights and sounds of the Istanbul harbor, the first major landmark along the European shore will be the long, white, and graceful row of buildings that constitute **Dolmabahce Palace.** This belongs to a different era and an altogether different spirit than Topkapi; its style has a greater affinity with Versailles and Sans Souci than with the domed and arched labyrinth of the older palace.

It was Abdülmecid who had the palace built, although his father Mahmud II (1808-39) had already abandoned Topkapi for various Bosphorus residences which no longer exist. The young Sultan was rather the epitome of a romantic Victorian gentleman: he suffered the love of various European ladies; wept to the music of Chopin; and appropriately died of consumption. He wished to make a clean break with the

The Dolmabahce Palace.

oppressive and bloodsoaked memories of his ancestors in Topkapi, and to remold his palace in a "civilized" European image.

The result sums up the dreams and paradoxes of an age. The palace is a self-conscious reaction against the Ottoman past, and an affirmation of the faith and will to revive the Empire in a new form. At the same time, the ruthless functionality of Topkapi has been replaced by a preoccupation with form and appearance that borders on the excessive. The opulence that is on display is spectacular, if sometimes overbearing, and does justice to the equivalent of a billion dollars that was spent on construction. The artistry is masterful, at times even eccentric. In addition to its 16 external pavilions, the place has 285 rooms, no less than 43 toilets, and 6 *hamams*, including one carved out of pure alabaster. The throne room is the largest in Europe, with a dome 117 feet (35 meters) above the floor, carrying a 9000-pound crystal chandelier that is reputedly the heaviest in the world. The staircase too have crystal balustrades, and some of the furnishings would turn Louis XV green with envy.

This last, fantastic display of the resources of the Ottoman Empire was also the setting of the end of its 620-year long saga. It was here that Mehmed VI Vahdeddin, the last sultan, fled at dawn on October 18, 1922, by rowboat to a British frigate that offered him asylum in Europe. His palace remained as the symbol of a brief era of hope that went sour, an experiment that failed to take root, repudiated both by diehard conservatives and the radical Republic.

Two other imperial residences of the same age are located within a short distance to Dolmabahce. The gutted edifice of **Çirağan Palace**, weathering the elements since a fire destroyed it, may have turned into a luxurious hotel by the time this book is published. Its halls once served as residence, then as prison-cell for the demented Murat V (deposed in 1876 after a brief reign), as his brother, Abdülhamid II (1876-1909) kept a paranoid eye on him from **Yildiz Palace** up the hill. At Yildiz, one can admire the creations of that tragic character, the last of the great Sultans, who became, amid the self-imposed solitude of his palace, one of the most accomplished carpenters of his empire. The perfectly reproduced Viennese and Swiss cafes in the vast park surrounding the palace once served him as their lone customer during the customary strolls he took to relieve his obsessive fear of conspirators. Now lovingly restored by Mr. Çelik Gülersoy—along with the imperial park and pavilions at **Emirgan**, further upstream, and the graceful patisserie on **Çamlica Hill**, on the Asian side—they provide a favorite spot for Istanbulite lovers to hold hands and exchange secret words, far away from the Abdülhamidian attentions of father, brother, spouse, neighbor and policeman.

Up the coast of Europe: Ortaköy is graced by a little pearl of a **mosque**, sprightly and mannered, created by the

Balyans at the same time and in the same spirit as Dolmabahce. The pleasant **quayside square** with open-air cafes and inexpensive fish restaurants next to the mosque has in recent years become a haven for the artists, bohemians, Greens, Bosphorus University students and sundry irregulars of Istanbul. Community events and the only open-to-all New Year's party to be found in the city are held here.

The spectacular **suspension bridge** which spans the skies above, surprisingly, contributes to the beauty of the spot rather than spoiling it. This was completed in 1973 as the fourth-longest bridge of its type in the world. The breathtaking views it offers from the driveway (pedestrians unfortunately not allowed) are matchless; but one must avoid at all costs the rush hour crush which has now necessitated the construction of a new bridge three miles upstream, with a third one already in the works.

Arnavutköy is one of the most pic-turesque of Bosphorus villages, rivaled only by Emirgan, the two Hisars, Anadolu Kavak, and perhaps a couple of others on the Asian shore. **Bebek**, by contrast, is distinguished by the conspicuous concentration of wealth that it contains, with side-effects like fancy shops, cafes, yachts, etc. Its attractions include the superb art-nouveau **Consulate of Egypt** which was once a summer residence of the Egyptian royalty (built in 1900), the unprepossessing **pastryshop** (Bebek Badem Ezmesi) which makes the best marzipan in the world, and the long roadside strand teeming with fish and fishermen from August onwards (rod and line available on the spot).

Asiyan and **Rumeli Hisar**, which occupy two flanks of the hill north of Bebek, deserve a long stroll up their narrow cobblestoned streets, through tranquil cemeteries and lilac-bedecked villas overlooking the Bosphorus, to fully appreciate their beauty. The seashore is dominated by the stupendous

Fishing boats lined up to bring in the evening's *lüfer.*

fortress built by Sultan Mehmed II in 1452 as a prelude to the conquest of the city. Plays are now occasionally staged at its open amphitheater, an experience that is not to be missed. The hill above is crowned by the campus of the former **Robert College**, built in 1863 by Yankee missionaries as a prelude, some say, toward the reconquest of the heathen by the gospel, then grown into the best academic institution of the country. Nationalized in 1971, it still retains some of its ivied dignity high above the fjord-like curves of the Bosphorus.

Emirgan offers a lively tea garden in the village square, and the fabled **tulip gardens** in the hilltop (formerly imperial) park, from where a specimen of that exotic flower first traveled to Holland in the 17th century. The village is named after the Persian prince whose scandalous liaison with Murad IV was the talk of Istanbul in the 1630s. A small adjunct of his erstwhile palace, the graceful *yali* which later belonged to Sherif Hüseyin (Ottoman MP from Mecca who in 1916 became the leader of the Arab revolt, and whose descendants reign in Jordan), is now open to the public. Its elegant beauty contrasts with the ostentatious "horsed" **mansion** of Mr. Sakip Sabanci, the wealthy industrialist, nearby.

Tarabya is distinguished by a gigantic hotel-casino much favored by Arabs, and a lively if somewhat showy restaurant-row whose outdoor tables clog the street and the quayside on summer evenings. To either side of the bay extends the row of the 19th century summer **residences** of the European embassies, with their magnificent parks and superbly preserved examples of old Istanbul wood architecture. It might pay to be brazen and try to get past the forbidding gates of one of them: it may be, after all, your tax money that keeps the place running. If that attempt fails, the next best choice is a visit to the **Sadberk Hanim Museum** past Büyükdere, further up the coast. This is a restored *yali* commemorating

A Bosphorus yali.

the late wife of Mr. Vehbi Koç, arch-competitor of Mr. Sabanci. The exhibit of antiques and artifacts is quite pleasant, and the building itself is lovely.

Sariyer, a first stop for trawlers returning from the Black Sea, boasts the most colorful fish market as well as the best **fish restaurant**—Urcan—in town. The alley between the market and restaurant contains some truly "authentic" fishermen's taverns, serving the freshest fish and strongest liquor on a rickety table by the sea, with a fiddle player and the occasional drunken brawl providing spice past midnight. The alley has been marked for "development", as such places tend to be; but the visitor should be consoled by the presence of similarly delightful establishments in the fishing village of **Rumeli Kavak**, as well as in **Beykoz**, opposite Sariyer on the Asian shore.

Down the Asian side: The northern end of the Bosphorus beyond both Kavaks is a restricted military zone. One happy effect of this arrangement, apart from keeping the Russians away, has been the preservation of **Anadolu Kavak**. This village is cut off on all sides by the restricted zone, and is normally accessible only by shuttle boat from the European (Rumeli) Kavak. Consequently, it has almost no motor traffic, the hills have not been invaded by apartment blocks, land prices have not skyrocketed, and the place has kept its bucolic charm, with colorful fish restaurants built on wooden stilts and fleets of ducks competing for the leftovers. The massive **Genoese fortress** looming above is theoretically off-limits, but it offers a stupendous view over the mouth of the Black Sea.

The famed walnut groves of Beykoz are now surrounded by factories, but the glassworks at **Paşabahce** are worth a visit for the excellent crystal and tableware manufactured there. Highly valued in Europe, where they are marketed under the Leonardo trademark, with no indication of their Turkish origin as that would presumably be a

The fog creeps in on little cat feet...

handicap, they can be bought here at a fraction of the price.

The section of the Asian shore further south, between Kanlica and Çengelköy, is arguably the most picturesque stretch of the Bosphorus. It is best appreciated by renting a motorboat from **Kanlica**, and cruising very close to the coast. A string of the original *yali's* survive along this shore, including that of **Şafvet Paşa** which is named after a prime minister of the 1870s although it dates from the mid-18th century; the little dilapidated gem of the **Amucazade Hüseyin Paşa** house, built for the powerful grand vezir of the 1690s; the home of **Count Ostrorog**, an important figure of the Russian-dominated 1830s; and that of Cypriot **Mehmet Emin Paşa**, thrice prime minister in the 1850s after having spent most of his life in London and Paris—all located between Kanlica and Hisar. Çengelköy is graced by the classic beauty of the **Sadullah Paşa** mansion, named for the brilliant young diplomat

of Abdülhamid's reign but built much earlier. A few yalis still belong to families of the original owners. One may even glimpse an old-time beauty wistfully looking through the latticed windows of a balcony, or the black nanny napping under a cupola in the shady garden.

Anadolu Hisar, where a peaceful lagoon hugs a storybook **castle** of the 14th century with a village of steep narrow streets and balconied houses, calls for a landing and a stroll. At **Kuleli**, the imposing "Parisian" edifice of the military lycee has replaced, since 1860, the Byzantine Empress Theodora's former convent for repentant prostitutes. **Çengelköy** calls for another stop to have tea in the pleasant village square dominated by the Greek church, a baroque fountain, and majestic plane trees.

Back at Kanlica, the choice is either to taste the fresh yogurt that has made the village famous, or to retrace one's steps to **Çubuklu** to dine amid the art

Leander's Tower at Haydarpasa.

nouveau luxury (reasonably priced) of the **Khedivial palace**, another of the summer homes of the Egyptian ruling family.

The cream-cake **Palace of Beylerbeyi**, like smaller **Küçüksu Palace** further up the coast, dates from the great mid-19th century imperial building binge. It epitomizes an ornate rococo style gone totally berserk, the overall effect of which is unexpectedly pleasing. In fact, the human scale of the architecture, combined with the absence of tourist crowds, makes Beylerbeyi an altogether more enjoyable palace to tour than its bigger cousin at Dolmabahce. Note the inlaid stairs of the Fountain Room, the hand-decorated doorknobs and the single-block carved table of the Harem, and try to imagine the gilded prison in which a raging Abdülhamid II, deposed in 1909, turned out his final masterpieces in walnut and rosewood.

The other Istanbul: **Üsküdar** is an old residential district, once a favorite of the Muslim "middle-class" of the capital, with countless little mosques, tranquil cemeteries, and nostalgia-laden streets. At least five of the principal mosques in the area were built for imperial mothers or daughters, with a noticeably "feminine" grace defining their style.

The seaward bluff below Üsküdar—Salacak—offers some of the most spectacular panoramas of central Istanbul across the Bosphorus. Sunset at **Huzur (Arap) restaurant** here may be an unforgettable visual, as well as gastronomic, experience. **Kizkulesi** presents its coquettish profile only 500 feet away at midsea. This landmark has been associated with Leander, the lover who braved the waves every night to meet his imprisoned sweetheart, like every other offshore tower around Turkey. It was in fact built as a lighthouse and guard tower, but the prosaic truth does not distract from its picturesque grace.

Enormous **Selimiye barracks** dominating the hill to the south are the scene of the invention of modern nursing by Florence Nightingale during the Crimean War of 1854, as well as of the less pleasant aspects of martial law regimes in 1971 and 1980.

Further south extends the apartment blocks of downtown **Kadiköy**, and the vast residential sections inland and along Baḡdat Caddesi that runs parallel to the Marmara coast. A third of the population of Istanbul live here; many commute daily to Europe, by boat or by the Bosphorus Bridge. Perhaps paradoxically, Asian Istanbul is by far the cleaner, greener, better organized—more "Western"—part of the city. For this reason, it holds little interest for the visitor seeking the exotic and the historic—though the **Fenerbahçe** shoreline which has become a center of teenage culture on summer evenings sometimes verges on the exotic, and the new **Kalamis marina** already claims some historic significance as "the largest yacht harbor in Europe".

Europe?

Left, garden at the Hidiv Kasri complex—a classic Bosphorus residence. Right, a city split between continents.

With lovely old Ottoman villas, and rustic fishing villages around every bend, the Bosphorus seems like a lazy stream meandering through the original Arcadia.

If geography has passed a magic wand over the straits, the same forces have conspired to make the Bosphorus one of the world's most strategic channels, and it has been coveted and conspired against by almost every power of significance.

The ancients, as cognizant as modern strategic thinkers of the military value of the 20 mile (32 km) long defile that divides Europe from Asia (sometimes by as little as 700 meters across) referred to the straits as the *symplegades*, or pair of facing cliffs which slammed together whenever a foreign vessel passed between them, crushing sailors and boat into flotsam. It took Jason the Argonaut of mythology to finally break the spell and secure free navigation.

When mythical characters were not wandering up and down the straits in pursuit of the Golden Fleece, very real historical conquerors were crossing the channel with their armies in search of an unified European and Asian Empire. Darius and Xerxes of Persia led their hordes over bridges of boats linking the two shores on their way to ultimate defeat in Greece, while Alexander the Great reversed this trend when he led his Macadonians across the sister strait of the Bosphorus—the Dardenelles, linking the Sea of Marmara with the Aegean—at the start of his epic conquest of Asia.

Control of the waterway was vital to the

health of the Byzantine state as well, a fact most dramatically underlined when the Turks built the facing fortresses of Rumeli and Anadolu Hisar in preparation for their conquest of Constantinople.

The Eastern question: As the Turkish empire crumbled, the city that commanded the straits became the grand prize for the European powers eyeing the sultan's domains. Czarist Russia, especially, was determined to control the straits. Without control of the Bosphorus, successive czars maintained, Moscow would not be in the possession of keys to its own backdoor.

The Ottomans, with the assistance of the western powers (and American mercenaries like John Paul Jones, who went down with his ship in the Black Sea in operations against the Russians) were able to foil Russian designs on the Ottoman capital throughout the 19th century. But the decision of the Ottoman Empire to enter the first world war on the side of the Kaiser Germany forced the Entente Powers to take on Russia as an ally, and, as part of the series of secret pacts aimed

tacit Turkish aid to Nazi Germany, once again demanded the right to station Russian troops along the straits. The "friendly visit" of the Battleship USS Missouri in 1946 sent the right message to Stalin, and led directly to Turkey's joining NATO—her major contribution being her possession of the straits, which remains the only warm water outlet for the Soviet Union's Black Sea fleet.

Soviet shipping: It is not difficult to understand Soviet apprehension with the status of

at parceling out the Ottoman Empire, Moscow was promised control of both the Bosphorus and the Dardenelles.

The failure of the allies to "force the straits" and reopen the waterway for Russian grain was a major factor in destabilization of czarist Russia and the revolution of 1917.

Although Turkey remained neutral during World War II, the Soviet Union, alleging

the Bosphorus. A cursory glance at *Janes' Book of Fighting Ships*—the bible of modern naval planners and watchers—reveals that more than half of the pictures of Soviet cruisers, destroyers, nuclear submarines and even its most modern aircraft carriers were casually snapped from the shores of the Bosphorus as the warships self-consciously steamed through the straits.

Soviet commercial shipping, too, is incredibly dependent on the Bosphorus, as are Romania and Bulgaria: over 7,000 ships flying East Bloc flags transit the straits every year.

Left, the castle at Rumeli Hisar. Above, Turkish sailors getting ready to guard the straits.

ETHNIC REMNANTS

Along the upper reaches of the Golden Horn lies **Balat**, one of the primary areas of settlement for the Jewish population of Istanbul during the Ottoman centuries. The descendants of Spanish Jews who escaped the Inquisition and accepted the invitation of the sultan to settle in Istanbul, most Jews today continue to speak a bastard form of Spanish known as Ladino—the Romance equivalent of Yiddish. Although Turco-Jewish relations have always been excellent (in sharp contrast to the treatment of Jews elsewhere), only some 25,000 remain in the city today, among them many prominent citizens of wealth and power.

Balat, oddly enough, contains only a few synagogues, most others being located in Pera and of fairly recent vintage. The most significant of the remaining ones is the **Ahrida**, the oldest synagogue in the city, with its altar shaped like Noah's Ark. It has been in operation since before the Ottoman conquest.

Other buildings of note in Balat are the Church of **St Stephan of Bulgars**, better known as the Bulgarian Church, located in a park along the shores of the Horn. Prefabricated in Vienna and shipped down the Danube in sections, the Gothic structure was mounted in 1871, at a time when the Bulgarian Church was attempting to assert its independence from Greek Orthodoxy. It still serves the tiny Bulgarian community on Sundays.

Nearby is the **Metochian of Mount Sinai**, a semi autonomous church under the control of Patriarchy of Alexandria in Egypt, which was responsible for St Catherine on Mount Sinai. The archmandrite, or spiritual leader, was expelled from Turkey in the late 60s and the building confiscated by the government in response to Nasser's siezure of Turkish owned property in Egypt.

Balat—the word is a corruption of "Palation," or "palace", also contains various Byzantine ruins of note, including the scanty remnant of the once splendid **Blachernae**, the last residence of the Byzantine emperors before the Turkish conquest, as well as the **Ayazma**, or Holy Spring; located near the walls, which was a place of minor pilgrimage during the Roman and Byzantine periods.

Kumkapi: Located along the Sea of Marmara, Kumkapi (or "Sand Gate") is a district best known for its fish restaurants—and well it should be, as it has long been the main fisherman's wharf of the city, with hundreds of colorful purse-sign fishing boats arriving every morning to deliver the nights catch of everything from bluefish for the Turkish table to tuna destined for the sushi bars of Tokyo.

But Kumkapi is more than just a big fish market. For one thing, it contains the **Armenian Patriarchate**, formerly the spiritual "see" of Armenians world-

wide, but now reduced to dependence on the mother church in Erivan, Soviet Armenia. The vast majority of Turkey's 70,000 Armenians are Georgian, and can trace their conversation to Christianity back to 301 AD—the first nation to have done so, and a full century before Constantine the Great declared the new religion to be that of his new state.

The Patriarchate and the associated **Church of the Virgin** are located on a side street off the colorful town square. The church was built in 1828, and is always open to the public. A little too open, some are tempted to add: during his errant youth, Kör Agop, the late proprietor of the restaurant by the same name on the town square, was known to hold cock-fights between his own prize rooster and those of the hopelessly outclassed competition on a Sunday afternoon in the church courtyard, with the priests turning a blind eye to the affair.

Off the main square again and next to the Post Office is the Armenian church of **St Harutyun**, built in 1834 by Harutyun Amia Bezciyan, who was influential at the Ottoman Palace at the time. The small chapel is better known as the "Fishermen's Church" because many of its early parishioners were Armenian fishermen. Many of the houses surrounding the church are at least 120 years old, but sadly in need of repair. This may happen sooner than expected, as Turkish Yuppies—like their First World counterparts, have begun discovering the joys of homesteading in the inner city.

Arnavutköy: One of the most pleasant villages in Istanbul—reflected in the surge in rent prices for "arty" abodes up cobble stone streets which remain impassable in winter and rained-out in summer—is Arnavutköy, a pleasant village located on the middle Bosphorus on the European side. It is famous for its fish restaurants, tavernas and winding hillside streets lined by quaint old houses—a touch of San Francisco

Old wooden houses at Arnavutköy.

circa 1850 in old Istanbul.

The name—literally "Albanian Village"—derives from the forced settlement of Albanians here during the reign of Mehmet II after his conquest of the Balkans. Although there are no identifiable Albanians in Arnavutköy today—the population was primarily Greek before 1964, who were replaced by Muslim Turkish settlers from the Black Sea in more recent times—the name nonetheless reflects the surprisingly good relations that Turkey has managed to maintain with modern Albania, arguably the most xenophobic nation in the world.

Scores of the once beautiful wooden houses, many in a sad state of dilapidation, cling to the hills of the village, several of which claim to be the oldest houses in the city. A bit of paint would make the argument more persuasive. There is an old Greek cemetery in the village, in addition to several churches, the most interesting of which is the **Ayi Strati Araksiarhi**, a large imposing building near the post office.

Dominating the hills of are the buildings of **Robert College**, a girls school established by American missionaries in 1871, with its counterpart for boys at **Bosphorus University** in the hills above Bebek, the next village up from Arnavutköy. Robert College went co-ed in 1971 when the boys' school was upgraded to university status and nationlized. The campus of either institution is well worth a visit, not only for the period architecture, but also the nearly sublime quiet after the hurly-burly of the city.

Kuzguncuk: A market village along the Asia shore of the Bosphorus, Kuzguncuk has one of the best preserved Greek, Armenian and Jewish houses in the city. Several mosques, churches and synagogues stand side by side along its quaint and narrow streets in a rare display of closeness between the religions.

Of particular interest in the village are the Armenian **Church of St. Gregory the Illuminator** built in 1835 (the only Armenian church in Istanbul that has a dome) and the Greek Orthodox **Church of St. Panpelemon**, situated on the main street. It is one of the oldest and most interesting Christian shrines found in Istanbul. Built during the reign of Justinian in the 6th century, the church became a convent after the Turk conquest.

A tiny bay situated between Kuzguncuk and Üsküdar is known as Paşa Limani. It was from this sight, some historians argue, that Io, goddess of mythology and mistress of Zeus, transformed herself into a cow to conceal herself from the jealous Hera. The cow plunged into the water and swam across the Bosphorus—thus the name for the waterway, meaning, in Attic Greek, "ford of the cow".

The strange feat was accomplished once again in 1866, when a cattle barge capsized and sank at the entrance to the bay, and several of the cattle broke loose and swam across, preferring distant Europe to Asia.

Fixing the nets near Kuzguncuk.

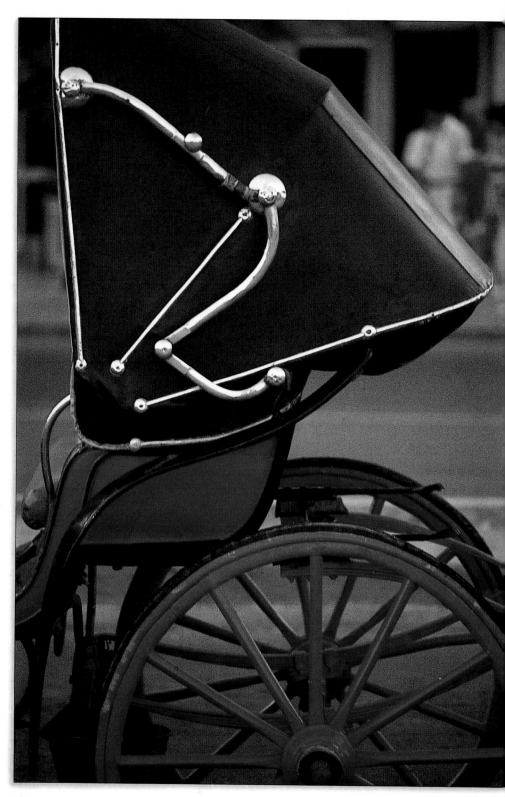

AWAY FROM THE CITY

Istanbul (Princes') Islands: The islands are nice. They are green, rich, and unhurried. Young bucks and wenches look ravishing in their minimal bathing suits. Ladies comment on each other's hairdo; gents smoke Havana cigars, and exchange their tough city sneer for a mellower, more generous face: the rabble may have taken over the city, but this is *their* home.

Above all, *there are no cars here.* This makes the islands so utterly unlike Istanbul—slightly eerie, in fact, for city-dwellers who have gotten used to the din of traffic and the smell of exhaust as part of their natural environment. Horse carriages—two-horse *phaetons* of 19th-century vintage— serve for public transport on Burgaz, Heybeli, and Büyükada; the vegetable-man does his rounds with a mule-cart, and construction material is carried to building sites by teams of donkeys. People walk: in the morning, hundreds of harried commuters rush to the boat landing, struggling with that goddam tie and trying to avoid as many "hellos" as possible. Around 5 p.m. everybody goes out "to do the *piazza*", to see and to be seen by everybody else. After dinner, one half go out again—the young to gather near the Square, the old to make housecalls—while the other half sit at their balconies to observe and chat with the half that's passing by.

One is born an "islander"; otherwise it is a difficult society for one to penetrate. An outsider is quickly noted and sized up—either a "nice type" (any third-generation Istanbulite qualifies; so does a member of the minorities; a westerner is welcome; wealth is a plus, but neither is necessary nor sufficient), or one of the rabble. The latter, to the great dismay of islanders, pour in in boatloads for weekend day-trips. Still, few city dwellers really know the islands; barely one in twenty can name

them in the correct order.

In winter, only a bottom layer of a few hundred workers, horse-keepers and fishermen inhabit them. In the summer, the four bigger ones get about 10 to 20,000 folks each. Most come for the duration of school break (June to September); the diehard and the childless stay "from May Day to Republic Day" (October 29), savoring the splendid tranquility of spring and early autumn. These are the best times to be there, while summer is good to go for swimming or watching island society in bloom—provided you avoid the weekend hordes. Boats leave and arrive at Sirkeci from Kinali in about 50 minutes, and take 15 minutes for each of the next three.

Kinali is not forested like the other islands. It is also somewhat over-crowded, and more "middle class". Its population has been at least two-thirds Armenian ever since two Armenian worthies bought the island to establish a Protestant utopian community in the

Left, pretty buggy on Büyükada. Right, when there are no cars, you can get a little fond of your horse.

middle of the last century, went bust, and sold it out in parcels. Turkish is spoken with an atrocious accent. Catching a well-positioned seat at **Cafe Bahar** at *piazza* time requires important skills; but the jazzier youth prefer **Nefi's**. Another "in" place is the Olympic **swimming pool**, though it is possible to swim just about anywhere in Kinali.

The Greek **convent** on the saddle of two hills is now an orphanage. Bits of Byzantine marble indicate this may have been where several mighties including Empress Zoe and Emperor Romanus Diogenes once served time. Periodic incarceration on the islands seems to have been one of the essential features of a Byzantine imperial or patriarchal career, whence the name "Prince's" islands.

Burgaz has a smaller, more select population of mixed background, with a predominant Jewish element replacing an earlier Greek majority. The domed Greek Church dominates the harbor, and the charming little **Monastery of St. George** set among cypresses on a bluff on the north coast rivals the best in Greece. The island also claims some extremely pleasant, quaint streets. But the top attraction is undoubtedly the two swimming-cum-social **clubs** to the left of the harbor. They offer an impressively high quotient of riches and well-appointed bodies per square inch, yet are surprisingly relaxed places for all that. City rabble is kept out, and goes to the naturally splendid but socially unfortunate beach at **Kalpazankaya** (Forgers' Rock) at the back of the island.

Heybeli has been a historical center of the Greek community, as witness the now defunct **theological seminary** that dominates one of the three hills—until 1973 one of the leading Orthodox religious institutions in the world. There are some six churches and monasteries as well, the most notable of which is the **Panaghia**, a well-preserved Byzantine work dating from 1431. This now

A little out of town retreat.

stands within the grounds of the **Navy Academy**, which also occupies the former palace of Patriarch Karadjas built in the 1770s, and the former Greek Commercial Academy which once used to be the equivalent of Harvard Business School in these parts. A distinctly Aegean atmosphere still pervades the very pleasant harborside **promenade** lined with sprawling cafes under cupolas and ancient plane trees.

Büyükada is the largest island, and—justly—the one visited by all tourists. It has extensive pine forests, and an excellent sandy beach at **Yörükali**. Above all else, it is a showcase of late 19th-century architectural extravaganza: the island probably contains a greater number of private buildings of architectural interest than the rest of Istanbul put together. **Nizam Caddesi** which has some of the poshest of them is one of the last redoubts of an old, cosmopolitan, Levantine-Ottoman class, with the occasional nouveau riche who broke in. Trotsky spent his

first two years of exile here. **Maden** district, one rung down on the social ladder, is inhabited by mostly Jewish, fewer Turkish and Armenian "old families" who keep their lovely wood mansions in much better repair than city folks. The **market** is what Istanbul markets used to be like before cars. **Hotel Splendid**, reeking with nostalgia, deserves its name and calls for a stay just to admire the beauty of the building.

Carriage Square is the world's most fantastic transport terminal where horse odors replace diesel fumes. Standard rates apply for the "Big Tour" (1 hour), "Small Tour" or the Yörükali ride. Atop the hill where the two tours diverge is **St. George's**, the only really working monastery (Greek) in Istanbul. Donkeys are available for those who find the climb too tiring.

The seaside restaurant row to the left of the boat landing will be one more reason to keep missing those boats you had planned to catch back. Old-timers

debate the relative merits of **Kapri** and **Milto**, though **Milano** is just as good. And no, these aren't Italian restaurants, but regular *raki-meze*-fish paradises.

Of the remaining five islands, two are private property. **Sedef**, accessible by boat from Büyük, is a very pleasant little colony whose beach and restaurant are open to outsiders. Being protected against the north by the hills of Büyük, the island has a strange semi-tropical climate. **Kaşik** (Spoon) can be viewed with distant envy in Burgaz harbor. **Yassi** (Flat) is a military base which continued a venerable Byzantine tradition by serving as prison for former government leaders after the 1960 coup. **Sivri** and **Tavşan** are uninhabited, although the latter, tucked behind Büyük, was until recently home to Mr. Kamil Kaya, alias Robinson, a colorful freak who was originally the Viennese biologist Franz Fischer, a refugee of 1938.

Black Sea beaches: Another possibility to get away from the city crowds is to go north toward the forests and beaches of the Black Sea coast. The road inland from Büyükdere on the European shore of the Bosphorus takes you into the birch and oak **forests of Belgrade**—named after a Serbian colony set up here in the 16th century, now disappeared. The many reservoirs in the area once supplied fresh water to the city, which explains the long, graceful aqueducts of 6th- and 16th century vintage which turn up at unexpected corners of the forest.

The road is lined with picnic grounds and open-air restaurants which get invaded over the weekends with hordes of non-nuclear families armed with samovars, barbecues, cassette-players, baby-carriages, outdoor pajamas, etc., though otherwise they are lovely places. Eventually you get to **Kilyos**, an old fishing village with an excellent sand beach that extends for miles. The Black Sea is one of the cleanest left in the world, but the season is rather short and the water often tends to be rough

Black Sea beach near Sile—miles and miles of sand.

because of the predominant north wind. Try to make your trip during the *lodos*, the hot and humid southwesterly which makes life unbearable in the city but is perfect for here.

Kilyos gets crowded on weekends, but for those who do not mind the lack of facilities, there are more than a hundred miles of unspoiled beaches to the north that are almost deserted beyond the first mile or two. You can drive a short distance west of Kilyos, or take the longer detour to **Terkos** (Durusu) where a freshwater lake also affords good opportunities for hunting fowl in season.

On the Asian side, the landscape is quite similar. A long, curvy drive from Beykoz leads to **Şile**, which has clean air, tall cliffs and good fish restaurants. You may check **Kumbaba Motel** for a night's escapade in a romantic setting.

Poland-in-Turkey: A detour on the way to Sile brings the visitor to an unusual corner of the Istanbul region: **Polonezköy**, "Poletown". The exiled Polish nobleman Adam Czartoryski set up a village here in the 1850s for Polish refugees who fought against Russia in the Ottoman army during the Crimean war. The place was initially called Adampol in his honor. Land was granted under the condition that it could not be sold to "outsiders". The community kept to itself, setting up dairy farms and cherry orchards and raising pork for sale in the city—a rare commodity in a Muslim country. There was no road until early this century, electricity arrived in 1973, and there is still no bus service to the village. Villagers first came into contact with state authorities in the 1920s, when they acquired Turkish citizenship. The obligatory bust of Atatürk was put up only in 1987, although the poet Adam Mickiewicz, the Pope and Lech Walesa still remain the true heroes of the inhabitants.

The delightful "Middle-European" farm atmosphere gradually turned Polonezköy into a favorite for outings, while the civilized attitude of the villagers made it especially attractive for outings that people would prefer to keep discreet. Most farmhouses began offering room and board, including typically a hearty lunch in bucolic setting and a room rented by the hour.

The interest of outsiders, however, eventually broke the isolation which made this place so special: the Polish character of the village has been eroding lately, and a five-storey hotel has already been built. Many who could tell the visitor about happier times have now moved to the quaint cemetery by the church. Zofia Rizi, who once entertained Baron von der Goltz, rests there; so do the many Dochodas, whose descendant, Edek, is still village headman. A living witness of the century is Madame Alwina who will reminisce over a few bottles of raki about the days in 1937 when her husband sent her away for the duration of a visit to the village by Atatürk. She now waits for the time when finally in Paradise she will make up for the lost chance to dance with the founder of the Republic.

The woods outside of Polonezköy.

TURKISH DELIGHTS

If civilizations are to be judged by the palate of the body-politic, the Turks—and especially those in Istanbul—may be among the most cultured urbanities in the world. One might even say that an Istanbulite's very existence revolves around the table—be it in the kitchen, or at the myriad restaurants, sofra's and meyhane's found around literally every corner of the city.

Breakfast: The first *ovun* in a day of the life of an Istanbulite is *kahvalti* (literally, pre-coffee) anytime between six and eight in the morning.

Cheese, black olives, butter, various jams and yoghurt are only accessorial to fresh bread, bought or home delivered in the early hours of the morning.

Istanbul enjoys over 900 bakeries, where over four million, unprocessed, non-factory loaves are produced daily. *Ekmek* is not only classified by its composition (the kind of flour—wheat, rye, corn, barley, chick-pea, etc.—and other, if any ingredients—milk, eggs, herbs, fats—used) but, also by the way it's cooked (on hot stone, concaved iron plate, pan) or baked (traditional charcoal oven, gas oven, electric oven) and whether it's leavened and to what extent. A day-old bread is considered practically inedible in Istanbul and nearly 500 tons are thrown away daily.

Up until the middle of the 19th century, cheese-making was strictly a part of home economics. Unlike Europe, cheese is mainly consumed at breakfast and placed in a quartered loaf of fresh bread (together with tomato and green pepper) is a meal in itself. Two main categories include those fermented with enzymes (obtained from lamb or weaned calf paunch) and those with vinegar essence (lesser quality). The first category includes dairy-fresh, *dil, lor* and *kaskaval*. Semi-matured *beyaz peynir* and *tu-*

lum are inseparable from *raki* tables, so chances are you'll meet them in every restaurant you go to. Hard crusted *kasler* and *mihalich* include up to 15 percent salt and are matured for no less than six months.

Jams are one of the richest aspects of Istanbul cuisine. Vegetables, like the eggplant; flowers, like the rose; nuts, like the unripened walnuts; berries, like the bird's rowan, raisins, like the mastic; and fruits ranging from green figs to bergamot go into

indescribably delicious jams. Some are made by placing the fruit (the vegetable, the rind) in boiling hot syrup and cooking; others are left under the sun (a layer of peeled, sliced fruit, a layer of sugar alternatively, placed in shallow dishes) to be cooked naturally. Some are mashed into marmalades, others have the viscosity of jelly, still some others are clear enough to count the number of strawberries in the container. Try Devecioglu, Tamek and Sultan Baci brands available in any foodstore.

Yoğurt is the last but certainly not the least item on our breakfast menu. In Ottoman

Preceding page: Bread—a basic. Left, the cook who conquered the castle. Above, breakfast on the beach.

Istanbul, the first and the last cry of the day belonged to the *yoğurtcu*, the peddler who sold his Kanlica or Silivri (the two very best!) door to door. There are not many left anymore, mass production having taken care of that, ruining the quality, say old Istanbulites. They should know, for yoghurt, as a staple, runs second only after bread. Quintessentially Turkish, (the word itself comes from the verb *yoğurtmak*, meaning "to coagulate") this versatile food is consumed plain, with confectionary sugar, with salt, garlic, grated cucumber and mint (a concoction called *cacik* and excellent with kebabs) or watered down to a salty, somewhat sour-milk like drink called *ayran*, the

secondary and optional. *Tarhana* (wheat flour, tomato paste, onion, paprika, yoghurt and herbs rolled into a dough, leavened, left to dry under the sun and crumbled into freeze-dry coffee size granules) and *Ezo Gelin* (beef broth, red lentils, rice, tomato paste, onion, mint, lemon or somak—plus coriaria,—) are the two favorites in this category usually consumed in the morning and often replacing cheese and olives for breakfast.

A second type of soup, usually consumed after a hard night's *Raki*-bout is offal-based. Lamb trotters and tripe are hard boiled down to jelly-like substances, thickened with white sauce and eggs (Istanbul style), and

most formidable competitor in the soft-drinks market, including world-known colas. Even the Istanbul McDonald's was obliged to make that concession to local tastes, and includes *ayran* on its otherwise standard McDonalds' menu. Try *Çoban* and *Tikveşli* brands for non-homogenized (therefore topped with clotted cream) and *Pinar* for homogenized varieties.

Soups: *Çorba*, or soup, comes in a rich variety of types, although cereals (bulgur, lentil, rice) and cereal flour are the main ingredients in about 50 percent. Yoghurt, milk, parsley, mint, fats and tomato paste are

served with lemon or vinegar and garlic. Known as *Işkembeçi's* the soup is found almost anywhere 24 hours a day. **Zuhal** near Taksim (Zambak Sokak, No. 6) is recommended. For the famous Beykoz Paça or trotter soup, you'll have to visit the 87-year-old establishment of **Tolon Usta** (Fevzi Paşa Caddesi, No. 8) in Beykoz, one of the last stops along the Asiatic Bosphorus.

The third soup category includes vegetable soups without meat. A recommended winter time *sebze çorbasi* is made with chicken or beef broth, carrots, leeks, potatoes, onion, egg, milk, flour and butter. In summer ingredients vary to include green beans, peas, zucchini and parsley. Another favorite is pumpkin soup, *balkabagi çorbasi*. The recipe will give an idea of what follows in the bowl: saute two medium size onions in butter, add finely cut pieces of medium size pumpkin, add beef broth, boil over moderate heat till tender, add salt. In a separate bowl, beat sour-yoghurt till creamy and fold into the pumpkin mixture when cool. It serves an army! With melted butter and cayenne pepper. Wedding, *düğün* and spinach soups are the two examples of soups with meat. Wedding soup is essentially a mixture of boiled and shredded pieces of lambs ribs (including chops) in broth thickened with bechamel sauce, served with melted butter, lemon and cinnamon. Spinach soup is prepared about the same way except that spinach, potatoes, rice and tomato paste are added into the broth.

Other soups include those whose main ingredients are milk and sugar. Tomatoes, rices, onion, celery, parsley, milk, sugar and salt will make a *soğuk domates çorbasi* (tomato soup) which is served cold.

Grills and kebabs: A menu starting with soup will have to continue with meat. If cooked over coals, it is called *izgaras*, like the succulent lamb chops, *şiş kebab* (always lamb; veal is for the foreigners), *döner kebab* (layers of meat on a revolving vertical spit, exposed to charcoal fire—nowadays electric and not so nice) or *kuzu çevirme*, lamb roasted on spit. If cooked in *tandir* (a 1-2 meter deep hole in ground, heaped with charcoal, where a whole lamb is dangled for five or six hours) or in a *firin* (oven method of cooking as above) you'll be having *tandir* or *firin kebab*. Kebab, then, is the generic name for meat cooked by direct exposition to fire—no sauces, no trimmings. The city is full of kebab houses (*kebabci*), but it is vital that you visit *Beyti*, one of the best meat restaurants in Europe (or so says William Saroyan) and the largest eating place in Turkey (Orman Sokak, No. 33, Florya) and Gelik (Sahil Yolu, No. 68-70, Atakoy). Try

the latter for their *kuyu kebab*.

Stews: *Yahni* is the generic name for meat cooked by indirect exposition to fire. Consider, for example, *kuzu yahni*: cubed pieces of lamb boiled tender, strained, rolled in flour, sauted in butter, returned into broth of onions, herbs and spices. To this essential receipe vegetables (potatoes, tomatoes, green beans, peas, okra, horse beans, you name it) and herbs are added to make such creations as *papaz yahni*, ("priest yahni") the *ayva yahni*, ("quince yahni") and others. One version is *kapama* where pieces of baby lamb are sandwiched between lettuce leaves with green onions, fresh dill, whole black pepper, butter, salt and cooked over very low

heat, no water added. When *yahni* stops being a meat dish and becomes a vegetable dish depends mainly on the meat—vegetable ratio. If the main ingredients are vegetables as in *turlu*, (a "hash" including eggplant, green beans, tomatoes, green peppers) or *kapuska* (cabbage, cauliflower) then you are having a *sebze* (vegetable) dish; skip the soup and salad and dip your bread in the sauce. If, however you are having *kabak*, *biber* or *patlican dolma* (zucchini, pepper or eggplant stuffed with ground meat in tomato sauce) it is hard to tell. Nor are vegetarians neglected: *zeytinyágli fasulye* (green beans

Left, fruit in abundance. Above, some like it hot—"arabesque" star Ibo with his favorite meal.

cooked with olive oil, served cold), *pilaki* (navy beans in olive oil, cold), *imam bayildi* (eggplant, onion, tomato, parsley, served cold), various *kizartma* (deep fried vegetables, served with yoghurt) and *yalanci dolma* ("fake" because green peppers, eggplant or wine leaves are stuffed with rice, not meat, and served cold) are the best bet.

Rice dishes: *Pilav* is a stately dish, often called the King of Turkish cuisine and even the Sacred Food of Mevlevi and Bektasi orders of Islam. Although the Turks owe *pilav* to China, it is in Turkistan that we see it enhanced far beyond mere rice. The very first recipes come from the time of Tamerlane (Timur), in the second half of the 14th

in Topkapi Palace is one of the oldest and best Istanbul restaurants. They have been specializing in pilavs since 1897. Another one is **Abdullah** (Emirgan Koru Caddesi, No. 11, Emirgan). No gourmet should ignore them.

Desserts: *Tatli* or "sweets", are another area of Turkish cuisine copied throughout the world. The two main categories are the *helva* (essentially, flour, semolina or sesame seeds browned in butter and cooked in hot syrup, with nuts and spices) and *hamur* (dough) desserts of which baklava is the best known. Made of buttered, see-through thin layers of unleavened dough, baklava is named after the kind of nut used in making it.

century. When used alone, the word *pilav* refers strictly to rice *pilav* (bulgur, boiled and pounded wheat and *kuskus*, egg dough made into small pellets and dried, are the two others). Most of the 104 recognized varieties are cooked with butter and served hot. Those cooked with oil (preferably olive oil) are special to Istanbul and served at room temperature. One must try *midyeli pilav* (with mussels), *patlicanli pilav* (with eggplant), *enginarli pilav* (with artichokes) and so-called *iç pilav* with pine nuts, currants and fried bits of chicken liver. **Konyali** restaurant (Ankara Caddesi, No. 223, Sirkeci) and

You have the pistachio (*fistikli*), hazel nut (*findikli*) and walnut (*cevixli*). Gulluoğlu in Karakoy (Rihtim Caddesi, No. 3) and **Haci Bozanoğullari** in Laleli (Ordu Caddessi, No. 218) are the two best bets. *Lokma* or "morsel", is one example of leavened dough based desserts. *Izmir lokma*, consists of morsel-sized bits of leavened dough deep fried and dumped in syrup and is served hot. Try **Izmir Lokmacizi**, (Kobasi Caddesi, No. 254—256, Yenikoy) but a warning: try on an empty stomach! Chances are you will find that it is a meal in itself.

Fish and Meze: Turks like variety in food

and *meze* or appetizers are an essential part of a proper meal. The current trend of "grazing food" restaurants in the United States, featuring small morsels of a variety of dishes, has been the way of life in the Mediterranean for centuries.

Cold *meze* generally are eaten first. *Haydariye* (white goat's cheese blended with yoghurt and thyme), *pastirma* (sliced, spiced, cured beef) which is the Middle Eastern pastrami and *tursu* (pickled vegetables) are common. *Cacik* (chopped cucumber and garlic in yoghurt), *kisir* (bulgar with onions, pepper and parsley) and *patlican salata* (eggplant puree) are tasty accompaniments to bread. Eggplant is the most

tavugu boiled chicken Circassian style with a sauce of crushed walnuts and paprika) can be made in a smaller portion and served as a *meze*. *Köftes* include the suggestive sounding *kadin budu* (woman's thigh or meatballs with rice). Any of the seafoods can be either fried or boiled and marinated to make a delicious starter.

Istanbul gourmets decry the lack of inventiveness in many modern restaurants which is reflected in the smaller selection of *meze*. Yet, with a little directive exploring, you can find many unusual dishes, many of which are specials not listed on the menu, so always ask or look in the kitchen. Istanbul chefs are famous for their creativity and even the

popular vegetable in Turkey and is prepared in an endless variety of hot and cold dishes. One which has an evocative name is *Imam Bayildi* or "the cleric fainted" named for an Islamic prayer leader who keeled over in ecstasy after eating this delectable combination of fried eggplant slices with onions, tomatos and lots of garlic.

Almost any main dish such as *çerkez*

humblest establishment often has a unique house speciality.

Mediterranean belief is that it is very damaging to ones constitution to drink alcoholic beverages on an empty stomach. Hence, many of the best *meze* can be found in the lively establishments known as *meyhanes*. *Meyhanes* were once wine shops and are now Turkish-style taverns where people drink *raki*, beer or wine and nibble on *meze*.

If you want to visit authentic *meyhanes*, go to the **Cicekpasaji** (Flower Passage) in the **Balikpazari** (Fish Market) in Beyoğlu. A

Left, pick your pickle. Above, *döner kebab lokantasi*.

constant stream of colorful characters fill a small passageway in the center of a row of once grand facades of derelict wrecks of dwellings. Merrymakers spill out into the arcade in warm weather, sitting at marble-topped beer barrels while feasting on fried mussels or *kokoreç* (grilled innards) sold by vendors or sampling the *meze* offered by the *meyhanes*.

In a few hours time, you may be entertained by a gypsy with a trained bear or rambling street musicians. You might join a group of boisterous celebrants who interrupt their raki consumption to bellow out some off-key tunes or spring into a tipsy dance. Eating *meze* should be done with great gusto

but at a leisurely pace. But beware; if you are imbibing *raki*, remember the innocent looking spirit, milky when diluted, carries a mean bite. For this reason, *meyhanes* used to provide the services of a kindly man with a large wicker basket on his back in which an inebriate could sit while being trundled back to his lodging. These days, you'll have to make it on your own steam.

Close to the fish market, on an obscure sidestreet off a rundown area of Tarlabasi is the charming establishment **Hasir** of Mr. Nikos Tas, the last of the Greek tavern owners in this section of town. The low-

ceilinged semi-basement has photos and memorabilia of past festivities covering the walls. The diminutive Mr. Tas presides over all of the operation, moving smoothly between the kitchen and tables with his ubiquitous worry beads in hand and a gentle smile on his face—just as he has done since 1948.

Hasir has a wide range of *mezes*; the cold ones are brought out on platters on a wooden tray for you to inspect. Most unusual is *topik*, an Armenian dish served only in the cooler weather and made from hen, *tahini*, chickpeas and sprinkled with cinnamon. *Kereviz* (celery) is creamed and cut in strips and the cheese souffle, perfectly puffed and browned in a ramekin, is superb.

Fish: The long coastline of Turkey, which includes the Aegean, Marmara and Mediterranean Seas, yields an incredible variety of fish. Istanbul, reaping the benefits of the cross flow between the cool waters of the Black Sea and the warmer Sea of Marmara, is said to have the tastiest fish and seafood of all.

The most popular fresh fish are *barbunya* (red mullet) or its smaller version *tekir*, *kalkon* (turbot), *lüfer* (bluefish), and *palamut* (bonito). *Kiliç* (swordfish) is in season during September, October and November. Swordfish used to be caught in *dalyans* (fisheries) along the Bosphorus and Sea of Marmara but these are used to catch other types of fish now. The swordfish is now harpooned from a boat while it naps on the surface of the water.

Seafood includes *yengeç* (crab), *karides* (shrimp), *ahtapot* (octopus), *istakoz* (lobster) and *midye* (mussels). The mussels are a popular delicacy of Istanbul that are fished from boats with a metallic trap with a net around it near the village of **Rumeli Kavagi**.

Really fresh fish needs little embellishment. For a simple but completely satisfying fish meal in a memorable setting, go to the floating restaurants at the edge of **Galata Bridge**. Fish are grilled over a charcoal fire which brings out its full flavor and then served simply with lemon and parsley. A salad and fresh bread complete this savory repast. The lower level of the Galata Bridge has other informal fish restaurants that offer a view of the ferries chuggings along the Golden Horn with the memorable skyline of

Stamboul as a backdrop.

Kumkapi is another earthy section in an old Istanbul neighborhood. It has recently had a face-lifting but despite the tasteful renovation and trendy additions such as wrought-iron lanterns, it has maintained much of its original unpretentious flavor. For your first visit, it is best to come in the late afternoon in order to visit the imposing Armenian Patriarchate church, the large open-air produce market on a side street or the bustling fish market on the ancient harbor of Kontoscalion which is the last Byzantine harbor on the Sea of Marmara. Porto Kontoscalion became known in Turkish times as Kum Kapi which means the Sand

of one sightless eye), was a legendary Kumkapi figure who died in 1983. According to Yassar Kemal in *The Sea-Crossed Fisherman*, he epitomized the crusty, independent nature of the area's innkeepers. "He was not in the world simply to cook fish and serve *raki* to boors." Instead, what he wanted was "friendly talk, warm comradeship, or otherwise you might as well push off."

Agop's son, Hayk Inciyan, now runs the restaurant which once allegedly featured seagull soup, a rare delicacy that none of the present management seems to recall. Kör Agop does offer an excellent cheesy *karides güveç*, a shrimp casserole with a spicy tomato sauce. In season, at least 20 varieties of

Gate, a name still used for the surrounding neighborhood.

Kör Agop, one of the most venerated establishments, recently moved to a modernized, two-story building at Ordekli Bakkal Sok. 7, where one will usually dine with a cross-section of Istanbul, from raffish street people to society matrons.

Kör Agop (Blind Agop, so called because

fresh fish are available. The house speciality is fish soup, large chunks of *kirlangiç* (tub fish) in a frothy, lemony base, all served in a huge ceramic cauldron. The din from the late night revelers and the music provided by a gypsy band (clarinet player, drums and violin) might seem festive to you. If it proves overwhelming, try one of the innumerable smaller restaurants in the vicinity such as **Kardeşler** at Capariz Sokak 18 or **Nezihler** at Ustet Sokak 17.

Arguably the best seafood is undoubtably served in **Üçler ("Three Guys") Restaurant**, which is owned by an Albanian Turk.

Left, a quiet corner. Above, an alfresco meal of mussels and fish.

When dining there, don't forget to ask for *pavurya*—crabmeat served as a *meze*, which is a house speciality.

The most delightful fish restaurants of Istanbul however are located at the Bosphorus. Every community has at least a couple of quayside eateries and others are often perched on hillsides with a glorious view of the twinkling lights of the many boats gliding through the waters and the connecting bridge. Those up for a challenge might want to try and start at the top villages nearest the Black Sea on either the European or Asian shores and proceed to eat and drink their way down to the bottom, taking taxis between communities and short strolls before settling

down for serious indulgence. Ferry boats also make the crossing between the European and Asian shores at various points, so if time permits, this could be an inter-continental outing.

Generally, the restaurants closest to the Black Sea tend to be less expensive and less pretentious. **Metin** in Rumelikavaği is a simple seaside restaurant in which to sample *midye tavasi* (fried mussels), shrimp casserole or any of a number of mouth-watering fresh fish. Near the town square is **Kösen**, a rustic inn with a fascinating display of nautical objects and starfish decorating fishing

nets and an old-fashioned pot bellied stove to warm oneself on a cold winters day. Across the Bosphorus, the chef at **Yosun Balik** in Anadolukavaği concocts a terrific fish soup.

Farther south, the fish market in **Sariyer** is fascinating and one can point out the fish or seafood desired and go inside one of the several harbor restaurants to watch the caiques unloading their catch on the quay. **Zadeler** which has a panoramic view of the Bosphorus from its site in the hills if Emirgan, is an amiable nightspot with belly dancers. Although the decor is strictly classic "kitsch", the food is distinguished. Besides the standard meat and fish dishes, interesting meze include *pirinç kofte* (chicken meatballs) and brain salad.

Iskele Balik in Yeniköy is a joyful explosion of color, from the fresh fruit and flower arrangements to the live crabs swimming in the little fountain. Stuffed mackeral is the speciality here but all the food is delicious and reasonable. **Yalim**, in Anadoluhisari on the Asian shore is noted for its *ispanakli levrek* (bass with spinach) and *kiremitte palamut* (bonito baked on a tile) and the charming Russian Baroness who plays the piano.

Both **Bebek** and **Arnavutköy** have disarmingly captivating waterfront restaurants in the gingerbread trim wooden houses. Sadly enough, the future of these houses is undecided, for a new highway built on a landfill will obscure the sea view. Nevertheless, the elegant **Ambassadeurs** in Bebek offers an international cuisine and the **Antik** in Arnavutköy serves tasty seafood dishes and an excellent *pastirma börek* (pastirma cooked in pastry) in a lovely house filled with appealing antiques. Nese, is situated on a hill below the Greek cemetery and next to a sixth century sacred wall. Run by Turks from Greece, there are an array of intriguing *meze* and fish dishes. The small band plays Greek music which may inspire you to let loose and smash a few plates along with the rest of the patrons.

Left, sometimes we all have a bit too much. Right, a typical fish restaurant along the upper Bosphorus.

MUSIC

Rather like Turkish Cuisine, Turkish music is a syncretic blend of a variety of cultures and styles, with elements ranging from the Chinese to the African, and all shades in between.

The Turkish tribes who moved in successive waves of emigration into Asia Minor and who later founded the two major empires (Seljuk and Ottoman) thereby exposed themselves mainly to two musical influences: Byzantine and Persian. No doubt they

the people living in the area. Some major composers of classical Turkish music were Armenians, Greeks and Jews, some of whom also composed especially religious music for their own communities.

European influence: New musical influences from the West began to appear in the 19th century. The Westernizing Palace played the leading role and the famous Donizetti's brother stayed in Istanbul for some time, instructing and conducting the

had their own background of Turkish folk music, and they encountered the folk music of many other peoples living in this part of the world. But at the root of what is known as classical Turkish music, Persian and Byzantine influences predominate.

Turkish music, like its Persian and Byzantine sources, was modal and kept this character until this century when some experimentations in a Turkish polyphony began. Especially in the Ottoman times, composers tried to develop new modes, enrich rhythms and create new forms. There is little doubt that there were reciprocal influences among all

Palace band and composing a few Ottoman marching-songs. The Ottoman market for the records by Odeon, His Master's Voice, etc, was surprisingly large and in a short time factories producing records were established in Turkey.

Towards the end of the 19th century a new song form called the *canto* was created, and this became the first form of urban entertainment in Istanbul. It more or less coincided with the growing popularity of the theater and was performed by non-Muslim performers of both sexes before a play. It was rhythmic and melodic, and, as it had no concern for "the purity of origins", it embraced a wide spectrum of the known types of music in the world, from Russian to Italian. The *canto*, in its day, was the closest thing to an indigenous vaudeville, with much shouting, shrieking and slapping of thighs as the singer would move around the audience, embarrassing husband in front of wife, friend in front of brother.

Modern tunes: With the establishment of the Republic, Western music was highly

Western pop songs also became popular, a trend best exemplified by such groups as M.F.Ö.—perennial candidates for the "Eurovision" song contest, on which Turkey stakes its national honor every spring.

At the end of the 1970s a new genre swept the country—*arabesque*. Combining the pathos of modern life in the *gecekondu* with the maudlin sentimentality of unrequited love, this is the music that blares out of every minibus, coffeehouse, restaurant or private

encouraged by the State, which at one time even banned Turkish music from the radio. The Charleston, the rumba and the tango all reached Turkey almost at the same time they were heard in the rest of the world. Here, of course, they really appealed to a very small minority, though the rest of the country couldn't remain entirely deaf.

After the 50s and 60s adopted versions of

Left, tuning in to the latest hits. Above, the "terrific trio" of M.F.Ö.

house in the land. Although certain intellectuals attempt to prove that *arabesque* is somehow a devious import from "Arabistan"—that amorphous sub-culture zone somewhere to the south of Turkey, this explanation is not very satisfactory, as the genre is very electic in its use of sources; besides, calling it *arabesque* suggests that the culprit has been found elsewhere, which is not intellectually very honest. The undisputed star of the genre is Ibrahim Tatlises, a former construction worker from Urfa, equally famous for his passion for women, and ice cream laced with red peppers.

ART AND CULTURE

Istanbul is not only the crossroads of a multitude of civilizations, but the cradle of a many-faceted cultural panorama in which art has always played an essential part be it in theater, ballet, opera, classical music, painting or sculpture.

Theater: Drama is one of the oldest art forms in Turkey. From the traditional impromptu epic play (*ortaoyunu*) and the shadow-theater reflected on a screen ("*Karagöz*") to Shakespearean productions and avant-garde output, Istanbul has always enjoyed a colorful theatrical scene. After the establishment of the Municipal Theater and State Theater several decades ago, the metropolis has witnessed the rise and development of a multitude of private theatrical companies.

Today over twenty different theaters raise their curtains every evening. One may see a classical Ibsen or Chekhov, light American comedies or French farces, Broadway-style musicals and modern productions by young Turkish playwrights. Theatrical companies mostly consist of actors and directors who are graduates of the drama departments of the Istanbul or Ankara State Conservatories. It is quite easy to come across several actors and actresses who have studied in various drama schools in Europe and in the United States. Some major groups, such as the Kenter Theater, the Ali Poyrazoğlu Theater, the Dostlar Theater, the Ankara Art Theater, the Comedy Theater and the Ostrich Cabaret Theater are extremely popular. Kenter and Ankara Art specialize in dramatic plays whereas the others tend to lean towards lighter stuff and comedy. Nevertheless, comedy or tragedy, the overall quality is good, if not always particularly innovative: what is sorely lacking is experimentation and research into new techniques and approaches.

Left, actress Yildiz Kenter performing *I Anatolia*. Above, Atatürk busts—the beginnings of Turkish sculpture.

For the visitor who does not speak Turkish, the International Istanbul Festival offers several drama productions by visiting English, French and Italian groups, often in the impressive setting of the Rumeli Hisar fortress, built in the 15th century. Major companies from Great Britain, France and Germany come to Istanbul quite frequently as the result of cultural exchange programs. Turkish companies do not generally perform in other languages.

There are, however, exceptions to that rule: most recently the Kenter Theater staged a production of Güngör Dilmen's *I, Anatolia* in English, a one-woman show describing the various cultural and historical periods of Anatolia through the eyes of several important women who had lived then. The play was staged by Yildiz Kenter, an eminent actress, and has played in England the United States, West Germany and elsewhere to good reviews.

Ballet: The development of classical ballet began in the 1930s in Istanbul, when Lydia Krassa Arzumanova, a Russian immigrant, established her own ballet school and staged performances throughout the city. The initial performance of the Arzumanova Ballet School took place at the Casa d'Italia in 1931, seventeen years before Ninette de Valois' Ballet Academy was founded. Ninette de Valois' Ballet Academy, operating between 1948 and 1950, went on to become the Ballet Division of the Ankara State Conservatory and thus formed the core of the Turkish State Ballet.

While Arzumanova's group dispersed due to lack of funds, another immigrant, this time the Hungarian Olga Nuray Olcay, arrived in Turkey in the 1940s and found the Ballet Department of the Istanbul Municipal

and Ballet and the Contemporary Ballet Group, both of which perform regularly at the Atatürk Cultural Center. Other dance companies crop up occasionally but are short-lived, primarily for financial reasons; the Ministry of Culture and Tourism finances prominent private theatrical companies each year but has no such funds for ballet groups. A visit by a foreign company is rare (except for the duration of the International Istanbul Festival) again because of financial matters as well as for the fact that only one well-equipped ballet stage exists in Istanbul, that of the Atatürk Cultural Center. As the above-mentioned stage is shared by the State Ballet, State Opera and State Thea-

Conservatory in 1953. Together with Rezzan Abidinoglu, an instructor and choreographer who joined that particular institution in 1955, Olcay began training would-be dancers. The City Opera of Istanbul was established in 1960 and moved to the Culture Palace in 1969, henceforth known as the Istanbul State Opera and Ballet. The tenure was short, as the Culture Palace burned down in 1970 and was not reopened to the public until 1978, under the name of the Atatürk Cultural Center.

Today, Istanbul boasts two permanent ballet companies: the Istanbul State Opera

ter, it is rarely available to visitors.

Current ballet productions range from typical classical works to neo-classical, avant-garde, modern and contemporary pieces. The standards are generally high but audiences at large feel that not enough experimental productions are staged. This is true, as both the Istanbul State Ballet and the Contemporary Dance Group tend to prefer classical and semi-classical works, thus not producing a sufficient number of modern pieces.

Opera and classical music concerts: It must be noted that opera was very popular in the

19th century in Istanbul: quite a few theaters staged operettas, visiting companies from Italy performed almost all of Verdi's operas and some were even presented on the palace grounds before the Ottoman sultan. During the first four decades after the establishment of the Republic in 1923, Istanbul witnessed very few operatic performances.

The City Opera of Istanbul was founded in 1960 and in 1969 moved to more spacious grounds, henceforth known as the Istanbul State Opera and Ballet. Each year the Istanbul State Opera offers a wide range of performances, from dramatic operas to light operettas; one may see Verdi's *Rigoletto* one night and attend a performance of

Seraglio may be found in the section entitled "The International Istanbul Festival"). The Istanbul State Symphony Orchestra shares the stage of the Atatürk Cultural Center with the Istanbul State Opera. For well over a decade the Istanbul State Symphony has given weekly concerts, the program extending from Beethoven to Mozart, from Tchaikovsky to Mahler, from Bach to Schönberg. The concerts are generally quite good, and the orchestra performs before an ever-increasing and appreciative audience each season.

Painting and sculpture: Painting flourished in Istanbul in the 19th century, after several select Turkish painters were sent to Paris by

Offenbach's *The Tales of Hoffmann* the following evening. Some excellent voices can be heard and the productions are staged by Turkish directors who have had extensive training in Europe. Mozart's *Abduction from the Seraglio* is performed yearly at the Topkapi Palace, with the participation of guest artists from major European opera companies. (Details on *Abduction from the*

Left, a young ballerina from the slums. Above, dance performance during Istanbul Festival.

the Ottoman sultans to study the art in all its aspects. The result was a passionate interest in painting and a boom in artists whose impact is still felt today. Indeed, Turkey boasts more painters now than it does actors and actresses, and it is impossible to list all painters. Suffice it to say that finding exhibits presents no problems; the city is sprinkled with countless art galleries, among which URART, B.M., SAN-FA, BARAZ and VAKKO carry the best collections.

Whereas in painting the abstract cubist and lyric abstraction styles became popular in the 1950s, to be later followed by the impressionists and primitivists, most Turkish sculptors still prefer the classical realistic style. After the establishment of the Turkish Republic, the Istanbul Academy of Fine Arts began. accepting students who wanted to train as sculptors. The initial products consisted mostly of statues and busts of Atatürk, the founder of the Republic, and those of other historical figures. Some promising young sculptors had the opportunity to study the latest forms of that particular art in Europe and upon their return, enlightened prospective artists on the subject. The tourist in Istanbul may visit several art galleries that specialize in sculpture exhibitions and may be pleasantly surprised to find some avant-

well as the Sports and Exhibition Palace which is mainly devoted to orchestral concerts. The International Istanbul Festival was the "brainchild" of a handful of pioneers who felt that Istanbul, once a truce crossroads of civilizations, cultures and arts, should once more become a center where artists, actors and musicians hailing from different countries and speaking different languages could come together and display their varied talents. These men and women, led by Dr. Nejat F. Eczacibaşi, a prominent industrialist, formed the core of what today is known as the Istanbul Foundation for Culture and Art. Their dream materialized in 1973, in commemoration of the 50th anni-

garde piece by a young artist sharing a stand with a classical statue by an elderly master. Some of the best galleries are mentioned in the section on painting.

The International Istanbul Festival: It takes place from mid-June to the end of July every summer, in a variety of historical locations throughout the metropolis: the St. Irene and St. Antoine churches, the famous Topkapi Palace (the one-time seat of the Ottoman sultans), the Rumeli Fortress and the Yildiz Palace, another dwelling of the sultans. Other locations would include the Open-Air Theater and the Atatürk Cultural Center, as

versary of the Turkish Republic; 1988 marks the festival's sixteenth year.

It is worthy of note that the festival, with its rich programs in symphonic and chamber music, classical ballet, modern dance, jazz, theater and opera attracts audiences from all over the world. Chick Corea, Miles Davis, Ray Charles and other celebrities of the jazz world may be seen in performance one evening while, less than a mile away, Merce Cunningham's company displays the latest in modern dance. Other eminent international figures and groups that have paraded across Istanbul stages in past festivals are

Yehudi Menuhin, Igor Oistrach, Rudolf Nureyev, the Bolshoi Ballet, the London Festival Ballet and the Royal Shakespeare Company, as well as the Paris Symphony, the Leningrad Philharmonic and the Berlin Symphony orchestras.

In addition to the international artists, one should not overlook the events based on traditional Turkish arts, particularly on music. For the visitor who is interested in "local color", the Ayangil Turkish Music Orchestra and Chorus, the Istanbul Municipal Conservatory Turkish Music Ensemble, the Istanbul University Fine Arts Department Turkish Music Research and Performance Group, the Ministry of Culture and

the *Sema* is one way of reaching total peace with oneself and with the universe at large. One must be aware that the *Sema* Ceremony, based on the philosophy of the Turkish mystic and poet Mevlana Jelaleddin Rumi, is definitely not a mere "performance" but a spiritual ritual dating back to the 13th century. One does not applaud.

The "highlight" of the International Istanbul Festival, however, is the production of Mozart's opera *Abduction from the Seraglio* in an original *seraglio*, the Topkapi Palace. When Mozart composed his opera about the kidnapping of two ladies from a pasha's harem, he set the scene in a Turkish palace. But *Abduction from the Seraglio* had

Tourism State Classical Music Chorus and quite a few others strive to present musical strains that have survived over the centuries.

Of particular interest to foreigners are the *Sema* Ceremonies of the so-called "Whirling Dervishes" who, through their mystical music and dance, reflect the transcendent value of the heart's purity, the image of the perfect human being, the poetic belief that

Left, "Whirling Dervishes" perform *Sema*. Above, a performance of Mozart's *Abduction from the Seraglio* in situ at the Topkapi.

its 1782 debut in Vienna, and has widely been performed in all opera capitals of the western world. Since 1973, the festival season in Istanbul has opened with a production of Mozart's "Turkish" opera in a Turkish setting by a mixed cast of international and Turkish stars. The idea of performing *Abduction* in Topkapi Palace came from Mr. Aydin Gün, a veteran of Turkish opera and director of the Istanbul Foundation for Culture and Art. Mr. Gün stages the opera himself and rightly claims that it is the major touristic attraction of the International Istanbul Festival.

HOTELS AND BARS

Accommodation in Istanbul comes in all shapes and sizes, ranging from hostels that can only boast lice and mice to those which offer ice for a price.

The lower end, naturally enough, are those hotels and pensions near the **Topkapi Bus Station**, the **Sirkeci Train Station** and **Sultan Ahmet Square** which cater to the back-packing crowd. Mid-range "family style hotels" dot the landscape of **Aksaray** and **Laleli**; the families they cater to, how-

with the Yeşil Ev offer the prospective lodger not only the best service to be had for a price in the city, but also a sense of architectural heritage.

The Ramada is the happy result of a major restoration by the NET Holding Group of a social welfare housing project dating from the 1920s, and boasts several restaurants, cafes, shops as well as the genuine belly-up-bar. The rooms, all built around central courtyards, are small but have all the ameni-

ever, are usually those of the extended Islamic type, with a healthy dose of East Bloc travelers thrown in to boot. Usually clean but lacking in most other amenities, the Laleli/Aksaray hotels are too numerous to mention. The advantage of staying in this area is the proximity of the major touristic sites of the city, as well as shopping opportunities in the Grand Covered Bazaar.

Special hotels: Also in the same general area are three up-market hotels: the newly restored **Ramada** in Laleli, the **Yeşil Ev** on Sultan Ahmet Square and the adjacent **Soğukçeşme Street Pensions** associated

ties, including cable television.

The Yeşil Ev (or "Green House") and its associated Soğukçeşme Street Pensions, both managed by Çelik Gülersoy's Touring Association, offer a similar historic setting, but with much less noise. Book well in advance, as both establishments are favorite hotels for upmarket travelers with a touch of class. Another touring establishment made for second honeymooners and those who want to stay far away from the madding crowd is the **Hidiv Kasri**, or Khedive's Castle, outside the upper Bosphorus suburb of Çubuklu on the Asian side of the city. The simultaneous attraction and detraction of this exquisite hostel is its distance from town.

Taksim Hotels: For those traveling on expense accounts, the five-star priced but four-star quality **Hilton, Sheraton** and **Etap** hotels in the Taksim area might be considered as a over-priced bed in which to rest one's head. All offer the standard internationally accepted mix of comfortable but characterless rooms, roof-top bars with room service for businessmen on expense accounts. In Istanbul—as throughout much of the developing world—luxury hotels also serve as a venue for circumcision parties and weddings replete with huge bouquets of flowers for those locals who have the cash to entertain hundreds of guests, but don't want their Isfahan carpets sullied by muddy shoes at home.

Hotel swimming pools, too, are a congregation point for well-heeled locals to show

commanding views of the city, conference halls, coffee shops, discos, communication rooms with telex, fax and direct dial telephones. This last may seem a little pedestrian, but should by no means be taken for granted, as anyone who has stayed in a hotel without direct dial can tell you.

Casinos and pools: The upmarket hotels, however, provide more than just shelter and

off the season's newest bikinis. Memberships are steep, but apparently worthwhile for the cruising crowd. The recent advent of computerized one-armed-bandits is an added attraction for newlyweds to test their prospects for future bliss. Live tables—black jack and roulette predominate—are found in every five-star hotel now, but are reserved for foreigners with hard currency.

Bars: The call of the *muezzin* to the faithful from one of the city's myriad mosques may be the first thing you hear in the morning, but the call of the bar-man for the last call in one of the hundreds of bars will no

Left, pool-side beauty. Above, newly-weds at a casino.

doubt be the last thing you want to hear before going to bed at night. The two, needless to say, do not mix well.

The most promising are the bars in the Taksim district. **Bilsak**, is a Mecca for cultural activities of every sort, ranging from day long seminars on the future of the city, to debates on homosexual (read: drag queen) rights. The building has a bar-cafe on the first floor, and a bar-restaurant on the roof, catering in general to that rare commodity, the Turkish Bohemian. The whole show moves to the **Bilsak outdoor bar**/garden at Yeniköy during the summer months.

Closer to Taksim Square is the **Arif's Place**. Allegedly a private club, it is open to

Valentino, a Victorian setting for Victorian encounters.

On the far side of the Taksim Square, hidden among the spare-parts outlet stores, is **Yeşil**, opened by one of the foremost names in Turkish entertainment, Ali Poyrazoğlu. Forget about going there on weekends without a reservation, when there is a cabaret show which directs irreverencies at the political elite. Food and drinks are a little stiff. Next door is the **Pub 14**, a favorite hangout for gays, of which Yeşil also has its share.

Uptown bars: The Maçka—Nişantaşi district also has its share of drinking establishments, although most are of the up-market

anyone who looks like he or she owns the place. Clientele consists in the main of film producers, their lovers, estranged wives, hangers-on, actors, critics, intellectuals, and would-be's of all of the above.

Closer to the square, is the **Taksim Sanat Derneği**, or Taksim Art Association. Mostly a theater-crowd bar, it has a piano, and serves decent food at reasonable prices. Although a basement (and more than a little humid) it is decorated like an alpine chalet. To either side of the TSD are the **PUB 1001**, a transsexuals' bar (ridiculously expensive) and the more subdued but equally gay

variety. **Kulis** and **Ziya** are two choices for a tranquil evening, which also have restaurants attached. **Zihni**, in Maçka, boasts the original bar of the Park Hotel, and is opened between 6 and 10 a.m. Pricey, it is packed daily nonetheless, so get there early.

Further on is the **Ece Bar** in Etiler, which also boasts live jazz. **W.O.M.** is nearby, with live music every night by the house band, Group Locomotive. Foreign bands are featured once a week, as well as cabaret-style entertainment ranging from plays to bodybuilding as the occasion presents itself.

Bosphorus Bars: Along the water at Ortakoy is **Ziya's Summer Bar**, situated right under the first Bosphorus Bridge. There is a large, outdoor area with a jazz band in the summer months, and two separate bars, an indoor section for the winter months, plus a year round restaurant. For the atmosphere and clientele, the prices are very reasonable, and if you want to get a good cross section of the people you'd never see at Hagia Sophia or the mosques, check out Ziya's. Further up the Bosphorus in Arnavutköy is the **Kedi Bar**, a pleasant place for drinks and snacks and live-old tunes a la 1967.

The Bosphorus suburb of Bebek boasts more bars per square inch than any other section of the city. Chief among these is the waterfront bar in the **Bebek Hotel**, with patio open in the summer months. The hotel manager, Metin Bey, insures that his prices are the lowest in town for a comparable bar, with a complete range of drinks to choose from. Across from the Chinese Restaurant is the **Kalem Bar**—a corridor like affair that caters to students from the nearby Bosphorus University, with soft piano music playing in the background. On the other side of the restaurant is the **Il Teatro**, managed by Korhan Abay, a prominent name in Turkish theater and also a TV host. It is frequented in the main by graduates of the French language Galatasaray Lycee, so if you like to hustle *Francais*, this is your place. Every Thursday evening is devoted to alumni. Ask for directions to the **3-12 PM**, down-Bosphorus from central Bebek. There is a live jazz band, playing moldy-oldies. The crowd is professional, with million dollar deals being discussed in the corners.

In the next suburb up-stream, Rumeli Hisar, there are a number of bar-restaurants, chief among which is **Han**, which also boasts a pleasant second story terrace in the summer months. Service is impeccable. Some 500 meters further on is the **Eskici**, or "Junk Store". The bar doubles as an antique shop, and one can purchase the chair one is sitting on, if wanted.

Far up the Bosphorus at Yeniköy (the summer home of the aforementioned

Bilsak) is the consciously exclusive **Park Şamdan** eatery-cum-bar-cum-disco. Set in a spectacular setting, it is worth forcing one's way into once, even if the normal drinks are on the spendy side. The well-heeled might take a stab at Metin Fadillioglu's **"29"** in Etiler. A heavy atmosphere, majestic decoration, a formal air and a collection of ministers and bonafide stars are there for the hobnobbing.

Discos: Istanbul has not received the word that discotheques are *passe* in the rest of the world, and the city—if it does not abound in them—boasts quite a few. Older establishments, like the **Hydromel**, **Regine** and **33**, are to be found along Cumhuriyet Caddesi

near Taksim, attracting a crowd of young bucks, cheap dates, off-work prostitutes and agents of the vice and narcotics squads. The **Plaza**, opposite Zihni's in Maçka, is small, pricey and crowded. **Studio 54**, right under the Ece Bar, has no other distinguishing quality aside from being the oldest in its category. The nearby **Airport**, in Zincirlikuyu, pioneered the "big space" concept in an old movie house, taken to its logical John Travolta-consequence in the **Discorium**, a laser-lit affair that holds over 1,000 dancing souls, with as many waiting outside to pay the $20 entrance fee on any given night.

Left, the stars come out at night. Above, floorshow at up-market club.

1001 Nights

Casinos: The sanitized clubs in the big hotels or up-market casinos around Taksim Square such as **Maksim's** or **Parisian** are essentially a family affair, their "authentic Oriental shows" consisting of a mixture of too-sweet "classical" Turkish music sung by an aging star, a prudish revue consisting of a slightly younger star performing play-back style, and a bellydancer who could be the girl-next-door. Entrance to such clubs can be pretty steep, although the obligation to tracted midnight eye is soothed by the neon glare of a hundred sleazy clubs featuring "*saz ve jaz*", or a mixture of arabesque-style music and disco hits. The shows usually include a couple of aspiring singers, voices enhanced by considerably more than adequate reverb and tremelo, a stripper, belly dancer and often an acrobatic show. Mid-market clubs occasionally provide "folklore" dancers as well as foreign dance troupes from England, Spain, Hungary,

spend more by stuffing paper money down the flimsy costumes of a dancer is still frowned upon in the better houses. Dancing with the bellydancer herself, more than being routine, is nearly expected in such establishments. The visitor will have a chance to hitch his shirt-up over his midrift, and, the ravages of age thus exposed, have a wandering photographer immortalize the moment on film for a modest fee.

For the real thing, needless to say, one must look elsewhere, and happily, not far away. Starting with the **Beyoğlu** district and moving toward **Taksim Square**, the dis-

Poland and Portugal—lost souls, in the main, working for their sweat-equity cards.

No self-respecting club expects anyone to show up before midnight at the earliest, and the potential denizen of the night is advised to wait for the bewitching hour, lest you be swamped by a small army of waiters/bouncers and two dozen whiskey dollies anxious for you to be the first to offer them an expensive drink for the pleasure of their company.

For the uninformed or novice in the milder vices of this world, whiskey dollies ("*konsomatris*" in Turkish) are ladies whose job it is

to try and make you buy them as many watered down gin-tonics as possible at inflated prices and then abandon you when it is clear you won't buy them another. The promise of sex, of course, is an essential part of the action. Clubs will often have a balcony or alcove with a couple of deep-cushioned couches for their more promising customers, where one might do a little necking with the girl of one's choice, but the ubiquitous waiters are there to insure that the hanky-

curious will have to experiment on their own.

Red light zones: Amsterdam may have its picturesque call girl shops along the canals; Paris, it is true, has its colorful Rue St Denis; Sweden, no doubt, has its own uniquely sanitized version of the world's oldest profession, and Thailand its frenzied dens of iniquity, if one can ever break through the crowds of sex-tour groups flown in from Germany and Japan. But in terms of sheer

panky doesn't get out of hand.

All the clubs are the same in all their essentials, so there is no need to mention any by name here. One possible difference suggested by students of the *saz ve jaz* scene is that clubs with stairs leading down only promise sex, whereas clubs with stairs leading up actually provide it. This has not been scientifically proven, however, and so the

raunchiness, the institution of the Turkish whorehouse (*Genelev*, or "common house") is one of a kind, and is a properly shocking part of any tour of the sleazy side of the city.

Located about half-way up **Yüksek Kaldirim Street** in Karaköy (about half way up hill from the Galata Bridge moving toward the Galata Tower) the brothel area is easy to find: just look for the knots of itinerant salesmen of watches, shoes, radios and rubbers. A constant stream of men walking in and out of a gate guarded by policemen lets you know that you are at the right place.

Two withered Armenian ladies—appar-

Left, belly-dancing girls from down-market club. Above, Beyoğlu-strip at night.

ently former bawds themselves—are the actual owners of most of the houses, and are honored every year by city-fathers for being in the top-ten tax paying bracket. All the houses are managed by burly pimps whose duty it is to periodically clear the crowded porches of vogeurs who regard the area as a free porno flick. Strolling salesmen lend a festive air to the debauched atmosphere. An itinerant hustler wanders around with a device for taking blood pressure, inviting all to let their excitement be officially registered and acted upon if too high.

The entire experience is made the more bizarre with the knowledge that a legal sex bazaar actually exists in a nominally Muslim

society, and even stranger with the knowledge that many of the girls actually marry their way out of sex-bondage, which, in more cases than not, they accept as their fate after having lost their virginity at an early age in a society that prizes female chastity above all else.

Sulukule: Another must for those obsessed with the seedier aspects of the city is the gypsy quarter of Sulukule near the **Edirne Gate,** where young (and not so young) ladies dance in their living room under the supervision of their parents before any group of strangers willing to pay. While

the band of musicians bleat and bang on fife and drum (the only song played seems to be *Mastika-Mastika,* which is the tune dancing bears also get excited by), the daughters of the house parade around in swimsuits while the brothers break big bills into smaller donatives for the convenience of the customer. Sulukule lives by tipping, and it is a rare visitor who does not feel more ripped off by the constant badgering for *bahsheesh* than if one had been honestly mugged.

For the insatiably curious: Strange as it may seem, Turkey—and especially Istanbul—has a substantial transvestite and transsexual community. One might speculate and attribute the fact to the traditional homosexuality practised by the Ottoman elite, mixed with the equally ancient tradition of eunuchs. Castration, even if illegal today, has been an essential part of the medical arts in Turkey for centuries. These are weak arguments at best, but nothing else really explains the phenomenon of men with breasts and sexual neuters who roam the **Taksim** area by night, nor the tolerance and even taste for them in a society that prides itself on its masculinity to a nearly obsessive degree.

Whole and half transsexuals are literally everywhere. The most famous in the "complete" category is the singer, Bülent Ersoy, who recently won a court-battle and now can reappear in concert after a hiatus of some six years, while in the silicon-alone group the most well known is one "Sisi"—an exquisitely beautiful half-man who hangs out with his/her fellow creatures at either the **PUB 1001** or **Valentino's** near the Square, and maintains that she/he delights in nothing more than seducing gold dealers in the Covered Bazaar and playing "butch" in bed.

Many of the drag queens also work as whiskey dollies in local bars, so beware that deep-throated darling cooing in your ear. The same goes for the apparent women cruising the main drag between Taksim and Harbiye in their cars on a Friday or Saturday night: the thick wrists and adam's apple, they say, give the game away.

Left, "Sisi", the king of the drag-queens. Right, belly-dancing in Beyoğlu.

TURKEY

The nearest way to reach these beautiful places is

**TÜRK HAVA YOLLARI
TURKISH AIRLINES**

For reservations please contact Turkish Airlines, Sales Offices or IATA travel agencies.

ISTANBUL SHERATON
HOTEL & TOWERS
TURKISH STYLE HOSPITALITY

Turkey
The best kept secret

Cafe Vienna
The informal alternative

Istanbul
The pearl of Turkey

Revan
Traditional Ottoman
cousine

La Coupole
A genuine International
dining experience

TRAVEL TIPS

DESTINATION ISTANBUL

GETTING THERE

Air: There are a number of daily flights from most European capitals to Istanbul's Atatürk Airport, which is modern and noted for its security precautions. Many of these flights have direct connections from the U.S. There are also an ever-increasing number of flights from the Middle East, the Far East and South East Asia. It is useful to know that there are duty-free shops in the arrival area, so that you need not carry duty free liquor with you on the plane. Banks are also available for changing money. Although there is an airport bus from the city Şişhane terminal to the airport, it is impractical to use it from the airport into the city because it departs from the domestic terminal, which is some distance from the international terminal. However, taxis are plentiful and have taximeters, so there is no need for bargaining. Be prepared for traffic jams on your way into the city; this approach from the airport takes you through some of the most crowded districts before you pass through the Byzantine walls and join the congestion of the inner city.

Sea: In addition to the cruise ships which call at Istanbul there is now a regular ferry boat service from Venice, via Piraeus, during the summer months. The ferry docks on the Asiatic side of the city and passengers are brought by launch to the European side, disembarking at Sarayburnu, below Topkapi Palace. From here you will be able to take a taxi to your hotel. The approach by sea is the most beautiful introduction to the city.

Rail: Trains from western Europe, via Bulgaria or Greece, arrive at Sirkeci in the old city, the original terminal of the Orient Express. Again, taxis are available to take you to your destination, plunging you into one of the most congested districts around the Galata Bridge. Trains from the east arrive at Haydarpaşa on the Asiatic side, with regular ferry boat connections to the European side of the city

By Bus: Because of the large numbers of Turkish migrants in some countries, especially West Germany, there are frequent buses between the major cities and Istanbul, of varying degrees of comfort and efficiency. This is the cheapest way to reach Istanbul from central Europe. Bus terminals are on the outskirts of the city and taxis are available to your final destination.

By Private Car: For those who enjoy driving, the journey across Europe is interesting, despite the hazards of the E5, especially in Yugoslavia. Remember to obtain a visa for Bulgaria in advance, unless you come via Greece. The ferry service from Venice also carries cars for those who prefer not to drive through Yugoslavia and Bulgaria. The approach by road from the east is only for the intrepid. Consult your local motoring organization about documents for your vehicle.

INSIDE ISTANBUL

GETTING ACQUAINTED

Istanbul is a city of over six million people. If you arrive by air you will be driven past about half of them on your way into the city through the crowded suburbs. Your hotel will probably be either the old city near the mosques and other ancient monuments, or the "new" city across the Golden Horn, the business center. Both of these sections of the city are in Europe. Opposite, across the Sea of Marmara and the Bosphorus Straits (*not* a river), is the Asiatic part of Istanbul, reached via the Bosphorus bridges or by ferry boats.

In the new city the central point for transportation is Taksim Square, where the Atatürk Cultural Centre is located, in which the State opera, theater and ballet groups perform. Across the Golden Horn in the old city, the main points to remember are Eminönü Square beside the Galata Bridge, Beyazit Square at the upper entrance to the Grand Bazaar and Sultan Ahmet Square around which more than 50 percent of the major tourist attractions are located.

The visitor's first impression varies according to the direction in which he has been travelling. Visitors from the U.S. and Europe tend to find the city confusing, crowded, bustling, antiquated, badly-lit, noisy and rather dirty. Those coming from Karachi or Cairo find it calm, clean and modern. The truth is that the city, which was clean enough for one to wear a white shirt for two days 20 years ago, has been suffering increasingly from congestion, noise and especially air pollution. This trend has fortunately now been reversed as factories are being moved out of the city and waste water is being controlled. A distinct improvement can already be observed.

Ultimately most visitors find the city a fascinating mixture of ancient and modern, chaos and calm, irresistible for the inexhaustible range of natural and man-made beauties around every corner, memorable for the hospitality of the people.

Visas: Visas are not required for the nationals of the following countries so long as they do not exceed the length of time indicated preceding each group.

3 months: Fiji, Finland, France, Gambia, Germany—Federal Republic of, Iran, Ireland, Korea— South, Lichtenstein, Malta, Morocco, Portugal, Switzerland, USA.

2 months: Australia, Austria, Bahamas, Barbados, Canada, Denmark, Grenada, Hong Kong, Italy, Jamaica, Luxemburg, Mauritius, Pakistan, San Marino, Spain, Sweden, Trinidad, Tunisia, Uganda, United Kingdom.

7 weeks: Afghanistan, Romania, Yugoslavia.

6 weeks: Belgium, Iceland, Japan.

Those who wish to extend their stay in Istanbul must apply to **Yabancilar Şube Müdürlügü** (Aliens Office, Cağaloğlu, Tel: 528 51 73.)

Customs Regulations: You are permitted to bring in all kinds of personal effects, including pets; 400 cigarettes or 1 kilo of tobacco or 50 cigars; 1 kilo of tea or coffee; five bottles of perfume and five (yes five) liters of spirits, duty free. Valuables such as fur coats, cameras, typewriters and electrical appliances must be noted in your passport to avoid complications when leaving.

Health Regulations: There are no vaccination requirements for visitors. Most medicines are sold freely at pharmacies, but it is a good idea to bring a supply of any particular brand you are accustomed to taking. Rabies is still a hazard and if you are bitten by an animal you suspect of being rabid, you should report as soon as possible to the **Kuduz Hastanesi** for a course of injections. Take the animal with you if possible, to be tested.

Before Departure: You should arrive at the airport 2 hours ahead of flight time, to allow for all security checks and formalities

Valuables worth up to US $3,000 may be taken out with no questions asked, and items worth more may also be taken out if a bank receipt is shown to prove that hard currency has been exchanged for the purchase.

Non-valuables worth up to TL 200 may be taken out however written permission is needed for items valued between TL 200,000 and TL 2 million.

Tea and coffee are limited to one kilo and spices to half a kilo.

If any valuables were endorsed in your passport on arrival it is essential to have these checked and cancelled when departing.

It is strictly forbidden to take antiques out of the country and you run the risk of being accused of smuggling if you try. If in doubt, ask the dealer you purchased from to obtain a customs clearance certificate for you.

Turkish Tourist Offices Abroad

Austria
Mahlerstrasse 3
1010 Wien
Tel: (0222) 52 21 28
    (0222) 52 21 29
Cables: TURKISCHES
INFORMATION
BURO-WEIN
Telex: 111281 TUINF

Belgium
42 Rue d'Arenberg
1000 Bruxelles
Tel: (02) 513 82 30
    (02) 513 82 39
Cables: TURKTANIT
BRUXELLES
Telex: 25973 TURKTA-B

Denmark
Vesterbrogade 11 A
1620 Copenhagen V
Tel: (01) 22 31 00
    (01) 22 83 74
Cables: TURKTANIT
COPENHAGAN
Telex: 22340

France
102 Champs-Elysées
75008 Paris
Tel: (01) 562 78 68
    (01) 562 79 84
    (01) 562 2611
Cables: TURKTANIT
PARIS
Telex: 290639

Germany (Federal Republic of)
Baseler Str. 37
D-6000 Frankfurt/Main 1
Tel: (0611) 23 30 81
    (0611) 23 30 82
Cables: TURKTANIT
FRANKFURT
Telex: 4170-081

Also: Kalsplatz 3/1
8000 München 2
Tel: (089) 59 49 02
    (089) 59 43 17
Cables: TURKTANIT
MÜNCHEN
Telex: 528190

Great Britain
170-173 Picadilly
1st Floor London
W1.V 9DD
Tel: (01) 734 86 81
    (01) 734 86 82
Cables: TURKTANIT
LONDON
Telex: 8954905 TTIORCG

Italy
Piazza della Republica 56
00185 Roma
Tel: (06) 46 29 57
    (06) 47 41 69
Cables: TURKTANIT
ROMA
Telex: 61 21 31 TURTANIT
ROMA

Japan
33-36 2-Chrome
Jingumae, Shibuya-ku
Tokyo 150
Tel: (03) 470 6380
    (03) 470 5131
Cables: TURKTANIT
TOKYO
Telex: 1-22856 EMBTURK

Kuwait
P.O. Box 15518
Deaya, Kuwait
Tel: (965) 42 42 48
    (965) 42 42 98
Cables: TURKISM/KT

Netherlands
Herengracht 51
1017 BS Amsterdam.
Tel: (020) 26 68 10
    (020) 24 40 06
Cables: TURKTANIT
AMSTERDAM
Telex: 1522

Saudi Arabia
Medina Road Kilo
6 Al Musaidiva Street
Jeddah
Or: P.O. Box 6966
Tel: (21) 5487-73
Cables: TURKTANIT
JEDDAH
Telex: 402631 CIBNEN-51

Spain
Plaza de Espana
Torre de Madrid
Piso: 13
Office: 1-3
Madrid 13
Tel: (01) 248 70 14
    (01) 248 71 14
Cables: TURKTANIT
MADRID
Telex: 44345 TUEL

Sweden
Kungsgatan 3
S-111 43
Stockholm
Tel: (08) 21 86 20
Cables: TURKTANIT
STOCKHOLM

Switzerland
Talstrasse 74
8001 Zurich
Tel: (01) 221 08 10
    (01) 221 08 12
Cables: TURKTANIT
ZURICH CH
Telex: 045—813752

U.S.A.
821 United Nations Plaza
New York
N.Y. 10017
Tel: (212) 6872194
Cables: TURKTANIT
Telex: 426428

Climate And Clothing: The best months to visit Istanbul are June and September if you want to indulge in swimming as well as sightseeing. May and October are lovely if you do not insist on swimming. July and August can be uncomfortably hot, with daytime temperatures reaching 30° celsius, but there is usually a cooling breeze, and the evenings are perfect. From November until April, it may rain and an overcoat is essential. Even in the height of summer a sweater may be necessary in the evenings, and a jacket is recommended in May and October. Contrary to general belief, it snows in Istanbul, usually in late January, February or early March. The best factor about Istanbul's climate is that it almost never stays the same for longer than three days and the sun shines on more than half the days of the year.

Whatever the season, rubber-soled walking shoes are necessary for the cobbled streets of the old city, and for negotiating ferry boats and castle walls. Istanbul's beaches are only topless for foreigners, but nightclubs are accustomed to any level of décolletage.

Customs: Hospitality is an intrinsic part of Turkish life. If you are offered glasses of tea and cups of coffee, accept gracefully. If a total stranger gives you a bus ticket, this is perfectly normal. If you should be invited to a Turkish home, it is customary to bring a small gift; flowers or chocolates are always acceptable. If your stay is short you are not expected to reciprocate until your host visits your own country.

When visiting mosques, tombs and churches, appro-

priate clothing should be worn; not shorts, skimpy tops or mini-skirts. Shoes must be removed on entering mosques or shrines and shawls may be given to those considered inadequately covered.

Traffic: Traffic does not stop for pedestrians unless forced to do so by a traffic policeman, by traffic lights (few) or by a large group of pedestrians. Follow the crowds and use the overhead pedestrian bridges whenever possible.

Tipping: This is an important way in which to express your appreciation of services, in a city where service is still an important factor of life. It is normal to tip around 10 percent of the bill in restaurants and bars, regardless of whether or not service is included in the total and of the quality of service. Of course you may increase this amount for extra attention. In hotels, special service should be tipped on the spot, not covered by a lump sum given to the reception desk.

Photography: It would be difficult to imagine a more photogenic city than Istanbul; the juxtaposition of old and new, drab and brilliant, together with the fabulous skyline, offer even the most amateur photographer a chance to impress friends back home.

However, you may occasionally be expected to pay for the privilege of photographing certain picturesque scenes, particularly dancing

bears. You may also be asked to send a copy to the subject of your photo—accept the address and send it or not, as you wish.

Of course you should not obviously photograph those praying or in similar circumstances. Avoid photographing military establishments, since this is strictly forbidden.

Film and batteries are available although somewhat expensive. You are advised to bring any special requirements with you. The full range of processing facilities is available.

Business hours: Banks and offices are closed on Saturday and Sunday, shops are closed on Sunday.

Banking hours are 9 a.m. to 12 noon, 1:30 - 4 p.m. but you may change money at major hotels at any time of the night or day, seven days a week.

Shopping hours are generally 9 a.m. to 7 p.m., Monday to Saturday. Few shops close for one hour at lunch time. All are closed on Sundays and National Holidays.

Public toilets: These are few and far between, therefore hotels and restaurants still permit their facilities to be used by outsiders.

Voltage: Istanbul is now almost exclusively 220v. 50 hz. although there are a few pockets of 110v. still waiting to be changed. Check before you burn out your hair dryer.

Weights and measures: Turkey uses the metric system of weights and measures. As a rough guide, one meter is equal to 39.7 inches and one kilo equals 2.2 pounds. Clothing measurements are similar to European sizes (not the U.K.).

Time: The time is 2 hours ahead of Greenwich Mean Time, 1 hour ahead of central Europe and 8 hours ahead of New York time, except Summer Time, it is in force from April to September and the time is GMT + 3 hrs.

Currency: The Turkish lira comes in coins of 5, 10, 25, 50, 100 lira value and notes of 100, 500, 1000, 5000 and 10, 000 TL.

V.A.T: Value added tax, (K.D.V.), is now added in the price shown on goods, not added on separately. It varies between 5% and 12%.

Tourist Information: Official tourist information offices are the best places to get brochures and maps of the different regions of Turkey. These offices are located at:

—Atatürk airport
—Karaköy sea port, where passengers disembark from cruise ships
—Sultan Ahmet Square, near St. Sophia and the Blue Mosque
—Hilton Arcade, at the entrance to the Hilton Hotel
—Meşrutiye Caddesi 57, Galatasaray, beside the British Consulate.

Advice and reservations for tours are best obtained from the following.

Airlines

A.A.—American Airlines
Kongre Tourism
Cumhuriyet Cad. 269/2-A
Harbiye, Istanbul
Tel: 130 2211

Aeroflot—Soviet Airlines
Mete Cad. 30
Taksim, Istanbul
Office Tel: 143 47 25-26

Air Afrique: Air France
Cumhuriyet Cad. 1
Taksim, Istanbul
Tel: 155 30 50
155 30 70

Air Algerie Rep
Miltur
Cumhuriyet Cad. 135/A
Elmadağ
Tel: 141 02 46-47

Air France
Cumhuriyet Cad. 1
Taksim, Istanbul
Tel: 155 30 50
155 30 70

ALTA—The Royal Jordanian Airlines
Miltur
Cumhuriyet Cad. 135
Elmadağ
Istanbul
Tel: 133 07 44
141 75 39

Alitalia
Cumhuriyet Cad. Erk Ap. 14/8
Elmadağ, Istanbul
Tel: 131 33 91-92
131 33 94
131 33 93

AUA—Austrian Airlines
Sheraton Hotel
Askerocagi Cad. 1
Taksim, Istanbul
Tel: 140 22 47-49

BA—British Airways
Cumhuriyet Cad. 10
Elmadağ, Istanbul
Tel: 148 42 35-38
148 50 17-19

Balkan—Bulgarian Airlines
Cumhuriyet Cad
Gezi Dükkanlar
8, Taksim, Istanbul
Tel: 145 24 56

BCA—British Caledonian Airways
Karavan Turizm
Cumhuriyet Cad. 131/3
Elmadağ
Istanbul
Tel: 148 06 91
148 36 99

CAAC Airlines—Civil Aviation
Administration of China
Cumhuriyet Cad. 235/1
Harbiye
Istanbul
Tel: 132 71 11-12

Cathay Pacific Airways
Arar Tours Tourizm
Sivritaş Sok
11 Mecidiyeköy
Istanbul
Tel: 167 46 49
172 29 22-27

CPAIR—Canadian Pacific Airlines
Sumer Tourism
Cumhuriyet Cad. 141/6
Elmadağ
Istanbul
Tel: 141 73 66-67

CTA—Cyprus Turkish Airlines
Cumhuriyet Cad. 111/2
Elmadağ
Istanbul
Tel: 133 00 55-56

CSA—Czechoslovakian Airline
Turkish Airlines
Cumhuriyet Cad. 131
Harbiye
Istanbul
Tel: 148 38 11

Eastern Airlines
Sumer Tourism
Cumhuriyet Cad. 141/6
Elmadağ, Istanbul
Tel: 141 73 66-67

EL-AL—Israel Airlines
Cumhuriyet Cad. 187
Hariye
Istanbul
Tel: 146 53 03-06

Egypt Air
Halâskârgazi Cad. 107/1
Harbiye
Istanbul
Tel: 146 71 91

Emirates Airlines
Çelebi Tourism
Halâskârgazi Cad.
Gürani 15 Han: 393/5
Sisli
Istanbul
Tel: 131 20 44
     131 32 48

Finnair
Cumhuriyet Cad. 26/A
Elmadag
Istanbul
Tel: 141 36 36

Gulfair
Cumhuriyet Cad. 213
Harbiye, Istanbul
Tel: 131 34 50-54

Iberia—Lineas Aeras Internacionales de Espana
Topçu Cad.
Uygun Ap. 2/2
Taksim
Istanbul
Tel: 150 54 78

Interflug
Halâskârgazi Cad.
3rd. Floor, Pangalti
Istanbul
Tel: 140 48 78
     146 62 23

Iranair—Airline of the Islamic Republic of Iran
Cumhuriyet Cad. 71
Elmadağ, Istanbul
Tel: 141 19 16-18

Iraqi Airways
Cumhuriyet Cad.
Gezi Dükkanlar
Taksim, Istanbul
Tel: 146 01 70-71

Istanbul Airlines
Incirli Cad.
50, Bakirköy, Istanbul
Tel: 570 34 00-03
     561 34 66-68

JAL—Japan Airlines
Sumer Turizm
Cumhuriyet Cad. 141/6
Elmadağ
Istanbul
Tel: 141 73 66-67

JAT—Yugoslav Airlines
Cumhuriyet Cad. 171
Elmadağ
Istanbul
Tel: 148 29 04

KLM—Royal Dutch Airlines
Abdi Ipekti Cad. 6-8
Nişantaşi
Tel: 130 03 11-16

Korean Airlines
Cumhuriyet Cad. 8
Elmadağ
Istanbul
Tel: 146 76 43
     150 85 85

Kuwait Airways
Halâskârgazi Cad. 41-45/1

Harbiye
Istanbul
Tel: 140 40 81-82
     142 78 78
     131 09 88

LAA—Libyan Arab Airlines
Cumhuriyet Cad. 169/2
Harbiye
Istanbul
Tel: 133 02 28-29

LOT—Polish Airlines
Cumhuriyet Cad. 91/2
Elmadağ
Istanbul
Tel: 140 79 27
     141 67 49

Lufthansa
Cumhuriyet Cad. 179-185
Elmadağ
Istanbul
Tel: 146 51 30-34
     146 84 41

Malev—Hungarian Airlines
Cumhuriyet Cad. 141-147
Elmadağ
Istanbul
Tel: 141 03 09
     148 81 53

MEA—Middle East Airlines
Cumhuriyet Cad. 30
Harbiye
Istanbul
Tel: 148 22 41-42
     148 37 23

Olympic Airways
Cumhuriyet Cad. 171/A
Elmadağ
Istanbul
Tel: 146 50 81
     147 37 01-02

Pan American Airways
Hilton Arcade
Cumhuriyet Cad.

215

Harbiye
Istanbul
Tel: 131 23 39-46

**PIA—Pakistan
International Airways**
Cumhuriyet Cad.
Nispet Sok. 2/3
Elmadağ
Istanbul
Tel: 146 94 09
     147 39 88

**Qantas—Australian
Airlines**
TGI Turizm Cumhuriyet
Cad. 155/1
Havapalas
Elmadağ
Istanbul
Tel: 140 31 00
     140 50 32
     146 34 66

**Sabena—Belgian
World Airlines**
Topçular Cad. 2/1
Taksim
Istanbul
Tel: 150 60 26
     150 67 62

**SAS—Scandinavian
Airlines System**
Cumhuriyet Cad. 26
Elmadağ
Istanbul
Tel: 146 60 75

**Saudi—Saudi Arabian
Airlines**
Cumhuriyet Cad. 31
Elmadağ
Istanbul
Tel: 156 48 05-06
Tickets: Cumhuriyet Cad.
33
Taksim
Istanbul
Tel: 156 48 00-04

Singapore Airlines
Halâskârgazi Cad. 59/3

Harbiye
Istanbul
Tel: 147 81 11
     148 86 20

Sönmez Airlines
Moris Seyahat Tünel Paşaji
11
Beyoğlu, Tünel
Istanbul
Turkey
Tel: 149 85 10-11
     149 30 36

**Syrianair—Syrian Arab
Airline**
Sheraton Hotel
Asker Ocagi Cad. 1
Taksim, Istanbul
Tel: 146 17 81
     146 63 04

Swissair
Cumhuriyet Cad. 6
Elmadağ
Istanbul
Tel: 131 28 44-48.
Reservation: 131 28 49-52

Talia Airways
Çekmece Cad. 20
Yeşilköy
Istanbul
Tel: 574 19 17

**Tarom—Romanian
Airlines**
Siraselviler Cad. 55
Taksim, Istanbul
Tel: 143 65 14
     145 70 55
     149 91 72

T.H.Y.—Turkish Airlines
Abidel Hürriyet Cad.
Vakif Isi Hani 154-156/2
Şişli, Istanbul
Turkey
Tel: 146 40 17
     147 13 38
Reservations Tel: 573 35 25
Group Reservations
Tel: 573 59 08-09

Charter Reservations
Tel: 573 59 80-81
Administration
Tel: 573 56 30
Promotion Tel: 148 26 31
Cargo Manager
Tel: 148 11 51
     148 45 72

**Torosair—Toros Airway
Syatem Trading Inc.**
Inönü Cad.
Gomosavyu
Istanbul
Tel: 151 74 60-63

Tunis Air
Cumhuriyet Cad. 309/1
Harbiye
Istanbul
Tel: 141 68 33
     141 71 17

**TWA—Trans World
Airlines**
Rep. Miltur
Cumhuriyet Cad. 193
Elmadağ
Istanbul
Tel: 141 02 46-47

UTA—Air France
Cumhuriyet Cad. 83
Taksim
Istanbul
Tei: 156 33 24
Variq: Rep. Miltur
Cumhuriyet Cad. 193
Elmadağ
Istanbul
Tel: 141 02 46-47

Yemenia
Antur
Büyükdere Cad. 42/C
Mecidiyeköy
Istanbul
Tel: 172 62 75

Consulates

Albania
Ömer Rüstü Paşa So

Your First Class choice.

In the finest traditions of First Class travel, we cater for your every need. Our cuisine is truly international with a wide selection of recipes from all over the world. Honoured by La Chaine des Rôtisseurs. Special diet meals can be pre-ordered to suit personal requirements.

The new-look interiors and luxurious sleeperseats give our cabin the stylish elegance you'll enjoy. Free stereo headsets provide musical entertainment to please all tastes, including the latest movies.

Our helpful courteous cabin crew are carefully selected to ensure they can converse in all the languages likely to be spoken by our executive passengers. We offer more flights to more places within the Gulf than any other airline.

For the smoothest connections west to east or east to west, Gulf Air serves you best.

طيران الخليج
GULF AIR
GOLDEN FALCON SERVICE

For further information contact your travel agent or local Gulf Air office.

BAZAAR 54

"Quality"

CARPET

The largest collection
of the top quality Turkish Carpets

- **İSTANBUL**
  Nuruosmaniye Cad.
  54 Cağaloğlu
  Tel. (1) 511 21 50

- **İZMİR**
  1373 Sok. 4/A,B,C
  Alsancak
  Tel. (51) 14 13 82 -14 86 35

- **KUŞADASI**
  Öküz Mehmet Paşa
  Kervansarayı
  Tel. (6361) 3411

- **MARMARIS**
  Yat Limanı
  Barbaros Cad. 1
  Tel. (6121) 2786

- **BODRUM**
  Neyzen Tevfik
  Cad. 186/A
  Tel. (6141) 2445

- **ANTALYA**
  Yat Limanı Kaleiçi 4
  Tel. (311) 10290

- **ASPENDOS**
  Alanya Yolu.
  Belkıs Harabeleri Serik
  Antalya Tel. (3221) 2900

- **CAPPADOCIA**
  Avanos
  Zelve yolu
  Tel: (4861) 1561

Bazaar 54 is an establishment of **NET GROUP of COMPANIES**

3, Teşvikiye
Tel: 161 57 26
Telex: 26042 arv-tr

Austria
Silahhane Cąd. 59/4
Teşvikiye
Tel: 140 54 77
146 37 69
Telex: 28026

Bangladesh
Honorary Consul General
Mr Pamir Bezmen
Ayse Sultan Korusu II
Bebek
Tel: 165 06 72
Telex: 27414/25 otx-tr

Belgium
Siraselviler Cad. 73
Taksim
Tel: 143 33 00-01
Telex: 25291 beis-tr

Bulgaria
Yildiz Posta Cad. 15
Gayrettepe
Tel: 166 26 05

Canada
Honorary Consul
Mr Yavuz Kireç
Büyükdere Cad. 107/3
Gayrettepe
Tel: 172 51 74
Telex: 26133 yvvz-tr

Chad
Honorary Consul
Mr Saeed Eabb
Yildiz Posta Cad. 17/4-5
Esentepe
Tel: 167 22 12
166 80 39
172 98 00
Telex: 26082 acer-tr
Cable: Cerrahoḡlullar

Chile
Honorary Consul
Mr Morda Dinar
Setüstü, Derya Han 1st

Floor, Room 101
Kabatas
Tel: 145 01 83-84
144 71 77
149 48 10
151 19 11
Telex: 25514 jur-tr

China People's Rep Of
Ortaklar Cad. 14
Mecidiyeköy
Tel: 172 52 00-01
Telex: 26906 ccgt-tr

Costa Rica
Honorary Consul
Mr Ender Kitap
Kocaainar,Köy Yolu
Sirinevler
Tel: 575 15 85-86

Czechoslovakia
Abdi Ipekçi Cad. 71
Maçka
Tel: 147 50 30-32
148 21 37
157 50 32

Democratic Rep Germany
Muallim Naci Cad. 118/4
Ortoköy
Tel: 160 48 77-38
Telex: 26349

Denmark
Silahhane Cad. 31/1
Maçka
Tel: 140 42 17
Telex: 26728 gkdk-tr
Cable: Danebiag

Dominican Rep
Honorary Consul
Mr Sahip Akosman
Akkavak Sok. 6
Nişantaşi
Tel: 148 36 13
131 30 05

Egypt The Arab Rep Of
Cevdetpaşa Cad. 173
Bebek
Tel: 163 60 33

165 24 40
Telex: 26087 aaf-tr

Federal Germany Rep
Selim Natun Cann Sok. 46
Ayazpaşa
Tel: 143 72 20
145 07 05
Telex: 24234 aais-tr

Finland
Inönü Cad. 69/6
Ayazpaşa
Tel: 143 37 75-76
144 80 00
Telex: 24521 fico-tr

France
Istiklâl Cad. 8
Taksim
Tel: 143 18 52-53
Telex: 24310-tr

Great Britain
Meşrutiyet Cad. 34
Tepebaşi
Tel: 144 75 40
144 75-49
Telex: 24122 brit-tr

Greece
Turnacibaşi Sok. 32
Galatasaray
Tel: 145 05 96-98
Telex: 24120 grek-tr

Hungary
Poyracik Sok. 35
Teşvikiye
Tel: 140 42 75
140 76 79
Telex: 22944 dips-tr

Iceland
Honorary Consul
Mr Nihat Hamamcioğlu
Büyükdere Cad. 13/A
Şişli
Tel: 146 31 43-44
147 24 89
Telex: 26974 hmmc-tr
Cable Address:
Hamamcioğlu, Istanbul

217

India
Consul General
Mr Nihat Boytüzün
Cumhuriyet Cad. 257/3
Harbiye
Tel: 141 73 72
    148 48 65
    147 85 25
Telex: 22528 hind-tr

Indonesia
Honorary Consul
Prof. Semih Tezcan
Seher Yildizi Sok. 22/11
Etiler
Tel: 163 80 08-09
Telex: 25351 buco-tr
    25695 bume-tr

Iran
Ankara Cad. 1/2
Cağaloğlu
Tel: 512 00 90-92
Cable: Iran Consulate
Istanbul

Iraq
Spor Cad. 124
Maçka
Tel: 160 50 20
    160 55 37
Telex: 26555-tr

Israel
Valikonagi Cad. 73/4
Nişantaşi
Tel: 146 41 25-27
Telex: 2341 hem-tr

Italy
Tomtonkaptan Sok. 15
Beyoğlu
Tel: 143 10 24-25
Telex: 25479 itco-tr
Cable: Italconsul
Beyoğlu

Japan
Inönü Cad. 24
Ayazpaşa
Tel: 145 02 90-91
Telex: 24127 ryoji-tr

Jordan
Honorary Consul
Mr Ismet Özbek
Valikonagi Cad. BM
Palas 63
Nişantaşi
Tel: 130 12 21-22
Telex: 27641 jor-tr

Lebanon
Teşvikiye Cad. 134/1
Teşvikye
Tel: 140 55 99
    147 37 87
Telex: 26729 coli-tr
Cable: Suliban
Teşvikiye

Libya
Miralay Befik Paşa Sok. 3
Ayazpaşa
Tel: 143 37 60-64
    143 61 82
    143 38 11
Telex: 24544 libu-tr
    24832 libu-tr

Malaysia
Honorary Consul
Dr Nusret Arsel
Halaokargazi Cad. 266/4
Room 7
Şişli
Tel: 147 17 28
    147 42 15
Telex: 233365 Toak-tr
    22768 aymar-tr

Malta
Honorary Consul
Mr Attila Artam
OTIM 2nd Floor
Ihlamur Beşiktaş
Tel: 172 58 37
    166 99 45
Telex: 26254 arit-tr
Fax: 172 02 95

Mexico
Honorary Consul
Mr Hüseyin Arif Akdogan
Hulusi Bay Wan 2-3

1st Floor
Karaköy
Tel: 144 06 91

Monaco
Honorary Consul
Mr Turan Çakim
(Also see under France)
Cevdetpaşa Cad. 164/17
Bebek
Tel: 163 02 54
    163 39 89

Nepal
Honorary Consul
Mr Hasan Behiç Onel
Valikonagi Cad. Yapi Kredi
Vakif Is Hanz 4/4
Nişantaşi
Tel: 140 53 35
    146 61 09

Netherlands
Istiklâl Cad. 393
Taksim
Tel: 144 90 96
    149 10-11
Telex: 24172-tr

North Cyprus Turk, Rep
Büyükdere Cad. 81/5
Room 9
Mecidiyeköy
Tel: 173 29 90
Telex: 28203 kied-tr

Norway
Honorary Consul
Mr L. Alex Dabkoviç
Rihtim Cad. 89/3
Karaköy
Tel: 149 97 53
Telex: 25290 norv-tr

Pakistan
OTIM
Blok A, 3rd Floor
Ihlamur
Beşiktaş
Tel: 172 16 36-37
Telex: 26850 pais-tr
Cable: Perap, Beşiktaş

Peru
Honorary Consul
Mr Sahap Kocatopçu
Ihlamur Youl 49/10
Nişantaşi
Tel: 146 88 09
   148 21 23
   141 21 80

Poland
Büyükçiftlik Sok. 5/7
Nişantaşi
Tel: 140 79 56
   147 74 94
Telex: 22895 hamp-tr

Portugal
Sehit Muhtar Cad. 43/3
Talinhane
Taksim
Tel: 150 11 30

Rumania
Siraselviler Cad. 55
Taksim
Tel: 144 35 55
   144 42 84
Telex: 24638-tr

Saudi Arabia
Yildiz Posta Cad.
Dedeman Ticaret Merkezi
52/7
Gayrettepe
Tel: 172 43 96-97
Telex: 26685 suud-tr

South Korea
Honorary Consul
Mr Ferda Kahraman
Aydede Cad. 24/70
Taksim
Tel: 146 76 43
   150 85 85

Spain
Teşvikiye Cad. 143/2
Teşvikiye
Tel: 140 34 44

Sweden
Istiklâl Cad. 497

Tünel
Tel: 143 57 70-72
Telex: 24250 tr
Cable: Svensk-Istanbul

Switzerland
Hüsrey Gerede Cad. 75/3
Teşvikiye
Tel: 148 50 70-71
Telex: 23327 suis-tr

Syria
Silahhane Cad. 59/5
Teşvikiye
Tel: 148 27 35
   148 32 84
   141 18 38
Telex: 23469 ary-tr

Thailand
Honorary Consul General
Mr Sahip Ihsan Tansuk
Honorary Vice-Consul
Mr Anthony J. R. Caouki
Cumhuriyet Cad. 349/1
Harbiye
Tel: 131 15 85-92
Telex: 22407 imto-tr
   22471 aese-tr

Tunisia
Honorary Consul
Mr Kenan Bulutoğlu
Hayriye Cad. 14/5
Galatasaray
Tel: 144 96 11

U.S.A.
Mesrutiyet Cad. 104
Tepebaşi
Tel: 151 36 02
Telex: 24306 usic-tr

U.S.S.R.
Istiklâl Cad. 443
Tünel
Tel: 144 16 93
   144 26 10
Telex: 25556 tr

Vatican
Ölçek Sok. 87

Harbiye
Tel: 148 08 1
   148 09 10

Yemen Arab Rep
Barbaros Bulvari
Güzel Konutlar
Ap. 32 Flat 10
Balmumcu
Beşiktaş
Tel: 166 35 88
Telex: 2834 amdn-tr

Yugoslavia
Valikonagi Cad. 98/A
Nişantaşi
Tel: 148 10 04
   148 11 33
Telex: 22048 tr

Travel Agencies

Anadol Tourism Co.
Cumhuriyet Cad. 261/4
Harbiye, Istanbul,
Tel: 146 80 84
   148 78 41
Telex: 22837 dolt-tr
Cable: Dolt-Tur

Bodrum Tourism
Cumhuriyet Cad.
Ka Han'16, Elmadag
Tel: 140 18 50
   141 65 18-19
   147 36 81
Telex: 27853 boto-tr
Cable: Bodrum-Tur
Owner: Mr Osman

Elegan Tourism & Travel Inc.
Valikonagi Cad. 111/6
Nişantaşi, Istanbul
Tel: 147 93 67
   147 93 86
   148 93 00
Telex: 27163 vakt-tr

Göksel Tourism & Travel Agency
Halâskârgazi Cad. 327/1

Şişli
Tel: 140 85 83
   146 31 67
Telex: 26127 nat-tr
Fax: 166 77 56

Gürkay Travel
Organization & Trade Inc.
Lamartin Cad. 11/2-3
Taksim
Istanbul
Tel: 150 27 00
   156 08 00-02
Telex: 24761 gurk-tr
Fax: 155 18 98

Istanbul Tourism
& Travel Office Inc.
Cumhuriyet Cad. 239/1
Harbiye
Tel: 140 84 47
   146 76 21
   143 03 57
Telex: 26617 itsb-tr

Kim Tour Travel &
Tourism Inc.
Cumhuriyet Cad. 167
Harbiye, Istanbul
Tel: 141 36 54
   141 74 90
   148 07 95
Telex: 26597 kimt-tr

Korur Tourism
Cumhuriyet Cad. 261/9
Elmadağ, Istanbul
Tel: 141 57 64
Telex: 27606

Kültur Tourism & Travel
Co. Ltd.
Cumhuriyet Cad. 243/4
Harbiye
80230
Istanbul
Tel: 141 52 53-54
Telex: 22108 ktt-tr
   27325 ktta-tr

Moris Travel & Tourism
Agency
Tünel Paşaji 11

Tünel
Istanbul
Tel: 144 68 96
   14930 35
   149 85 10-11
Telex: 24214 aris-tr

Roy Tourism & Travel
Agency
Topçu Cad. 3/B
Taksim
Istanbul
Tel: 155 08 15-6-9

Sultan Tourism & Travel
Trade Inc.
Cumhuriyet Cad. 87
Elmadag
Istanbul
Tel: 140 37 71
   148 60 98-99
Telex: 22583 star-tr
Cable: Sultantur

Tantur Travel & Shipping
Agency
Sheraton Hotel Lobby
Askerocagi Cad. 1
Taksim
Istanbul
Tel: 147 40 23
   147 80 48
   147 85 65
   148 43 40
   148 90 00
Telex: 27760 tor-tr

TGI Travel Agency
Cumhuriyet Cad
Havapalas 155/1
Elmadag
Istanbul
Telex: 27559 hait-tr
   22698 tai-tr
Fax: 141 55 52

Turamco Tourism
Industry Co. Inc.
Cumhuriyet Cad. 43/2
Taksim
İstanbul
Tel: 155 00 03
Telex: 24019 turc-tr

Unitur   International
TourismServices &
Investments Inc.
Inönü Cad. 31/8
Taksim, Istanbul
Tel: 144 08 36
   144 56 53
Telex: 25692 untr-tr

VIP Tourism Pirinççioḡlu
Inc.
Cumhuriyet Cad. 269/2
Harbiye,
Istanbul
Tel: 141 65 14-16
   130 22 06
Telex: 22417 vid-tr

Viking Tourism & Trade
Inc.
Mete Cad. 24
Taksim
Istanbul
Tel: 143 53 47-48
   149 35 00
   149 96 78
Telex: 31282 viki-tr
Cable: Peri-Istanbul

Information Offices

Istanbul Deniz Iicaret
Odasi
(Istanbul Marine
Transport Chamber
of Commerce)
Istiklâl Cad.
Odakulp Is Merkezi
Floor 10
Beyoḡlu
Istanbul
Tel: 143 54 95-97
Telex: 24727 dio-tr
   25774 dzod-tr
Cable: Denizoda

Törkiye Turing e
Otomobil Kurumu
(Touring & Automobile
Club of Turkey)
Halâskârgazi Cad. 364
Şişli
Istanbul

Tel: 131 46 31-35
Telex: 27800 ring-tr

Türsab—Türkiye Seyahat Acenteleri Birklig (Turkish Travel Agencies Association)
Cumhuriyet Cad. 187
Elmadağ, Istanbul
Tel: 146 02 36
    146 02 37
Telex: 27823 isba-tr
Cable: Türsaba

Uluslarasi Nakliyatçilar Derneg
(International Land Transporters Association)
Büyükdere Cad. Sivritas Sok
Elbiris Han, 18/4
Mediciyeköy, Istanbul
Tel: 172 70 40-43
Telex: 26658 und-tr

Credit Cards: Most of the best-known international credit cards are valid in Turkey even though they do not all have offices.

Access
Anadolu, Turiza, Cumhuriyet Cad. Ceylan Ap, 27/2, Taksia, Istanbul
Tel: 150 60 70-75.

American Express
Valikonagi Cad. 69/1, Nişantaşi, Istanbul
Tel: 140 95 58-140 95 54.

Barclaycard
No office in Turkey.

Carte Blanche
No office in Turkey.

Diners Club
Setur, Cumhuriyet Cad. 131/2, Elmadağ, Istanbul
Tel: 130 09 18-25.

Eurocard
Anadolu Turizm, Cumhuriyet Cad. Ceylan Ap. 27/2, Taksim, Istanbul, Tel: 150 60 7075.

Interbank
No office in Turkey.

JBC
Tantur, Sheraton Hotel, Asker Ocagi Cad. 1, Taksim, Istanbul, Tel: 146 44 81.

Mastercharge
Anadolu Turizm, Cumhuriyet Cad. Ceylan Ap. 27/2. Taksim, Istanbul
Tel: 150 60 70-71.

Visa
Imar Bankasi, Büyükdere Cad. Dogus Han, 42-46, Medcidiyeköy
Tel: 166 06 20-172 17 29-30.
Also: Iktisat Bankasi, Büyükdere Cad. 56/13, Mecidiyeköy, Istanbul
Tel: 172 70 00.

Holidays and Festivals

*January 1
New Year's Day. Banks, offices and some shops are closed.

February 9-13
International Textile & Fashion Festival.

April 6-10
Annual Fashion Shows.

April 6-19
International Film Days.

*April 23
National Sovereignty and Children's Day.
It is celebrated with parades and processions by school children. Banks and public

offices are closed.

April 23-May 1
Tulip Festival. It is traditional to visit Emirgan Park and see the display of tulips during this week.

**May 16 noon-19 (1988) Seker Bayrami
Ramadan Feast, when visits are made and gifts exhanged, especially sweets.

May 18-30
International Jazz Festival.

*May 19 Youth & Sports Day Atatürk Commemoration
Marked by sports displays in stadiums and parades. Banks and public offices are closed.

May 28-30
International Marmara Folk Dancing Festival.

May 29
Fatih Festivities, commemorating the conquest of the city in 1453 by Sultan Fatih Mehmet.

May
Silivri Yoghurt Festival.

June 15-July 31
International Istanbul Festival. This is the high point of the cultural year and features concerts of all types of music, theater, opera, ballet, traditional and folk arts, lectures and exhibitions.

July-August
Sultanahmet Culture and Arts Festivities.

July
Sile Silebezi (cheesecloth) Festival.

July 14-15
Culture Festivities.

July 15-September 15
Drama Festival.

**July 23 noon-July 27 (1988) Kurban Bayrami
Holy Sacrifice Feast, when sheep and other animals are sacrificed. Banks and public offices closed throughout, shops closed for at least two days.

August (first week)
Adalar (Princes' Islands) Culture Festival.

August 19-26
Yalova Festival.

***August 30
Victory Day**
Marked by parades through main streets, an opportunity to see the few surviving veterans from the War of Independence. Banks and public offices closed.

September (second week)
Çatalca Milk & Fruit Festival.

September
Sariyer Festival

October 14-November 8
Istanbul Bi-Annual Arts Festival.

***October 28 noon-29
Republic Day**
Celebrated with parades, public speeches, firework displays, etc. Banks and public offices closed.

* Public holidays, during which all banks, public offices, schools and most private offices are closed, but many shops remain open.

** Religious holidays, during which families and friends exchange visits and gifts. Food shops and shops selling consumer goods usually open on the second or third day of the holiday. These holidays move forward by 10 or 11 days each year.

Radio and Television: These are state owned and known collectively as TRT (Turkish Radio and Television). There are currently two television channels and the main news in Channel 2 is followed by a news summary including a weather report in English every night. Radio has just added a fourth programme for Turkish music only, but it is the third programme (TRT 3 or FM) which gives news summaries in English, French and German following the Turkish summary at 9 a.m., noon, 5 p.m., 7 p.m. and 10 p.m. daily. The third programme broadcasts nothing but music all day, popular and classical, jazz and folk, with no commercials.

Video rental shops are proliferating all over the city and some hotels have closed circuit video channels as well as radio broadcasts.

Newspapers and Magazines: *The Daily News* is the only daily English language newspaper published in Turkey and gives basic coverage of Turkish and foreign news. An English language weekly, *Dateline* also available on news-stands. Newspapers from abroad are generally available the following day, while the *Financial Times* is sometimes obtainable the evening of the day of issue.

Notable local newspapers in languages other than Turkish or English are *Apoyevmatini* (Greek, founded in 1924), *Jamanak* (Armenian, founded in 1908) and *Shalom* (Jewish, founded in 1947).

The Turkish Press: All nine of the Turkish national dailies are published in Istanbul. They are colorful (apart from the highbrow *Cumhuriyet*), powerful, and not necessarily reliable. Travelers with pretty legs may wish to avoid photoreporters from the less scrupulous newspapers such as *Tan* and *Günaydin*. *Hüurriyet* and *Sabah* are the top sellers; *Milliyet* and *Günes* claim to represent liberal opinion; *Tercüman* and *Türkiye* tilt toward Islamic conservatism.

Postal Services: Post offices are marked by PTT signs with black letters on a yellow background. The main post office, Büyük Postane, in Sirkeci is open 24 hours as is the Kadiköy Post Office in Asiatic Istanbul. Some large post offices such as the one at Galatasaray remain open until 8 p.m., while most close at 6 p.m. Stamps may be purchased from hotel reception desks, which is easier than queueing at the post office. Letters and cards may be posted in the yellow post boxes or in the post offices, as well as in major hotels.

222

Letters may be sent "Post Restante" to any post office; if addressed to "Post Restante Istanbul" they will be kept at the main post office in Sirkeci. Letters are held for two months before being returned to the sender.

Telephones: Public telephones are operated by *jetons* (tokens) which can be purchased in post offices or from kiosks near telephone booths. *Jetons* come in three different sizes according to the distance of the call. Phone cards are also available in post offices and represent approximately the equivalent of 120 small *jetons*. It may be easier to get your hotel switchboard to place calls for you. Many small shops will allow you to use their phone for a little more than the normal charge, too. Direct dialing is now possible to most countries of the world.

Telex And Fax: These services are available at the main post offices but it is generally much easier to use the facilities of the major hotels, even though this may cost more.

Pharmacies: Each district of the city has one pharmacy which remains open throughout the night for emergencies. The name of the pharmacy on duty is posted in the windows of other chemists in the district and they are listed in daily newspapers. Most medicines apart from addictive drugs can be obtained without prescription. Pharmacists will also check your

blood pressure and give injections when necessary.

Hospitals: The best equipped are those owned by the State or Municipality and these are recommended for emergencies. Private hospitals patronized by foreigners include the American Hospital (Admiral Bristol), the Armenian (Surp Agop), the French Hospital (Pasteur) and the German Hospital which is noted for its high standards. Of the private Turkish hospitals, the oldest and largest in the country is Vatan, in the old city, which is very near to one of the newest, the Topkapi, also in Akasaray. Perhaps the best-known private hospital is still the Hayat in Şişli, with its Diners Club sign on its door.

State Hospitals

Çap
Millet Cad., Çapa.
Tel: 525 9230-59.

Cerrahpaşa
Kocamustafapaşa Cad.
Cerranhpaşa.
Tel: 585 2100.

Haseki
Millet Cad., Haseki.
Tel: 523 6000.

Haydrapasa Nümune
Selimiye Tibbiye Cad.
Haydarpaşa.
Tel: 338 1010-18.

Private Hospitals

Amerikan Hastanesi
(Admiral Bristol Güzelbahçe Sok., Nişantaşi. Tel: 131 4050.

Surp Agop Hastanesi
(Armenian Hospital):
Cumhuriyet Cad. 6,
Elmadag.
Tel: 148 4762.

Pasteur Hastanesi
(French Hospital)
Taskisla Cad.,
Elmadağ.
Tel: 146 1020.

Alman Hastanesi
(German Hospital)
Siraselviler Cad. 119,
Taksim.
Tel: 143 8100.

Balikli Hastanesi
(Greek Hospital)
Hastaneler Yolu Cad.,
Yedikule.
Tel: 528 7330.

Hayat Hastanesi
Büyükdere Cad., Şişli.
Tel: 166 4916.

Italyan Hastanesi
(Italian Hospital)
Defterdar Yokusu, Tophane.
Tel: 149 975.

Tesvikiye Saglik Yurdu
Sakayik Sok. 38, Teşvikiye.
Tel: 148 5020.

Topkapi Hastanesi
Vakif Guraba Cad.,
Bexm-i Alem, Sok. 22,
Gapa., Tel: 542 1919.

Vatan Hastanesi
Vatan Cad. 19, Aksaray.
Tel: 525 9395.

Diagnosis Clinics: There are several diagnosis and check-up centers with very modern equipment, including computers. The best-known is perhaps Intermed at present, while Saykon offers a 24 hour service.

Medical Check-up Centers

Intermed
Tesvikiye Cad.143,
Nişantaş. Tel: 141 7096.

Medica
Büyükdere Cad. 4,
Şişli. Tel: 133 0525.

Sakykon
19 Mayis Cad. 5,
Şişli. Tel: 146 0480.

Ambulances: Although there are several private ambulance services and free services run by the State and Municipal hospitals, most of these are not fully equipped to handle emergencies and are not always staffed by fully trained personnel. Therefore it is usually better to get to a hospital as quickly as possible in emergencies, rather than waiting for an ambulance.

Doctors: A great many good doctors and dentists speak English and even other languages. Major hotels also have house doctors who are always on call. Prices are reasonable by U.S. standards, especially for dental treatment.

Nurses: Turkey suffers from a severe shortage of nursing staff. However, private nurses can be found via hospitals or from an organization called Hasbak.

Hasbak
Semsettin Günaltay Cad.,
Evren Sok.,
Intas Sitesi D-Blok, D.13,
Erenköy.
Tel: 350 8727-356 8621.

IN TRANSIT

WHERE TO STAY

Hotels: Selecting a hotel in Istanbul depends largely on what district you prefer to be in. For the tourist determined on seeing every major ancient monument, the old city is the best choice. Here the newest hotel is the Ramada, the most attractive the Yeşil Ev in Sultan Ahmet Square, the most interesting the Ayasofya Pansiyonlari on the outer walls of Topkapi Palace, while others worth noting in the area include the Sokullu Paşa and the Kalyon. The Olcay, on the road to the airport, just inside the city walls, is also well-placed for touring and the Çinar, near the airport, is spectacularly situated with excellent views and a swimming pool. In the "new" city across the Golden Horn are the main international hotels, of which the best by far is the Hilton. Unfortunately it is being spoilt by new buildings being added on all sides. The Hilton is the oldest hotel in this category, built before space was counted in dollars per square meter, it has an excellent tradition of management. Others include the Sheraton, the Etap Marmara and the Etap Istanbul, while several additional international hotels are currently under construction. The best of the other hotels is certainly the Divan and the most interesting historically is the Pera Palas, in operation since 1892, the rendezvous spot for international spies during the First World War.

There is a great variety of hotels to choose from but one must not forget those situated on the Bosphorus such as the Tarabya and those on the Asiatic side. Consult the list below for a selective listing of hotels.

Special/Historical

Ayasofya Pansiyonlari
Sogukçeşme Sok.
Sultan Ahmet
Tel: 512 57 32
     512 50 58

Hidiv Köskü
Çubuklu, Istanbul
Tel: 331 6 51-52
Telex: 23346 ring-tr

Perapalas Oteli
Meşrutiyet Cad. 98-100
Tepebaşi
Tel: 151 45 60-71
Telex: 24152 per-tr

Sokullu Paşa
Mehmetpasa Sok. 10
Sultanahmet

Tel: 512 37 53-58

Yeşil Ev
Kabasakal Cad. 5
Sultanahmet
Tel: 528 67 64
    511 11 50
Telex: 30470-F

Five Star

Büyük Sürmeli Hotel
Saatcibaviri Sok. 3
Gayrettepe
Tel: 172 05 15-24
    172 11 60-24
Telex: 26656 suot-tr

Büyük Tarabaya Oteli
Kefeliköy Cad. Trarbya
Tel: 162 10 00
    162 07 10
Telex: 26203 htrb-tr

Çinar Oteli
Fener Meykii
34800/Yesilköy
Tel: 573 29 10-19
Telex: 28861 çin-tr

Divan Oteli
Cumhuriyet Cad. 2
Elmadağ
Tel: 131 41 00-11
    131 40 70-72
Telex: 22402 dvan-tr

Etap Marmara Oteli
Taksim Meydani 80090/
Taksim
Tel: 151 46 96-(30 lines)
Telex: 24137 etma-tr

Hilton Oteli
Cumhuriyet Cad.,Elmadağ
Tel: 131 46 46 (70 lines)
Telex: 27027 hiis-tr

Ramada Otel Istanbul
Ordu Cad. 226
Laleli
Tel: 519 40 50-89
    512 81 20

---

    512 63 90
Telex: 30222 rahn-tr

Sheraton Oteli
Asker Ocagi Cad. 1
Taksim
Tel: 131 21 21-80
Telex: 22729 sher-tr
Fax: 131 21 80

Four Star

Etap Istanbul Oteli
Meşrutiyet Cad
Tepebaşi
Tel: 151 46 46-63
Telex: 24345 bot-tr
Fax: 149 80 33

Fuar Oteli
Namik Kemal Cad. 26
Aksaray
Tel: 525 97 32-35
    525 98 59-62

Istanbul Dedeman Oteli
Yildiz Posta Cad. 50
Esentepe
Tel: 172 88 00-19
Telex: 28217 akd-tr

Maçka Oteli
Eytam Cad. 35
Maçka
Tel: 134 32 00-22
Telex: 28002 mako-tr

Olçay Oteli
Millet Cad. 187
Topkapi
Tel: 585 32 20-23
Telex: 23209 loca-tr

Riva Oteli
Aydede Cad. 8
Taksim
Tel: 156 44 20-31
Telex: 25246 rvht-tr

Three Star

Bebek Oteli
Cevdetpaşa Cad. 113-115

Bebek
Tel: 163 30 00-01
Telex: 27201 hobe-tr

Büyük Keban Oteli
Gençtürk Cad. 47
Aksaray
Tel: 512 00 20-23
Telex: 22022 büke-tr

Dilson Oteli
Siraselviler Cad. 49
Taksim
Tel: 152 13 05-09
Telex: 25689 duho-tr

Eresin Oteli
Topçu Cad. 34
Taksim
Tel: 150 44 76
    150 33 67
Telex: 24235 ntt-tr

Harem Oteli
Ambar Sok. 1
Selimiye
UuskUudar
Tel: 333 20 25
Telex: 22482 hrm-tr

Istanbul Büyük Oteli
Spor Cad. 98
Beşiktaş
Tel: 160 78 60
    158 08 57
    158 29 77

Kalyon Oteli
Sahil Yolu
Sultan Ahmet
Tel: 511 44 00-09
Telex: 23364-22999 klyn-tr

Keban Oteli
Siraselviler 51
Taksim
Tel: 143 33 10-13

Kennedy Oteli
Siraselviler Cad. 29
Taksi
Tel: 143 40 90
    145 27 90

Kilim Oteli
Millet Cad. 85/A
Findizade
Tel: 586 08 80-82
Telex: 2211 tr

Konak Oteli
Cumhuriyet Cad.
Nispet Sok. 9,Elmadağ
Tel: 148 47 44-45

I.M.I. Oteli
Büyükdere Cad. 84
Gayrettepe
Tel: 167 33 34
Telex: 31102 tr

Yenişehir Palas Oteli
Asmali Mescit Oteller Sok.
113
Tepebasi
Tel: 144 13 00
   144 45 47
   148 88 10-12
Telex: 24404 rahi-tr

Washington Oteli
Gençtürk Cad. 12
Laleli
Tel: 520 69 90-93
Telex: 22094 was-tr

Zürih Oteli
Vidinli Tevfik Paşa Cad
Harikzadeler Sok. 37
Laleli
Tel: 512 23 50-54
Telex: 30154 zrh-tr

Two Star

Bale Oteli
Refik Saydam Cad
Akarca Sok. 55
Tepebaşi
Tel: 150 49 12-16
Telex : 25515 balf-tr

Büyük Londra Oteli
Meşrutiyet Cad. 117
Galatasaray
Tel: 145 06 70-71
   149 10 25

Çiragan Oteli
Müvezzi Cad. 3
Çiragan
Beşiktaş
Tel: 160 02 30-33

Gezi Oteli
Mete Cad. 42
Taksim
Tel: 145 21 67-69

Inka Oteli
Meşrytiyet Cad. 225
Tepebaşi
Tel: 143 17 28-29
   154 59 83

Nazar Oteli
Yeşiltuumba Sok. 17
Aksaray
Tel: 526 80 60-61

Oriental Oteli
Cihangir Cad. 60
Taksim
Tel: 145 10 67-68

Plaza Oteli
Siraselviler Cad
Arslan Yatagi 19-21
Taksim
Tel: 145 32 73-74
   145 79 89

Santral Oteli
Siraselviler Cad.
Billurcu Sok. 26
Taksim
Tel: 145 41 20-24
Telex: 24625 sant-tr

Star Oteli
Saglik Sok. 11/13
Gümüssuyu Taksim
Tel: 145 00 50-52

Service Flats: These are a new development in Istanbul, mainly aimed at long term summer visitors from the Middle East, but also useful for businessmen from all over the world. Of these,

Family House, very near Taksim Square, is particularly recommended.

Hostels: The demand for inexpensive lodgings by younger tourists has led to a few reasonable hostels being established in the Sultanate area. The oldest of these is the Yücel, just next to St. Sophia and another well-known hostel is Sultan in Yerebatan Caddesi, also near St. Sophia.

Motels

Kilyos
Turban Kilyos Motel
Kilyos, Tel: 142 02 88
Telex: 23770 tr.

Kumburgaz
Marin Hotel
Silivriyolu
6th ka., Kumburgaz
Tel: 4102.

Küçükçekmece
Baler Motel
Avcilar Ambarli,
Küçükçekmece
Tel: 591 17 56.

Yeşilköy
Yeşilköy Motel
Havan Sok. 4., Yeşilköy
Tel: 573 29 95.

Camping sites

Class 1
Ataköy Mocamp
Sahilyolu, Ataköy
Tel: 572 49 61-572 08 02-03,
Telex: 28894 esat-tr.
Yeşilyurt Kamping
Sahilyolu 2, Yeşilköy
Tel: 573 55 82-573 84 08

Class 3
Kervansaray Kartaltepe

Mocamp
Çobançesme Mevkii
Tel: 575 19 91.

Residential flats

Bosphorus Residence

Besaret Sok. 17,
Gümüssuyu
Taksim
Tel: 144 61 46-47.

Family House
Kutlu Sok. 53

Taksim
Tel: 149 73 51-149 96 67.

Istanbul Residence:
Bağdat Cad. 401, Suadiyel:
350 71 59-359 50 02
Telex: 29403 kzdh-tr.

ON THE MOVE

TRANSPORT

Buses: The cheapest method of transportation, but very crowded on some routes, especially at rush hours. Tickets are all one price and obtainable from kiosks at main bus stops, in any quantity, or from unofficial sellers at a slightly higher price. Destinations and routes are shown on the front and side of each bus, but if in doubt, don't hesitate to ask someone for advice—even the locals do this frequently. Drop the ticket in the box as you enter, and press the button above one of the exit doors just before the stop where you wish to alight.

Dolmuş: This is a shared taxi operating only on certain routes, with fixed fares for specific distances. The shortest distance costs the same as a bus ticket, but rates increase rapidly thereafter. It is easiest to get on at a terminal where you simply queue and wait. Otherwise you have to wait by the roadside and negotiate when one slows down. Make sure the car you get into is not a taxi, by saying "Dolmuş?" as you step in. Generally taxis have a sign on the roof and are yellow in color, whereas dolmuses have plain stripes around.

Minibuses: Minibuses operate on long distance routes, carrying commuters to and from the outskirts of the city. They are definitely not recommended, being crowded and dangerously driven, but can be useful when there is no dolmus to a distant place, or when bus services are infrequent. Cheaper than dolmuşes.

Taxis: Now that all taxis have meters, there is no longer any need to bargain and dispute over prices with the driver. If your driver is courteous and helpful, it is a good idea to tip him about 10 percent since most drivers these days are full of (legitimate) complaints about traffic conditions. Prices are higher after midnight and you can tell by the starting price indicated on the meter whether you are being charged daytime or nighttime rates. If you have reason to believe you are being overcharged, write down the number of the taxi and make it clear that you intend to complain to the traffic police about this incident. This should result in speedy correction and if not, you still have the option of lodging a complaint.

Recently, because of the horrendous traffic condiions in certain districts, taxis have been refusing to take passengers to some destinations. This is understandable but not correct and again you may complain.

Ferry Boats: This is by far one of the most pleasant form of public transportation, if you are lucky enough to need to travel between Üsküdar and Beşiktaş, Kadiköy and Karaköy or Kadiköy and Berşiktaş. Otherwise you will find yourself using the ferry boats to visit the peaceful Princes' Islands in the Marmara Sea, to visit Eyüp at the far end of the Golden Horn and most important of all, to travel up the Bosphorus on the seas on one of the special trips that leave from Eminönü once, twice or three times daily according to the season. The trip takes almost 3 hours to the last calling point, where you may want to disembark for lunch or tea, returning approximately 2 hours later by boat, or by land if you prefer.

Water Bus: The new excellent high speed water bus service operates between Bostanci on the Asiatic side of the city and Kabatas, with a free bus sevice from Kabataḡ to Karaköy and Taksim. More of these catamaran water buses are on order and the service will be extended to include the Princes' Islands and other destinations in future.

Car Rentals: Self-drive cars and chauffeur-driven limousines can be rented from various agencies located in the city. The cost in Turkey is high in comparison with other European countries but the condition of the cars is good. Your national driving licence is valid for three months after you enter Turkey.

Plane and Helicopter Hire: Relatively new in Turkey, it is used almost exclusively by businessmen. However the helicopter hire service offers touristic trips to see Istanbul by air, and there is a helicopter service between the airport and the Hilton Hotel forecourt, for VIPs who are allergic to traffic. Sancak and Nesu are the primary companies involved in this area.

Underground Railways: There are many current projects for light-weight rail systems and full scale metros, but at present the only underground railway is the single stop connection between Tünel and Karaköy. This was built in 1877 and is the oldest underground railway in the world, worth riding for its curiousity value.

FOOD   DIGEST

WHERE TO EAT

There is no doubt that food is high on the list of Istanbul's pleasures. Restaurants not solely devoted to eating fast, which have their own atmosphere, cuisine and clientele, can be roughly classified into (a) Bosphorus and Kumkapi restaurants serving fish and *meze*, (b) international restaurants offering a selection of Turkish and other dishes, and (c) national restaurants which at present include German, Russian, Chinese, Japanese, Korean, French, Iranian, Greek and Italian. Restaurants in museums and art galleries are useful at lunch time, especially the Konyali inside Topkapi Palace and the Gar Restaurant at Sirkeci railroad station, which is well placed for sightseeing.

Good Turkish food in the old tradition can be enjoyed at Abdullah's in Emirgan, at Pandeli's at the entrance to the Spice Bazaar (lunch only), Liman Lokantasi overlooking the harbor at Karaköy (lunch only) and in the restaurant of the Divan Hotel. Fashionable places for special evenings at the time of writing include the Plaza, Park Şamdan and Ziya in the Nişantaş/Maçka district, Şamdan and 29 in Etiler, "S" which is the most expensive and situated on the Bosphorus road between Arnavutköy and Bebek, Ziya in Ortaköy, Bebek Süreyya in Istiniye, Les Ambassadeurs in Bebek and Le Chalet in Tarabya. All of these serve international food as well as Turkish specialities. The Divan Hotel has a late-night after theater restaurant attached to the elegant bar.

Mention should be made of bars which have restaurants for the drinker. These include Avni's in Harbiye, Papirus and Eski Kulis in Beyoḡlu, Zihni's in Maçka.

Turkish Food: Turkish cuisine justifies its reputation of being one of the three great culinary traditions of the world. The essentially nomadic cooking tradition was enhanced and enriched by contact with the varied civilizations which the Ottoman Empire comprised. This rich heritage combined with the superb freshness of the fish (but see the fish and check for this), fresh fruit and vegetables in a country which is self-sufficient in foodstuffs, results in a truly memorable experience for visiting gourmets.

Lamb is still the basic meat, usually grilled in the form of shish kebab or döner kebab, dishes which are now familiar all over the world, or *pirzola* which are tiny lamb chops. The best meat is often found in **Kebabci's**, which are restaurants specializing in kebabs.

Istanbul is particularly famous for its seasonal fresh fish. Take the waiter's advice on the day's selection or inspect it yourself.

The aubergine, or eggplant, is the king of vegetables and is prepared in a great variety of ways. Vegetables cooked in oil are one of the great delights of Turkish cuisine. Hors d'oeuvres, *meze*, should always include *dolma* (stuffed vegetables) and *börek* (savoury pastries) although these are also served as main dishes.

Turkish desserts are justly famous, particularly the syrupy pastries with or without nuts. The best baklava can be found at Güloğlu in Karaköy. Milk puddings such as *sütlac* and *kazandibi* are generally found in Muhallebici, together with *tavuk gögsü* (chicken's breast), yoghurt and ice cream. Kaymak, a delicious form of clotted cream should also not be missed.

Finally, mention must be made of the *Iskembeci,* or tripe soup, of kitchens mainly aimed at all night drinkers and which are therefore open all night long.

However, apart from curing hangovers, tripe soup is enjoyed by many people, served thin or creamy and garnished with garlic flavored vinegar. Tripe restaurants often serve other delicacies enjoyed by the minority such as brains, roast lamb's head, guts and trotters and even eyes.

Restaurants: Classified by main cuisine—however most restaurants have at least a small selection of both Turkish and international dishes. Price indications are given according to three categories: Expensive, Medium or Moderate.

Turkish

Expensive
Reyan
Sheraton Hotel
Asker Ocagi Cad. 1
Taksim
Tel: 131 21 21-79 ext. 32 76
Hours: Midday-3 p.m.
7.30 p.m-11.30 p.m.

Medium
Abullah
Emirgan Koru Cad. 11
Emirgan
Tel: 163 64 0
Hours: Midday-3 p.m.
7 p.m.-midnight
Closed: Tuesdays.

Kamilica Karfez
Korfez Cad. 78
Kanlica
Tel: 332 01 08

Hours: Midday-3p.m.
8 p.m.-midnight
Closed: Mondays.
(Fish)

Liman
Rihtim Cad.
Karaköy Boat Terminal
3rd Floor, Karoköy
Tel: 144 10 33
Hours: Midday-4 p.m.
Closed: For dinner and weekends.

Pandeli
Misir Carsisi
1, Eminönü
Tel: 522 55 34
527 39 09.
Hours: Midday-3 p.m.
Closed: Everyday for dinner, Sundays.

Moderate
Beyti
Orman Sok. 33
Florya.
Tel: 573 93 73
Hours: Midday-midnight.
Closed: Mondays.
(Meat).

Gelik
Sahilyolu 68-70
Ataköy.
Tel: 571 37 32
572 08 06-07
Hours: Midday-midnight
*Zeytinburni-Kennedy Cad.
Sahilyolu.
Tel: 582 84 76
558 19 18
Hours: Midday-midnight.
(Meat)

Hasir
Feneryolu Cad. 25
Yeşilyurt Camping
Yeşilyurt
Tel: 574 42 30-33
Hours: Midday-midnight.
*Nişantaşi-Valikonagi Cad.
117

Tel: 130 16 36
    130 14 84
(Meat)

Konyali Saray
Mecidiye Köskü
Topkapi Saraya
Sultan Ahmet
Tel: 526 27 27
Hours: 11 a.m-3 p.m
Only open for lunch. And
closed on Tuesdays.

International

Expensive
Lale
Ramada Hotel
Ordu Cad. 226
Laleli
Tel: 519 40 50-89
Hours: 6 a.m-midnight.

Park Şamdan
Min Kemal Oke Cad. 18
Nişantaşi
Tel: 140 83 68
Hour: Midday-3 p.m.
        7.30 p.m-midnight.

Plaza
Abdi Ipekçi Cad. Bronz Sok
Maçka
Tel: 141 63 56
    147 54 96
Hours: Midday -3 p.m.
    8 p.m.-midnight.

Şamdan
Nispetiye Cad. 30
Etiler
Tel: 163 48 98
Hours: Every restaurant
    12.30 p.m-2.30 p.m.
    8.30 p.m-1 a.m.
Closed: June-30 September
*Yeniköy-Báglar Sok. 57
Sabanci Korusu
Tel: 162 13 13
    162 23 93
Hours: 8 a.m.-3 p.m.,
1 June-30 September.

Closed: 1 October-30 May.

Sarnic
Ayasofya Pansiyonlari
Soğukçeşme Sok.
Sultan Ahmet
Tel: 5 57 32-37
Hours: 12.30 p.m.-midnight
1 January-30 December.

29
Nispetiye Cad. 29
Etiler
Tel: 163 54 11
Hours: Every restaurant 9.30
    p.m.-11.30 p.m.
Closed: Everyday for lunch
    and 1 June-1 October
* Çubuklu
Tel: 332 34 81
Hours: 8.30 p.m.-midnight
    15 June-30 September
Closed: 1 October-14 June.

Medium
Ambassadeurs
Bebek Hotel
Cavdetopasa Cad. 113
Bebek
Tel: 163 30 02
Hours: Midday-midnight.

Çift Nal
Ihlamur Cad.
Süslü Karakol
Beşiktaş
Tel: 160 42 49-161 31 29
Hours: Midday-midnight.

Divan Hotel
Cumhuriyet Cad. 2
Elmadağ
Tel: 131 40 70-131 41 00-11
Hours: Midday-3p.m.
    7 p.m.-1 a.m.

Hidiv Kasri
Çuburklu
Tel: 331 26 52
Hours: Midday-3 p.m.
    7 p.m.-midnight.

La Soupee

Divan Hotel
Cumhuriyet Cad. 2
Elmadağ
Tel: 131 41 00-11
Hours: 11 a.m-2 a.m.

Yesil Ev
Kabasakal Cad. 5
Sultahahmet
Tel: 528 67 64
Hours: 8 a.m-10 a.m.
    Midday-2.30 p.m.
    7 p.m.-11 p.m.

Ziya
Mim Kemal Öke Cad. 21
Nişantaşi
Tel: 147 17 08
Hours: Midday-3 p.m.
    7.30 p.m.-midnight.
* Ortaköy
Muallim Naci Cad. 109/1
Tel: 161 60 05-06
Hours: 11 a.m.-1 a.m.

Moderate
Four Seasons
Istiklâl Cad. 509
Tünel
Tel: 145 89 41
Hours: Midday-3 p.m.
    6 p.m.-midnight.

Gar
Inside Sirkeci Railway
Station
Sirkeci
Tel: 522 22 80
Hours: 11 a.m.-midnight
Closed: Sundays.

Le Chalet
Yeniköy Cad.
Pastaci Halil Sok. 280/3
Tarabya
Tel: 162 33 15-16
Hours: Midday-midnight.

Park
Maçka Hotel
Eytan Cad. 35
Maçka
Tel: 140 10 53

o r 140 31 03
Hours: Midday -3 p.m.
6 p.m.-midnight.

Sokullu Paşa
Sokullu Paşa Hotel
Mehmetpaşa Sok. 10
Sultan Ahmet
Tel: 5 37 53-58
Hours: 11.30 a.m.-2.30 p.m.
7 p.m.-10 p.m.

French

Expensive
La Bouffe
Karakol Bostan Sok. 13
Nişantaşi
Tel: 146 99 43-148 95 22
Hours: Midday-2.30 p.m.
5.30 p.m.-midnight
Closed: 1 June-1 September.

Orient Express
Etap Marmara Hotel
Taksim Square
Taksim
Tel: 151 46 96-30 ext. 706
Hours: Midday-3 p.m.
7 p.m.-1 a.m.
Closed: Mondays.

Medium
Fondue
Istinye Cad. 92
Istinye
Tel: 165 55 77
Hours: 7 p.m.-1 a.m.
Closed: Everyday for lunch
and Sundays.

Russian

Medium
Süreyya Bebek
Istinye Cad. 26/1
Istinye
Tel: 177 58 86
177 68 25
Hours: Midday-3 p.m.
7 p.m.-1 a.m.

Moderate

Russian
Inönü Cad.
Miralay Sok. 1
Ayazpaşa
Tel: 143 48 92
Hours: Midday-3 p.m.
6 p.m.-10 p.m.

Rejans
Olivo Çikmazi 15
Galatasaray
Tel: 144 16 10
Hours: Midday-3 p.m.
6 p.m.-11 p.m.

Italian

Moderate
Rosa
Cumhuriyet Cad. 131
Tel: 141 28 27
Hours: 11 a.m.-midnight.

C. Fisher
Inönü Cad. 51
Ayazpaşa
Tel: 145 33 75
Hours: Midday-3 p.m.
6 p.m.-11 p.m.
Closed: Sundays.

Yekta
Valikonagi Cad. 39/1
Harbiye
Tel: 148 11 83
Hours: Midday-3 p.m
6 p.m.-1 a..m.

Ristorante Italiano
Cumhuriyet Cad.
Elmadağ
Tel: 147 86 40
Hours: Midday-3 p.m.
7 p.m.-11p.m.

German

Waldhotel Hilde
Bahçeköy-Kilyos Yolu
Bahçeköy, Büyükdere
Tel: none
Hours: Midday-3 p.m.
7 p.m.-11 p.m.

Chinese

Expensive
Dragon
Hilton Hotel
Cumhuriyet Cad.
Elmadağ
Tel: 131 46 46 (70 lines)
ext. 88 78-88 00
Hours: 12.30 p.m.-2.30 p.m.
7 p.m.-11.30 p.m.

Moderate
China
Lamartin Cad. 17/1
Taksim
Tel: 150 62 63
150 84 34
Hours: Midday-3 p.m.
6.30 p.m.-11p.m.
Closed: Sundays.

Peking
Aytar Cad. 3
Levent
Tel:169 90 17
Hours: Midday-3 p.m.
6 p.m.-11.30 p.m.

Oriental

Dynasty
Ramada Hotel
Ordu Cad. 226
Laleli
Tel: 519 40 50-89
Hours: Midday-2.30 p.m.
7 p.m.-11.30 p.m.
(Expensive).

Seoul
Niapetiye Cad. 41
Etiler
Tel: 163 60 87
165 47 38
Hours: 6 p.m.-1 a.m.
(Moderate).

Japanese
Yumeya
Cumhuriyet Cad. 39/1
Taksim

Tel: 156 11 08
Hours: Midday-2 p.m.
 7 p.m.-10 p.m.
Closed: Sundays
(Moderate).

Bistros

Kral Ve Ben (The King & I)
Turnacibaşi Sok. 10
Galatasaray
Tel: 143 36 41
Hours: 11 a.m.-10 p.m.
Sundays Midday-7 p.m.
* Çittehavuzlar
Bağdat Cad. 236
Tel: 358 66 86-358 31 97

Sultan
Divanyolu Cad. 2
Sultan Ahmet
Tel: 526 63 47
Hours: Midday - 4 p.m.
 6 p.m.-11 p.m.

Fast Food

McDonalds
Taksim Gezi
Dükkanlari 5
Taksim
Tel: 144 75 30
 144 86 00
Hours: 11 a.m.-11 p.m.

DRINKS

It is not the custom to drink alcohol without eating or at least nibbling on something; hence the only pure bars in town are those in international hotels, catering to the habits of foreigners. The best bars in Beyoğlu are all restaurants on the side and you will never be served a drink in Turkey without a few nuts or a slice of cucumber as accompaniment. Even in the beer houses which have sprung up since the late 70s (and which have brought drunks to the streets of Beyoğlu for the first time since the end of Pera's "belle epoque" in the early 20s) a variety of snacks are served. Ece Bar in Etiler is fashionable at the time of writing and there is a pleasant bar at Bilsak, listed elsewhere under cultural associations. Arif's (sometimes called "Çiçek" and not to be confused with the famous bistro—row known as the "Çiçek paseji") and the Taksim Sanat Evi in Taksim are where the art crowd hangs out, while the Club 1001 is Istanbul's primary gay and drag-queen bar. The Bebek Hotel's bar is the best of the upper-Bosphorus trendy establishments, although there are several other watering holes in Bebek as well.

Turkish Drinks: The most famous alcoholic drink is *raki* (a form of anisette), a spirit which clouds when water is added. Turkish wines are excellent young wines, but no reliable vintage wines have been marketed yet. The most common and reliable brands of red wine are Doluca, Kavaklidere (Yakut is their best wine), and the wines of the State Monopoly (Tekel) of which the best currently are Buzbag and Güneybag. White wines usually found in restaurants are again Doluca and Kavaklidere (Çankaya is recommended), while Kulüp white wine is very good if you can find it. The rosé wines of Doluca, Kavalidere (Lâl), Kulüp and Doruk are all easy to drink. The best beer is that produced by the State Monopoly (Tekel) but it is hard to find in restaurants. Efes Pilsen, Tuborg and Löwenbrau are all German-type beers, of which the Tuborg Special is worth asking for but is only available around the New Year.

Of the non-alcoholic drinks, apart from non-alcoholic beer, ayran, made from a mixture of yoghurt and water, is wonderfully refreshing in the summer.

Turkish coffee is thick and dark, served in small cups with considerable sediment at the bottom. The amount of sugar desired must be specified in advance as it is cooked together with the coffee. *Şekerli* is with lots of sugar, *Orta* is medium sweet, *Az Şekerli* means a little sugar and *Sade* is without any sugar.

Meyhane: The meyhane is the traditional Turkish tavern, of which very few remain. This was where one stopped for a drink on the way home from work, the place where one met friends to discuss the topic of the day, politics, theater, gossip, but never business. Nowadays only the impoverished bohemians frequent them, but they may regain their fashionable status one day. The remaining Meyhanes are to be found around the Balikpazari (the so-called cicele paşaji) at Galatasaray and in the district of Koca Mustafa Paşa in the old city.

Bars
Bebek: Bebek Hotel, in

Bebek Tse Bilsak Cicek, Tel: 163 30 00, Hours: 5 p.m.-midnight.
Ece Bar: Nisbetiye Cad. 24, Levent, Tel: 168 66 60-61, Hours: 5 p.m.-4 a.m.
Eski Kulis: Istiklâl Cad. 209/A, Beyoğlu, Tel: 143 20

46-149 48 00, Hours: Midday-midnight.
Closed: Sundays.
Papirus: Alyon Sok. 5, Beyoğlu, Tel: 151 49 97, Hours: Midday-midnight.
Pub Avni: Cumhuriyet Cad. 239, Harbiye, Tel: 146 16

11, Hours: 11 a.m.-midnight.
Zihni Nin Yeri (Deko): Bronz Sok. 1/B, Maçka, Tel: 146 90 43, Hours: Midday-3p.m.,5p.m.-10p.m. Closed: Sundays and 20 May-20 September.

ACTIVITIES

WHERE TO SHOP

Shopping is one of the greatest pleasures for visitors to Istanbul, in addition to eating and sightseeing. The fashionable and sophisticated shops of the new city, in the districts of Nişantaş, Teşvikiye, Şişli, Beyoğlu and Etiler sell jewelry and clothing of top quality at fairly reasonable prices. Shops in and around hotels tend to be both the most selective and the most expensive. Souvenir and carpet shops can also be found around major hotels. However, the great Covered Bazaar (Kapali Çarşi) in the old city is the most exciting place to shop for rugs, kilims and carpets, gold and silver jewelry, leather garments, blouses and scarves, slippers, copper vessels, hand-painted ceramics, onyx, meerschaum, antiques, handicrafts, all sorts of souvenirs and in fact almost anything you have in mind. There are more than 4,000 shops in the Bazaar, which is open until 7 p.m. except on Sundays. Bargaining over prices is expected and it is helpful to get an idea of prices in advance by visiting the shops in your hotel first.

Another source of typically Turkish items to take home with you is the Egyptian or Spice Bazaar (Misir Çarşisi) in Eminönü, which sells a wide variety of spices, dried fruit and nuts, as well as traditional Turkish sweets. The aroma of this enticing market will be remembered with nostalgic delight.

Department Stores

Ufi: Namik Kemal Cad. 4, Aksaray, Tel: 525 93 85-87.

Yeni Karamürsel: Kadiköy—Söğütlüceşme Cad, Kadiköy Palas Paşaji 18. Tel: 336 11 17.

Siracevizler: Siracevizler Cad. 132, Tel: 141 79 08.

Sultanhamam: Sakaçeşme Sok. 2 Vakif Han 12. Tel: 526 82 50.

Şişli: Halâskârgazi Cad. 368. Tel: 48 41-23.

Üsküdar: Ahmedive Mevdani, Üsküdar Palas Paşaji 1. Tel: 333 39 41.

Men's Fashion Stores

Beymen: Halâskârgazi Cad. 230, Osmanbey. Tel: 146 00 27.

Beyoğlu: Istiklâl Cad. Gökçek is Ham 2, Beyoğlu. Tel: 145 25 14.

Discontinued Line Shops at Çarşi: Incirli Çikisi, Olgunlar Sok. Ömür Duragi, Kartaltepe, Bakirköy, Tel: 572 84 06 and **Sultanhamam.** Tel: 526 64 08.

Mudo: Bahariye—Bahariye Cad. Onur Is Hani 29/17, Kadiköy. Tel: 337 28 76.

Bakirköy: Yakut Sok. Üstün Paşaji 26-28. Tel: 571 82 25.

Beyoğlu: Istiklâl Cad. Fitas Paşaji 24/11-12. Tel: 145 77 92.

Erenköy: Bağdat Cad. 306. Tel: 358 77 69.

Levent: Nispetiye Cad. Melodi Paşaji 23. Tel: 168 16 53.

Mecidiyeköy: Ortaklar Cad. Bahçeler Sok. 10. Tel: 173 08 30.

Misirçarşisi: Misirçarşisi 63, Eminönü. Tel: 522 90 99.

Osmanbey: Rumeli Cad. 44. Tel: 146 59 77.

Vakko: Istiklâl Cad. 123-125, Beyoğlu. Tel: 144 75 30.

Kadiköy: Söğütlüçeşme Cad. 74-78, Kadiköy. Tel: 338 12 47.

Vakkorama: Etap Marmara Hotel, Taksim Square, Taksim (entrance also Osmanli Sok.). Tel: 145 34 21.

Suadiye: Bağdat Cad. 407, Suadiye. Tel: 356 12 37.

Yargici: Bağdat Cad 313/1, Erenköy. Tel: 350 28 73.

Nişantaşi: Valikonagi Cad. 30. Tel: 141 08 54.

Osmanbey: Halâskârgazi Cad. Ebekizi Sok. 1. Tel: 140 45 30..

Women's Fashion Stores

Ali—Alta Moda: Halâskârgazi Cad. 334, Şişli, Tel: 147 71 28.

Allegria: Nispetiye Cad. 27, Etiler. Tel: 164 04 26.

Atalar: Halâskârgazi Cad. 202, Osmanbey. Tel: 148 17 97.

Beymen: Halâskârgazi Cad.

230, Osmanbey. Tel: 146 00 27.

Beyoğlu: Istiklâl Cad. Gökçek Is Hani 2. Tel: 145 25 14. Excellent designs. Excellent Quality. Very Expensive but worth it.

Discontinued Line Shops at the **Çarşi**: Incirli Çikisi, Olgunlar Sok. Ömür Duragi Kartaltepe, Bakirköy. Tel: 572 84 06

Colpan: Halâskârgazi Cad. Yilmazlar Paşaji 20/21 Şişli. Tel: 140 57 01.

Caddebostan: Bağdat Cad. 294, Caddebostan. Tel: 358 45 54.

Dükkân—Dükkân: Kuyulu Bostan Sok. 6, Nişantaşi. Tel: 147 84 11.

A.D.V.D.: Karakol Sok. 3, Teşvikiye. Tel: 148 45 57.

Handan & Hayat: Teşvikiye Cad. 113/1, Teşvikiye. Tel: 146 55 90.

Levent: Çalikusu Sok. 9, 1 **Levent**: Tel: 164 09 86.

Mudo: Bahariye—Bahariye Cad. Onur Is Hani 29/17. Kadiköy. Tel: 337 28 76.

Bakirköy—Yakut Paşaji 24/11-12. Tel: 571 81 25.

Erenköy—Bağdat Cad. 306. Tel: 358 77 69.

Levent—Nispetiye Cad. Melodi Paşaji 23. Tel: 168 16 53.

Mecidiyeköy—Ortaklar Cad. Bahçeler Sok. 10.

Tel: 173 08 30.

Misircarşisi—Misircarşisi 63, Eminönü. Tel: 522 90 99.

Osmanbey—Rumeli Cad. 44. Tel: 146 59 77.

Sevil: Min Kemal Öke Cad. 15/1. Nişantaşi. Tel: 148 64 06. Caddebostan: Bağdat Cad. 291, Caddebostan. Tel: 350 02 60.

Titiz: Rumeli Cad. 123-125, Beyoğlu. Tel: 144 75 30. Kadirköy: Söğütlüçeşme Cad. 74-78, Kadiköy. Tel: 338 12 47.

Vakkorama: Etap Marmara Hotel, Taksim Square, Taksim (entrance also at Osmanli Sok.) Tel: 145 34 21.

Suadiye: Bağdat Cad. 407. Tel: 356 12 37.

Zeki Triko: Rumeli Cad. 64/2, Osmanbey. Tel: 140 38 97.

Jewelry

Adler: Hilton International Hotel, Cumhuriyet Cad. Harbiye. Tel: 147 59 90.

Bazaar 54: Nuruosmaniye Cad. 54, Cagaloğlu. Tel: 520 11 27.

Diamond: Valikonagi Cad. Demir Han 30/B, Nişantaşi. Tel: 146 43 00.

Mücevher: Rumeli Cad. Villâ Is Hani 4-6, Nişantaşi. Tel: 141 34 61-141 78 90.

Urart: Maçka Hotel, Eytam Cad. 35/A, Maçka.

Tel: 148 2781-140 10 53.

Leatherware

Derimod: Kennedy Cad. 28, Sahilyolu Zeytinburnu. Tel: 582 84 00-06.

Erenköy—Bağdat Cad. 303. Tel: 357 53 10.

Osmanbey—Halâskârgazi Cad. 222. Tel: 147 74 81.

Derishow: Valikonagi Cad. Akkavak Sok. 18/A, Nişantaşi. Tel: 140 37 15-141 43 38.

Kosar: Meydan Sok. 8, Kazlıçeşme. Tel: 582 42 03-06.

Şişli—Halâskârgazi Cad. 366/1. Tel: 140 59 20.

Teşvikiye—Silahhane Cad. 38. Tel: 146 85 93.

Modello: Nispetiye Cad. 2/1, Etiler. Tel: 165 09 62.

Discontinued Line Shop: Valikusu Sok. 4, Aralik 12/1, 1. Levent. Tel: 169 56 96.

Teodem: Rumeli Cad. Safak Sok. 27, Nişantaşi. Tel: 147 22 16-166 90 09.

Souvenirs And Gifts

Bazaar Alibaba: Fesciler 47, Kapalicarşi (Grand Bazaar). Tel: 527 09 75.

Bazaar 54: Nuruosmaniye Cad. 54, Cagaloğlu. Tel: 520 11 27.

Havana Pazari: Halâskârgazi Cad. 216. Osmanbey. Tel: 148 14

TURKISH BATHS

Hamams orginally purified the soul as well as the body and baths have always been an important part of the Turkish culture. If you decide to sample this sensual experience, select a hamam which caters for your sex on the right day and at the right time. After undressing, you will be given a large towel and will move into a warm room (30°) and then to the hot room, where you will be left to perspire before being massaged by the *tellak* or *natir* with a *kese*, a special rough bath glove. When you have had enough of this, you return to the warm room for fresh towels and refreshments before facing the world as a new person.

Hamams

Cagaloğlu Hamami: Hilâl-i Ahmer Cad. 334, Cagaloğlu. Tel: 522 24 24.

Galatasaray Hamami: Suterazi Sok. 24, Beyoğlu. Tel: 144 14 12 or, just look down any side-street for a sign saying "Hamam". Neighborhood hamams are usually just as clean and much cheaper.

TOURS

The following is a list of suggested itineraries based on what a resident in Istanbul would suggest to a good friend for the first time in town. It assumes the visitor stays at a hotel in the Old City, possibly in the Sultan Ahmet area which is preferred by most tourists. Accommodations here range from youth hostels to the upmarket Soğukçeşme rowhouses.

One Day Tour

The Hagia Sophia, The Topkapi Palace Museum, The Hippodrome and the Sultan Ahmet (Blue) Mosque are all located within shouting distance. A whirl-wind tour of the Bazaar in the afternoon, capped with dinner at a fish-restaurant in Kumkapi. (Whew! Spend another day!)

Two Day Tour

Same exhausting routine for the first day. A leisurely boat-ride up the Bosphorus the next day (boats leave from Sirkeci near the Galata Bridge) getting off for lunch in Sariyer or another village that hits one's fancy. Drive back along European shore (don't miss Rumel Hisar!) Catch a glimpse of night-life in Beyoğlu, with a drink or two at Çiçek Pasaji.

Three Day Tour

Give the monuments around your hotel their full due, adding the Archaeological Museum, the Yerebatan Cistern, and the Ibrahim Paşa Museum. End the day in Kumkapi. Spend most of the second day in the Bazaar and the market streets around it (a quick side trip to the Süleymaniye Mosque), gradually working your way down to the Egyptian Bazaar and Yeni Camii. Watch the sun set over the mosques before having dinner under the Galata Bridge. Devote the third day to the Bosphorus as in the 2-day tour.

Five Day Tour

Same as above for the first three days. On day four, wander through old city neighborhoods from Fatih, through Fener, to Kariye Museum and walls. Proceed up the Golden Horn to the Eyüp Mosque, and a glass of tea at the Pierre Loti Cafe. In the evening, try one of the meat restaurants lining the shores of the Sea of Marmara. "Beyti" or "Gelik" are recommended. On day five, take the ferry to the Princes' Islands (boats leave from Sirkeci), getting off at Büyük Ada for a horse-and-buggy tour and lunch. Return to the city for one night on the town, possibly spend it at the huge Discorium in Gayrettepe or a bar in Bebek.

Over A Week

For those who stay longer, the Asian shore of the Bosphorus calls for a day trip including visits to the Hidiv Kasri, the villages of Kanlica and Anadolu Hisar, the Beylerbey Palace, the heights of Camlica and a dinner in Salacak. For those with still more time, a visit to Polonezköy or Sile (with an overnight preferred) provides a nice break from the din of the city.

SPORTS

Most major hotels have some sports facilities, usually sauna and swimming pool, sometimes tennis and gymnastics. Otherwise there are a few sports centers recently opened which allow non-members to use their facilities on a daily basis. Skiing is possible from mid-December until March at Bursa, Mt. Uludağ and Kartalkay near Bolu. Fishing is a relaxation available to all, by boat in the Marmara Sea or from the shores of the Bosphorus. The annual Asia to Europe Marathon takes place on a Sunday in November and starts by crossing the Bosphorus Bridge.

The main spectator sports are football, basketball and horse racing.

Recreational clubs are a new and welcome development. The first is Korukent, situated between Levent and Ortaköy, which has facilities for basketball, bowling, mini-football, table-tennis and tennis, as well as swimming pools, an ice-skating rink, sauna and Turkish bath. This establishment is open to non-members on a daily basis, and is worth knowing about since most other swimming pools in the city are only open to members of hotel residents. The last alternative is to make friends as quickly as possible with someone who is a member of one of the exclusive swimming clubs such as Galatasaray, Lido or Yüzme Ihtisas Kulübü, in order to be able to go with them as a guest.

Sports Centers

Istanbul Golf Club (Istanbul Golf Ihtisas Kulübü): Büyükdere Cad., Ayazaga. Tel: 164 07 42.

Istanbul Atlispor Kulübu (Istanbul Riding Club): Binicilik Sitesi, Üçyol, Maslak. Tel: 176 14 04.

Penguen (Ice skating): Yedikuyular Cad. 12, Elmadag. Tel: 141 02 54 or 148 82 83.

Istanbul Tennis Club (Istanbul Tenis Kulübü): Bayildim Yokusu 2, Taslik. Tel: 160 17 39.

Istanbul Hilton Dinlenme ve Spor Tesisleri: Hilton Hotel, Harbiye. Tel: 131 46 46. (Tennis, gymnastics, squash, swimming pool, sauna, etc.)

Kerukent Rekreasyon Merkezi: Ortaköy Yolu, Levent. Tel: 166 49 26-166 44 93. (Tennis, ice skating, swimming pool, ice hockey, sauna, etc.)

Beaches: Although Istanbul is surrounded by water on many sides, it is extremely difficult to find a satisfactory place to swim. Beaches on the Marmara Sea are dangerously polluted and therefore not recommended; the Bosphorus is also polluted as well as being rather cold except in late summer; this leaves swimmers with the Black Sea beaches of Kilyos and Gümüşdere on the European side and Sile on the Asian side. The sea water here is clean enough for swimming although the sand is sometimes polluted by tar.

CULTURAL EVENTS

The State theater, ballet, opera and orchestras perform at the Atatürk Cultural Centre in Taksim Square and it is worth collecting their current programme from the box office. There are many other theaters in the city of which the main ones are listed in daily papers. There is no such thing as a theater ticket agency in Istanbul yet, but travel agencies and hotel personnel may be helpful in advising and purchasing tickets.

There are several international fair centers in Istanbul and some of the fairs may be considered cultural, such as the annual book fair in November. The main fair centers are the Hilton Exhibition and Convention Center and the TÜYAP Exhibition Center at Tepebaşi. A permanent trade exhibition is maintained at OTIM (Middle East Trade and Export Center) and occasional exhibitions are mounted in the Chamber of Industry.

There is an occasional Istanbul International Jazz Festival. Meanwhile, jazz can be heard at Bilsak and at changing locations elsewhere. Several Western nations maintain cultural offices which offer concerts, film shows and other national and educational displays. Of these the most active are the Austrian, British, French, German, Italian and Spanish. The United States cultural activities have recently been restricted to se-

lected guests, presumably for security reasons.

Films are shown both at the Atatürk Cultural Centre and at the cultural associations mentioned above. There are also a few centers at which films are shown in the original version with Turkish subtitles (dubbing is the normal practice in Turkey and the standard is very high). At the time of writing, these are limited to Bilsak, near Taksim Square, the Ortaköy Sanat Merkezi in the village of Ortaköy on the Bosphorus and the Sinema Kültür Merkezi at Moda on the Asiatic side of the city. Films shown at the International Film Festival are always screened in the original language.

Sound and Light shows are presented in Sultan Ahmet Square, between the Blue Mosque and St. Sophia, in English, French, German and Turkish, during the summer months. Be sure to check beforehand for times and languages.

Cultural Associations, Film Clubs, Jazz Centers

Austrian Cultural Office: Silahhane Cad. 101/12, Teşvikiye. Tel: 147 50 91.

British Council: Cumhuriyet Cad. 22-24. Ege Han 2nd Floor, Elmadağ. Tel: 146 71 25-26.

Casa D'Italia: Mesrutiyet Cad. 161, Tepebaşi. Tel: 144 08 95.

French Cultural Centre: Istiklâl Cad. 2, Taksim. Tel: 149 48 95.

Istanbul Turco-British Association (ITBA): Cumhuriyet Cad. Adli Han 1st Floor, Harbiye. Tel: 141 05 18.

Italian Cultural Centre: see under Casa D'Italia.

Spanish Cultural Office: Tomtom Kaptan Sok. 37, Beyoğlu. Tel: 144 27 38.

Turkish-American University Association: Rumeli Cad. 60-62, 1st Floor, Osmanbey. Tel: 147 21 88.

Turkish-German Cultural Centre: Istiklâl Cad. 286. Odakule, Galatasaray. Tel: 149 20 09.

U.S.I.S. (United States Information Services): Meşrutiyet Cad. 108, Tepebaşi. Tel: 143 62 00.

Ortaköy Sanat Merkezi: Dereboyu Cad., Barbaros Paşaji No. 110, Ortaköy. Tel: 161 79 43 (Films in original language.)

Moda Sinemasi Kültür Merkezi: Bahariye Cad., Adliye Yani, Moda. Tel: 337 01 28. (Films in original language.)

Bilsak: Soganci Sok. 7, Cihangir. Tel: 143 28 79-143 28 99. (Jazz)

Jazzino: Yildiz Posta Cad., Ayyildiz Paşaji, Gayrettepe. Tel: 167 13 12.

PLACES TO VISIT

Art Galleries: There are

many respectable galleries selling works by contemporary Turkish artists, almost all in the Beyoğlu-Harbiye-Nişantaş-Maçka areas of the new city. A few names to watch out for are Gülsün Karamustafa, Oya Katoğlu, Cihat Burak, Belkan Naci Islimyeli, Nur Koçak, Filiz Basaran Özayten and Yüksel Arslan. Paintings are considered safe financial investments these days, hence an escalation in prices to the point where it is difficult for the average individual to purchase paintings while millionaires are prepared to pay unrealistic sums.

Exhibitions are listed on Mondays in the main daily papers and a list of galleries worth visiting can be found below.

Occasional international exhibitions such as the 1st International Istanbul Contemporary Art Exhibitions in 1987 are particularly exciting as they make maximum use of the beautiful spaces available throughout the city, such as restored imperial baths, to mention only one.

Galleries

Akbank
Bahariye-Bahariye Cad. 42, Tel: 337 96 29-236 18 49

Bebek-Cevdet Paşa Cad., Nispetiye Cad. 36/1. Tel: 165 75 15.

Nişantaşi-Teşvikiye Cad. 141. Tel: 146 74 78.

Osmanbey-Halâskârgazi Cad. 289, Osmanbey.

Tel: 147 34 27-140 12 50.

Also: Rumeli Cad. Tel: 146 54 84-140 79 28.

Silivri-Ali Çetinkaya Cad. 128, Tel: 1360-2350.

A.K.M.-Atatürk Kültor Merkezi (Atatürk Cultural Centre)
Taksim Square, Taksim. Tel: 143 54 00.

Anadolu
Belyoz Sok, Yeni Han. 4, Galatasaray. Tel: 151 44 18.

Artisan Ortaköy
Iskele Cad. 3, Ortaköy.

Baraz
Kurtulus Cad. 19/f, Sinemköy. Tel: 140 47 83.

Hilton International Hotel, Cumhuriyet Cad., Harbiye. Tel: 146 97 23.

Bilsak
Siraselviler Cad. Soganci Sok. 7, Cihangir. Tel: 143 28 99.

Caddebostan
Bağdat Cad. 256/3, Caddebostan. Tel: 358 87 98.

Cumali
Sakayik Sok. 45/3, Teşvikiye. Tel: 148 31 65.

Destek
Abdi Ipekçi Cad. 75, Maçka. Tel: 146 03 54.

Dolmabahce Palace
Dolmabahce Cad. in Dolmabahce. Tel: 161 02 25.
Open: 9 a.m.- 4 p.m.
Closed: Mondays and Thursdays.

Edpa
Hüsrev Gerede Cad. 126, Teşvikiye. Tel: 141 27 11.

Garanti
Halâskârgazi Cad. 36, Harbiye. Tel: 140 13 60-146 20 41-148 96 19.

Göztepe-Bağdat Cad. 250/13. Tel: 358 01 72.

Nişantaşi-Teşvikiye Cad. 141. Tel: 133 01 20.

Hobi
Valikonagi Cad. Paşaji 85, Nişantaşi. Tel: 146 72 81.

Istasyon
Teşvikiye Cad. Maçka Palas 41/11, Maçka. Tel: 140 56 50.

Is
Istiklâl Cad. Meselik Sok. 2/6, Yürekli Han, 2nd Floor, Parmakkapi. Tel: 144 20 21.

Erenköy-Bağdat Cad. 296/A. Tel: 356 01 68.

Kazim Taskent
see under Yapi ve Kredi Bankasi.

Kile
Cevdet Paşa Cad. 376, Bebek. Tel: 165 74 96.

Kolesiyon
Sheraton Hotel Lobby, Asker Ocagi Cad. 1, Taksim. Tel: 148 90 00-ext. 31 52.

Lebriz: Mim Kemal Öke Cad. 8/3, Nişantaşi. Tel: 140 22 82-141 09 84.

Maçka
Eytam Cad. 31/1, Maçka. Tel: 140 80 23.

Mimar Sinan Universitesi (Mimar Sinan & Osman Handi Galleries)
Meclis-i Mebusan Cad., Findikli.
Tel: 145 00 00 ext. 296.

Neriman Erkut: Matbaaci Osman Bey Sok. 35/2, Osmanbey. Tel: 146 05 47.

Nev: Silahhane Cad. 33/B, Maçka. Tel: 131 67 63.

Opera
Saglik Sok. Opera Han 43/16, Taksim. Tel: 149 92 02.

Pamukbank:
Bebek-Cevdet Paşa Cad. 182, Küçük Bebek.
Tel: 165 80 58-59.

Levent-Gül Sok. 1.
Tel: 164 23 34.

Pangalti-Halâskârgazi Cad. 84. Tel: 146 67 84-146 89 95-147 45 41.

Suadiye-Bağdat Cad. 417.
Tel: 356 99 57-358 20 11.

Yeşilyurt-Sipahioğlu Cad. 19.
Tel: 573 41 32-573 41 46.

Ramko: Atiye Sok. 8/2, Teşvikiye. Tel: 141 77 09.

Resim ve Heykel Müzesi (Halil Dikmen & Seker Ahmet Paşa Galleries)
Dolmabahce Cad., Beşiktaş. Tel: 161 42 98.

Taksim
Gezi* Dükkanlari 21, Taksim. Tel: 145 20 68.

Tem
Kuyulu Bostan Sok. 44/2, Nişantaşi.

Tel: 147 08 99-147 97 56.

Teşvikiye
Abdi Ipekçi Cad. 48/1, Teşvikiye.
Tel: 141 04 58-147 74 75.

Tiglat
Kücük Bebek Cad. 2/2, Bebek. Tel: 163 10 31.

Ümit Yasar
Istiklâl Cad. Terkos Çikmazi Yapi-Kur Is Hani,
1st Floor, 27, Tünel.
Tel: 144 96 33.

Urart
Abdi Ipekçi Cad. 21, Nişantaşi. Tel: 148 03 26 (Main gallery): Yalliboyu Cad. Koruluk Sok. 1, Beylerbevi. Tel: 333 33 06.

Ürün
Asmalimedcit Sok., Çagin Han 13/3, 2nd Floor, Tünel.

Vakko
Istiklâl Cad. 123-125, Beyoğlu. Tel: 144 75 30.

Yapi ve Kredi Bankasi
Kazim Laskent (Galatasaray), Istiklâl Cad. 285, Galatasaray.
Tel: 144 30 70.

Bebek-Cevdet Paşa Cad. Ragerasi Sok. 1.
Tel: 163 31 10.

Etiler-Nispetiye Cad. 35.
Tel: 163 51 55.

Kadiköy-Söğultüçeşme Cad. 2. Tel: 337 85 25.

Osmanbey-Rumeli Cad. 85.
Tel: 140 89 02.

Yeşilköy Sanat Merkezi
Istasyon Cad. Yeşilyali Sok.

Altinay Paşaji, Yeşilköy.
Tel: 574 14 41.

Yonca
see under Garanti.

Ziraat
Erenköy-Bağdat Cad. 310.
Tel: 358 91 37.

Kiziltoprak-Bağdat Cad. 72.
Tel: 338 19 01.

Üsküdar-Hakimiyet-i Milliye Cad.
Tel: 333 07 01.

Museums
(Unless otherwise stated, museums are normally closed on Mondays)

Adam Mickievcz House
Tatlibadem Sok. 29, Tarlabaşi, Istanbul. Tel: none.

Aeronautical Museum
Yeşilköy Hava Harp Okulu, Yeşilyurt, Istanbul.
Tel: 574 11 00.
Closed Mondays and Tuesdays.

Al
Haydar Üstay Hunting Museum: Dulkadiroglullari Sok. 2, Arnavutköy, Istanbul. Tel: 165 74 49.

Asiyan Museum
Rumelihisar, Istanbul.
Tel: 163 69 86.

Atatürk Reforms Museum
Halâskârgazi Cad. 250, Şişli, Istanbul.
Tel: 140 63 19.

Calligraphy & Associated Arts Museum
Hünkar Kaşri, Sultan Ahmet Mosque, Sultan Ahmet, Istanbul. Tel: 528 53 32.

Construction Arts Museum
Amcazade Hüseyin Paşa Külliyesi, Fatih, Istanbul. Tel: 525 12 94.

Divan Literature Museum
(in Galata Mevlevihanesi, temple of the Mevlevi sect) Galip Dede Cad. 15, Tünel, Istanbul, Tel: 143 50 45-145 41 41.

Florence Nightingale Museum
Selimiye, Istanbul, Tel: 333 00 20.

Health Museum
Divanyolu Cad. 132, Sultan Ahmet, Istanbul. Tel: 522 08 61.

History of Medicine Museum
Cerrahpaşa Faculty of Medicine, Cerrahpaşa, Istanbul. Tel: 585 21 00 ext. 569 & 575.

Horse Racing Museum
Veliefendi Hippodrome, Veliefendi, Istanbul. Tel: 570 24 80.

Hüseyin Rahmi Gürpinar Museum
Demirtas Sok. 19, Heybeliada (Princes' Islands), Istanbul. Tel: 351 84 03.

Istanbul Archaeological Museum
Sultan Ahmet, Istanbul. Tel: 520 77 40-41.

Military Museum
Harbiye, Istanbul. Tel: 140 62 55.

Municipal Musuem
Kovacilar Cad. 12, Saraçhane, Istanbul.

Tel: 521 12 64.

Museum of Oriental Antiquitie
Sultan Ahmet, Istanbul. Tel: 520 77 42.

Naval Museum
Beşiktaş, Istanbul. Tel: 161 00 40.Closed Mondays and Tuesdays.

Printing & Sculpture Museum
Carağan Cad., Beşiktaş, Istanbul. Tel: 161 42 98-99.

Rumelihisari (Fortress also Museum)
Yahya Kemal Cad. 42, Rumelihisari, Istanbul. Tel: 163 53 05.

Sadberk Hanim Museum
Büyükdere, Istanbul. Tel: 142 38 13. Closed Wednesdays.

Sait Faik Abasiyanik Museum
Burgaz Çayifi Sok. 15, Burgaz Adasi (Princes' Islands), Istanbul, Tel: none.

St. Irene Museum
Sultan Ahmet, Istanbul. Tel: 528 45 00.

St. Sophia (Ayasofya) Museum
Sultan Ahmet, Istanbul. Tel: 528 45 00-522 17 50.

St. Saviour in Chora (Kariye) Museum
Edirnekapi, Istanbul. Tel: 523 30 09. Closed Tuesdays..

Tanzimat (1839 Reforms) Museum
Gülhane Park, Sultan Ahmet, Istanbul.

Tel: 512 14 25.

Topkapi Palace-Harem:
Sultan Ahmet, Istanbul. Tel: 512 04 80-91. Closed Tuesdays.

Topkapi Palace Museum
Sultan Ahmet, Istanbul. Tel: 512 04 80-91. Closed Tuesdays.

Transport Museum
Söğütlüçeşme, Kadiköy. Tel: 336 06 43.

Turkish & Islamic Arts Museum
Ibrahim Paşa Palace, Sultan Ahmet, Istanbul. Tel: 522 26 43.

Türbeler (Mausoleums) Museum
Sultan Ahmet Mosque, Sultan Ahmet, Istanbul. Tel: 522 26 43.

Yahya Kemal Museum
Yeniçerililer Cad. 43, Çemberlitas, Istanbul. Tel: 522 95 17.

Yedikulu Golden Gate & City Walls Museum
Yedikule, Istanbul. Tel: 585 89 33.

Ancient Churches

Church of Christ-Pantepoptes (Eski Imaret Mosque): in Fatih. Built by Anna Dallasens, mother of Emperor Alexios I, it is one of the important works of the Golden Age of Byzantine architecture.

Church of Peribleptos (Sulu Manastir or Surp Kevork): in Florya Coastal Road. Built around 1031 by

Romanos III Argyros. Rebuilt in 1722 after a fire. Only the cellars remain as parts of the original Byzantine structure.

Convent of Women of Mirelaoin (Bodrum Mosque): in Aksaray. Exact construction date unknown. Became a convent during 6th century Iconoclast Constantine Coprnyme (741-775) closed it in 8th century Was restored in 10th century by Roman Lecapen II (959-963) who with his wife Theodora is buried here. Converted into a mosque in 1574 by Mesih Pasha, Governor of Egypt, during the reign of Mahmut III.

Dominican Church (Arab Mosque): in Galata. Originally built as a mosque by Arabs who beseiged the city in 717 and captured Galata. Byzantians converted it into a church for Dominican Friars. When Arabs (expelled from Spain in 1455) took refuge in Istanbul, it was once again converted into a mosque.

Monastery of St. John Studios (Imrahor Mosque): in Yedikule. Built in 5th century by a Byzantine nobleman. Today a roofless structure. Converted into a mosque by Imrahor Bey, Master of Horses of Sultan Beyazit II, following conquest of the city.

Pantocrator (Zeyrek Mosque): in Zeyrek. Built 1120-1136, it is a composite building consisting of two churches and a chapel in between. Founded by the Empress Eirene, the monastery to which these churches belong was the most renowned in Byzantium.

Saviour in Chora (Karlye Mosque): in Edirnekapi. (Tel: 523 30 09). Built outside city walls before reign of Theodosius II (408-450). Restored as a basilica in 527-565 by Justinian, its murals were destroyed by Iconoclasts and repaired by Alexy Commen I in 1081-1118. Latin Crusaders destroyed it once again in 1204 and Paleologue II (1283-1328) spent all his fortune on its renovation. Mosaics of Christ, Virgin Mary, angels, saints, prophets and miracles make this church a fascinating gallery of early Christian history. It was converted into a mosque by Atik Ali Pasha (1495-1511). It is now a museum.

St. Andrew in Crisal (Koca Mustafa Paşa Mosque): in Koca Mustafa Paşa. Though built as a church, it was used as a convent for women and is therefore also known as the Girls' Monastery. Converted into a mosque by Koca Mustafa Paşa, Grand Vizier of Beyazir II (1481-1512).

St. Benoit: in Kemeralti Cad. Karaköy. Originally constructed by Latins in 1427 on remains of a Byzantine church.

St. George (Austrian Church): in Bankalar Cad.

St. George's (The Patriarchatel): Sadrazam Ali Paşa Cad. 35, Fener. Tel: 521 25 32. Services: Everyday 8.30 a.m., Sundays 9 a.m.-11 a.m.

Easter services: April 11th-18th. Founded during Byzantine era. Rebuilt in 15th century. Restored: 1720.

St. Irene: in Sultan Ahmet. (Tel: 528 45 00). Built in 4th century by Constantine the Great and dedicated to St. Irene (The Divine Peace). Restored by Justinian following Nika revolt of 532 and later in 740. Recent findings indicate existence of three pagan churches in the same site prior to erection of the present building. Never converted into a mosque.

St. Joannes Profromos (Ahmet Paşa Mosque): in Yaviz Selim. Built in the 12th century. Converted into a mosque in 1590 by Hirama Pacha. Bus: 86.

St. Mary Panmakaristors (Fethiye Museum): in Fener. Situated on the fifth hill of the city. Built in 8th century but entirely restored in 1315 by Michael Glabas Tarchaniotis as a women's convent. Remained the seat of Patriarchy until 1574 when it was converted into a mosque by Murat IV to commemorate conquest of Georgia and Azerbaidjan. Most of the Byzantine Emperors are buried here. Open: Saturdays and Sundays only 9.30 a.m.- 5 p.m.

St. Nicholas (Kefell Mosque): in Karagümrük. Built in the 9th century. Converted into a mosque in 1627.

St. Paplyos (Ayos Minas Church): On Florya Coastal Road. Built in 1833.

St. Peter: in Bankalar Cad. Built in 1604 by (Dominican Friars on site of an earlier wooden chapel. Burnt down twice in 1660 and 1731. Present building designed by Swiss architect Fassati built in 1841.

St. Saviour Akataleptos (Kalenderhane Mosque): in Şehzadebaşi. Dates from the 9th century. Converted into a mosque after the conquest of Istanbul in 1453.

St. Sergius and Bacchus (Kiliçik Ayasofya Mosque): in Sultan Ahmet. Built in 550 by Emperor Justinian. Its plan resembles St. Sophia, hence it is called 'Little St. Sophia' in Turkish. Converted into a mosque during the reign of Beyazit II.

St. Sophia: in Sultan Ahmet (Tel: 528 45 00). *Hagia Sophia* in Greek means Holy Wisdom. Its building was started by Constantine the Great who erected a small basilica church in 325 over a pagan temple. It was rebuilt in 415 by Theodosius II but was totally destroyed during Nika revolt in 532. Present building started between 532 and 537 by Justinian, was designed by architects Arthemius of Trolles and Isidorus of Miletus.

St. Theodorus (Kilise Mosque): in Beyzit. Exact date of construction remains vague but the monastery walls nearby go back to 5th century.

St. Theodosius (Gül Mosque): in Balat. Built in 9th century to honour a woman persecuted and killed by Iconoclasts during reign of Leon III the Isaurian (717-741). Ottomans upon conquering Istanbul, found the church full of roses which is why it was named Gül Mosque (Mosque of Roses) when transformed into a mosque by Sultan Salim II (1566-1574).

Theoctocus de Petra (Odalar Mosque): in Karagümrük. Built around 12th century.

Theotocus Panagiotissa (Moukhiliotissa Greek Orthodox Church): in Fener. Built in 13th century on ruins of an older 11th century building. One of the few ancient Orthodox temples still active.

Mosques

Atik Ali Paşa Mosque: in Çarsikapi. One of the oldest mosques in Istanbul. Built by Ali Pasha, a Grand Vizier of Beyazit II in 1497.

Atik Valise Mosque: Üsküdar. Built by the architect Sinan in 1583.

Beyazit Mosque: in Beyazit. Built in 1501 during the reign of Beyazit II. One of the oldest mosques in Istanbul and the least altered.

Cerraphasa Mosque: in Cerrahpaşa. Fine example of 16th-century Turkish architecture.

Davut Paşa Mosque: in Davut Paşa. Built for Davut Paşa, Grand Vizier of Sultan Beyazit II, in 1485.

Dolmabahce Mosque: in Dolmabahce. Built in 1853 by Sultan Abdul Medjid I.

Eyüp Mosque: in Eyüp. The most celebrated mosques in Istanbul renowned throughout the Islamic world. Halit Bin Zeyd, the standard bearer of Umayyids who beseiged Istanbul in 669, fell and was buried at an unknown grave near this site called Kosmidion or Little World. In 1453 before the conquest of the city, Mehmet II the Conqueror had a dream about the incident and guessed the exact spot. Excavations proved him right. As a result, a tomb was built for him as well as a mosque: The Eyüp Mosque. During Ottoman rule coronation ceremonies for the Sultan, also Caliph, the protector of the Faith, were held at this mosque. It is still customary to pay a visit to Eyüp on the way to Holy Pilgrimage in Mecca.

Fatih Mosque: in Fatih. At this site, the fourth hill of the city, there once stood a church dedicated to the Apostles and which was once the seat of the frequently relocated Patriarchate. The building of one of the oldest mosques in Istanbul was begun in 1462. The dome fell due to the earthquake of 1766 and was rebuilt by Mustafa III in four years.

Haseki Mosque: in Haseki Built in 1539 for Hürrem

Sultana (better known as Roxelana) by architect Şinan as the first of his masterworks.

Hekimoglu Ali Paşa Mosque: in Koca Mustafa Paşa. Built in 1735 on order of Hekimoglu Ali Pasha, Grand Vizier of Sultan Mahmut I.

Kiliç Ali Pasa Mosque: in Tophane. Designed by the architect Sinan, and built in 1580 on order of Chief Admiral Kiliç, Ali Pasha.

Lalei Mosque: in Lateli in 1763.

Mirhrimah Mosque: in Edirnekapi. Built in 1555 by architect Sinan for Mirhrimah Sultana daughter of Süleyman the Magnificent and wife of Grand Vizier Rüstem Pasha.

Murat Paşa Mosque: in Aksaray. One of the first mosques built after the conquest. It was erected in 1468 by Murat Pasha, Grand Vizier of Sultan Mehmet II the Conqueror.

Nuruosmaniye Mosque: in Cagaloğlu. Started during the reign of Mahmut I in 1749, it was designed by Simeon Kalfa and was completed by Osman III in 1755.

Ortaköy Mosque: in Ortaköv. Built in 1870 by Sultan Abdul Medjid I.

Piyale Paşa Mosque: in Kasimpaşa. It was built by architect Sinan in 1573 for Admiral Piyale Pasha.

Rüstem Paşa Mosque: in Eminönü. Built in 1581 by architect Sinan in memory of Rüstem Pasha.

Semsi Paşa Mosque: Uskirdar. Built by Sinan on the waterside , in 1580.

Sokullu Mehmet Paşa Mosque: in Sultan Ahmet. On South West corner of Hippodrome. Built by architect Sinan in 1572 for Admiral Sokullu Mehmet Pasha.

Sultan Selim Mosque: in Yavuz Selim. Situated on fifth hill of the old city, this mosque was built between 1520 and 1522.

Sultan Ahmet (Blue) Mosque: in Sultan Ahmet. Best known of all Istanbul mosques, it was built by architect Sedelkat Mehmet Agha, pupil of Sinan, for Sultan Ahmet I.

Süleymaniye Mosque: in Süleymaniye. Named after Süleyman the Magnificent. Built between 1550 and 1557, it is regarded as the masterwork of architect Sinan. The Sultan with his wife Roxelana lie in separate tombs in a mausoleum to the east of the mosque. Architect Sinan's tomb is on the north west side of the building.

Şehzade Mosque: in Şehzadebaşi. Built in 1544-1549 by Süleyman the Magnificent in memory of his youngest son. One of the minor works of architect Sinan.

Valide Mosque: in Aksaray. Started in 1597 by

architect David Agha. Was completed in 1663.

Yeni Mosque: in Eminönü. Built during 17th century.

───────────────

Palaces

Aynalikavak Kasri: Aynalikavak Cad. Kasimpaşa. Tel: 150 40 94. Closed Mondays and Thursdays.

Beylerbeyi Palace: Beylerbeyi. Tel: 333 69 40. Closed Mondays and Thursdays.

Boucoleon-Justinian's Palace (also known as Justinian's House. The palace complex where it is situated also includes remains of Studios Basilica): Imrahor, Fatih. Tel: none.

Dolmabahçe Palace: Dolmabahçe, Beşiktaş. Tel: 161 02 25. Closed Mondays and Thursdays.

Göksu Palace: Kücüksu. Tel: 332 02 37. Closed Mondays and Thursdays.

Hünkar Kaşri: Eminönü, Tel: none. Presently closed to public.

Ihlamur Kasri: Müzhetiye Cad. Beşiktaş. Tel: 161 29 91. Closed Mondays and Thursdays.

Küçüksu Kasri: See under Göksu Palace.

Maslak Kasirlari: Levent-Istinye Road, next to Maslak Military Hospital, Maslak. Tel: 176 10 23. Closed Mondays and Thursdays.

Tekfur Sarayi (Palace of

Constantine Porphyrogenitus): Edirnekapi.
Tel: none.

Topkapi Palace: Sultan Ahmet. Tel: 528 35 47. Closed Tuesdays.

Yildiz Sale Köskü: Yildiz, Beşiktag. Tel: 161 20 43. Closed on Mondays and Thursdays.

Parks

Abrahim Paşa Korusu (Grove). Near Beykoz.

Belgrade Forest. Bahçeköy.

Emirgan Park. Emirgan. Tulip Festival in early May.

Gülhane Park. Sultan Ahmet. Next to the Archaeological Museum.

Yildiz Park. Beşiktag. It has several cafeterias, artificial lakes and restored Ottoman buildings.

Trade And Exhibition Centers

Chamber of Commerce (Istanbul Ticaret Odasi): Gümüspala Cad., Unkapani. Tel: 526 62 15-528 18 00.

Chamber of Industry (Istanbul Sanayi Odasi): Meşrutiye Cad. 118, Tepebaşi. Tel: 145 41 30-39.

Interteks (Hilton Convention & Exhibition Centre): Mim Kemal Öke Cad. 10, Nişantaş. Tel: 133 08 94-95-140 19 76-77-141 65 50-51.

OTIM (Middle East Trade and Export Center): Ihlamur, Beşiktaş. Tel: 166 99 45.

Tüyap Istanbul Exhibition Palace: Tepebaşi. Tel: 167 67 04-05.

Libraries and Bookshops: There are few libraries and bookshops catering to Eng-lish language readers. The major hotels have branches of Hachette (Haset) whose main shop is on Istiklâl Caddesi near Tünel. Nearby is another source of English language books, the ABC bookshop. Apart from these, the Redhouse bookshop in Sultanhamam has a very good selection. Deniz Kitapevi in Bebek caters to foreigners living in the district; and Tülin Zambakoğlu in Ayazpaşa, opposite the Japanese Consultate, offers a valuable selection of books and magazines, as well as interesting ceramics. The only library open to the general public worth visiting is the British Council, now in the BP building beside the Hilton Hotel, which resembles a small British public library and is invaluable for newspapers, magazines and British books. The U.S.I.S. library has an excellent reference collection but it is difficult to get in, again for security reasons.

WORSHIP

CHURCHES

Greek

Panaghia
Istiklâl Cad. Olivo Çikmazi 26, Galatasaray. Tel: 144 11 84. Built: 1804. Service: Sundays 9 a.m., midday.

**St. George
(Partiarchy of Phanar)**
Sadriazam Ali Paşa Cad. 35, Fener. Tel: 521 25 32—521 19 21. Built: 1720. Service: Sundays 9 a.m., 11 a.m.

St. Triada
Meselik Sok. 11/1, Taksim. Tel: 144 13 58. Built: 1880 Service: Sun 9 a.m., noon.

Apostolic Armenian (Gregorian)

Patriarchate: Sarapnel Sok. 20, Kumkapi. Tel: 527 82 20. Built: original 1641, present 1913.

Surp Yerrortutyun (3 Horan): Sahne Sok. 26/1, Balikpazari, Beyoğlu. Tel: 144 13 82. Built: original 18th century, present 1838. Service: 10.30 a.m. Sundays and Tuesdays.

Catholic

**Armenian rite
St. Mary (Astvadzadzin):** Sakizagaci Cad. 31, Agacami, Beyoğlu. Tel: 144

12 58. Service: Sundays 10 a.m. Built in 1866.

Latin rite
St. Antuan
(Antonio di Padova)
Istiklâl Cad. 323, Beyoğlu. Tel: 144 09 35. Service: Sundays 10 a.m. (English).

St. Esprite
Cumhuriyet Cad. 205, also entrance: Ölcek Sok. 82, Harbiye. Tel: 148 09 10. Service: Sundays 10 a.m. (English).

Anglican

Crimean Memorial Church

Serdar-i Ekrem Sok. 82, Tünel. One of the largest modern churches in Istanbul, it was designed by **C.E. Street**, architect of London Law Courts but is presently closed. Built in 1868.

St. Helena
British Consulate grounds, Galatasaray. Tel: 144 42 28 Service: Sundays 10 a.m. (English). Built in 1870.

German Evangelical

Deutsche Evangelische Kirche
Emin Camil Sok. 40, Aynaliçeşme, Beyoğlu. Tel:

150 30 40. Service: Sundays 10.30 a.m. (German). Built in 1861.

Interdenominational

Dutch Chapel
Istiklâl Cad. 485, Beyoğlu. Tel: 144 52 12. Service: Sundays 10 a.m. (English). Built: Early 18th century.

Synagogues

A s h k e n a z y : Yüksekkaldirim Cad. 37/1, Karaköy. Tel: 144 29 75.

Neve Salom: Büyük Hendek Cad. 61, Sishane. Tel: 144 75 66-144 15 76.

SURVIVAL TURKEY

TURKISH LANGUAGE

Pronunciation: ç is pronounced as j in English; ç is ch; ş is sh; ğ is pronounced as y when it is in the middle of a word, or not at all; ö and ü have shortened sounds as in German and French.

Useful Vocabulary

Madame! Sir!
Efendim!

Please
Lütfen

Thank you
Teşekkür ederim

Thank you
Merşi

Hello
Merhaba

Yes
Evet

No
Hayir

Bath(room)
Banyo

Car, vehicle
Oto, araba

Taxi
Taksi

Driver
Şoför

Museum
Müze

Bank
Banka

Money
Para

Check
Çek

Foreign exchange
Döviz

Attention!
Dikkat!

Help!
Imdat!

Busy/occupied
Meşgül

Free/available
Serbest

Man/Mr.
Erkek/Bay

Woman/Mrs.
Kadin/Bayan

Toilet *Tuvalet*	Tea *Çay*	Today *Bugün*
Where? *Nerede?*	Coffee *Kahve*	Big/small *Büyük/küçük*
When? *Ne Zaman?*	Instant coffee *Nescafé*	Bill/check *Fatura/hesap*
How much? *Ne Kadar?*	Beer *Bira*	Get well soon! *Geçmis olsun!*
What is this? *Bu nedir?*	Wine *Şarap*	Good appetite! *Afiyet olsun!*
All right/O.K. *Taman/Peki*	Ice *Buz*	Good morning *Günaydin*

There is (something) *Var*	Sugar *Şeker*
There is not (something) *Yok*	Post office *P.T.T.*
Too much *Fazla*	Stamp *Pul*
Not enough *Az*	Grocery *Bakkal*
Restaurant *Lokanta. Restoran*	Chemist/Pharmacy *Eczane*
Hot *Sicak*	Doctor *Doktor*
Cold *Soğuk*	Hospital *Hastahane*
Open *Açik*	Stop *Dur*
Closed *Kapali*	Quick/fast *Çabuk/hizli*
Bread *Ekmek*	Slow *Yavaş*
Water *Su*	Left/right *Sol/sağ*
Milk *Süt*	Now *Şimdi*

FURTHER READING

Akurgal, Ekrem: *Ancient Civilizations and Ruins of Turkey;* Ankara, 1983.

Brosnahan, Tom: *Turkey: A Travel Survival Kit*; Lonely Planet, 1985.

Davidson, Alan: *Mediterranean Seafood*; Penguin, 1972.

Der Haroutunian, Arto: *A Turkish Cookbook*; Ebury Press, 1987.

Freely, John: *Blue Guide Istanbul*; Benn & Norton, 1983.

Goodwin, Godfrey: *A History of Ottoman Architecture*; Thames & Hudson, 1971.

Harrell, Betsy: *Mini Tours Near Istanbul*; Redhouse, 1975—1978.(2 vols.)

Hotham, David: *The Turks;*

John Murray, 1972.

Kelly, Laurence: Istanbul: *A Travellers' Companion*; Constable, 1987.

Kinross, Lord: *Atatürk; The Rebirth of a Nation*; London, 1966.

Kinross, Lord: *The Ottoman Centuries*; Jonathan Cape, 1977.

Lewis, Bernard: *The Emergence of Modern Turkey*; Oxford, 1961.

Pauls, Michael and Dana Facaros: *Turkey,* Cadogan Books, 1986.

Penzer, N. M.: *The Harem*; Spring Books, 1966.

Roden, Claudia: *A Book of Middle Eastern Food*; Nelson, 1968.

Summer Boyd, Hilary and John Freely: *Strolling Through Istanbul*; Redhouse, 1972.

Toker, Biltin: *Spot on Istanbul*; 1986.

ART/PHOTO CREDITS

Cover	Çakir/FOG	41	Şemsi Güner	77	Martini Collection
Front piece	Kismet/FOG	42/43	Martini Collection	78	Şemsi Güner
5	Keribar/FOG	44	Cengiz Civa	80	Şemsi Güner
6/7	Çakir/FOG	46	Cengiz Civa	81	Şemsi Güner
8/9	Şemsi Güner	47	Marcus Brooke	83	Murat Öcal
10/11	Çakir/FOG	48	Kismet/FOG	84	Şemsi Güner
12/13	Albert Martini	49	Cengiz Civa	85	Isa Çelik
14/15	Kismet/FOG	50	Kismet/FOG	86	Emin Hakkarar
16	Tony Stone	51	Ugur Ayyildiz	87	Keribar/FOG
18	Marcus Brooke	52	Çakir/FOG	88	Martini Collection
19	Marcus Brooke	53	Martini Collection	89	Çakir/FOG
22/23	Marcus Brooke	54	Keribar/FOG	90	Yildiz
24	Martini Collection	57	Muharrem Simsek	91	Şemsi Güner
25	Çakir/FOG	58	Keribar/FOG	92	Mihrimah Üzel
26	Nermi Erdur	59	Keribar/FOG	94/95	Çakir/FOG
27L	Isa Çelik	60	Keribar/FOG	96	Keribar/FOG
27R	Tony Stone	61	Keribar/FOG	97	Çakir/FOG
28	Mehmet Erkan	62	Çakir/FOG	98	Şemsi Güner
29	Keribar/FOG	63	Çakir/FOG	99	Michele Macrakis
30	Isa Çelik	65	Cengiz Civa	101	NET
31	Çakir/FOG	66/67	Çakir/FOG	102/103	Cengiz Civa
32	Çakir/FOG	68	Martini Collection	104	Isa Çelik
33L	Keribar/FOG	69	Çakir/FOG	107	Martini Collection
33R	Cengiz Civa	71	Martini Collection	108	Şemsi Güner
34	Çakir/FOG	72L	TKB	109	Şemsi Güner
35	Keribar/FOG	72R	TKB	110	Albert Martini
36	Michele Macrakis	73L	TKB	111	Martini Collection
37L	Mehmet Erkan	73R	TKB	112	Martini Collection
37R	Cengiz Civa	74/75	Martini Collection	113	Çakir/FOG
38	Şemsi Güner	76	Martini Collection	115	Martini Collection

INDEX